Diabetes and Your Diet

A Diabetes Diet Cookbook with Nutrition and Lifestyle Tips for Reversing Diabetes

By Nancy Addison

This book contains raw, vegan, and gluten-free recipes.

Diabetes and Your Diet: A Diabetes Diet Cookbook with Nutrition and Lifestyle Tips for Reversing Diabetes

Volume One of the *Healing Diet* Series

ISBN-13: 978-0996108577
ISBN-10: 0996108572
Library of Congress Control Number: 2016916738

Nancy Alisa Gibbons Addison
www.OrganicHealthyLife.com

Limits of Liability and Disclaimer of Warranty
The author and publisher are not liable for misuse of this material. This book is strictly for informational and educational purposes. Nancy Addison offers information and opinions, not a substitute for professional medical prevention, diagnosis, or treatment. Please consult with your physician, pharmacist, or healthcare provider before taking any home remedies or supplements, or following any treatment suggested by Nancy Addison or by anyone listed in the books, articles, or other information contained here. Only your healthcare provider, personal physician, or pharmacist can provide you with advice on what is safe and effective for your unique needs or diagnose your particular medical history.

Warning & Disclaimer
The purpose of this book is to educate and entertain. The author and publisher do not guarantee that anyone following these techniques, suggestions, tips, ideas, or strategies will become successful. The author and publisher shall have neither liability nor responsibility to anyone with respect to any loss or damage caused, or alleged to be caused, directly or indirectly by the information contained in this book.

Let food be thy medicine, and let medicine be thy food.

—Hippocrates

Testimonials

"As a healthcare trustee of the largest healthcare system in North Texas, diabetes is one of main issues our patients are struggling with. I truly believe Nancy's book can help heal a person with Type 2 diabetes, and can reduce the amount of insulin needed if a person has Type 1 diabetes. I followed a raw, vegetarian food diet for 4 months and lost 84 pounds, and then incorporated a healthier, plant-based diet to maintain my weight. I highly recommend Nancy Addison's book for diabetes management!"

—**James Y. Wynne**, Certified Texas Healthcare Trustee.

"Healthcare in North America and many parts of the world has struggled for several decades to address the advancing rates of heart disease, obesity, diabetes, cancer, and hypertension. Expenditures on these conditions are escalating at rates that neither individuals nor payor agencies can sustain.

Finally, in Nancy Addison's book *Diabetes and Your Diet,* both the healthcare provider and lay person have an easy-to-understand resource for reversing the course of preventable disease. Increasing your lifespan and the quality of your daily activities through better dietary choices is an easily afforded recipe. Better dietary choices are vital to preventing and reversing today's chronic illnesses.

Nancy offers an authoritative, well-researched book that is easy to follow and apply to even the most hectic of lifestyles. Nancy's style and presentation of expert content are inviting and hospitable. For both the healthcare provider and the lay person, reading this book will provide new insights for a long and healthy life for yourself and the lives that you affect!"

—**Michael W. Hall, DC, FIACN**, has been providing chiropractic services for the past 20-plus years. He is the Executive Director for the NeuroLife Institute on the campus of Life University. He is an international speaker on the management and prevention of neurological disorders, a Fellow of the International Academy of Chiropractic Neurology, and a Diplomat of the American Board of Chiropractic Neurology.

Contents

"Nearly 100 percent of Type 2 diabetics can be successfully cured without drugs. You just might be surprised to know that you can eat, exercise, and live your way to recovery."[1]

—Dr. Joseph Mercola

Acknowledgments

Heartfelt Thanks to Amanda Gibbons Addison and Frederick Gibbons Addison. You, my wonderful children, are the loves of my life. You have hung in there with me through thick and thin. You have been my foundation and support over the years as I experimented with food and life in all its aspects. You were my original taste testers! You have helped me prepare, develop, refine, and taste test all my new ideas all your lives. You are my biggest fans, and I am yours. I am so blessed to be able to call myself your mother. My heart overflows with love for you, and I thank you for a lifetime of your unwavering support and love.

Thank you to my wonderful family and especially my mother, Junia Gibbons. Thank you to my sister Jane, her husband David, their child Claire and her husband Stefan, and their children Audrey and Reid. Thank you to my sister Liz, her husband Layne, and their children: Jack and his wife Amber, and their children Annie, Ford and Mary; Clayton and his wife Lynsie, and their children Scout and Gwen. Thanks to my brother Patrick and his son Ryan; to my sister Mary, her husband Rusty, and their children, Carter, Katie, and Rebecca. Your love and support for my children and me has been a godsend. You enrich my life every day. I'm so fortunate to be a part of this family.

Thank you to my precious daughter-in-law Edy, my son Gibbons, and their son, Shepherd. Thank you to my daughter-in-law's wonderful parents, Chip and Cynthia Jones. I am honored with your love, generosity, encouragement, friendship, and support. I love your family, and I am thrilled to share my son with you.

A special thank you to Dr. Gary Massad for contributing the foreword to this book. I am deeply honored by your contribution, and I am very grateful for your time, effort, faith, generosity, and support. Please know how greatly it is appreciated.

A special thank you to Michael W. Hall, DC, FIACN and your wife, Cara Hall, DC, for all your help, support, encouragement and faith in me and my work through the years. Please accept my heartfelt thanks.

A warm thank you to Linda Gray. You have been an incredible friend ever since we met. Thank you for your friendship, support, encouragement, and belief in me.

Thank you to James Wynne for encouraging me to write this book.

Thank you so much to Kaaydah Schatten, Merrilee Jacobs, Belinda and Jim Buddrus, Maryann DeLeo, Roy Teeluck, Suann and Ralph Davis, Mark Pharo, Charlotte Ammerman, Susan and Joe Doyle, Grimanesa Amoros, Bill Fleischer, Leeann Lavin, Lauren and Blake Massad, Rhina Valentin, Autumn, Vasquez, Sharyn Wynters, Deanna Sweet, Adele Good, Cindy Williams, Stephanie and Michael Askew, Leeann Lavin, Gary Corona, Todd and Katie Wynne, Fallon and Wes Way, Leslee Feiwus, Denise Stringer, Elizabeth Naylor, Sheila Fitzgerald, Dean Vanderslice, Dr. Mary Warren, Jane Phillips, Mia Davis, Carol Kirby, Carol Egan, Steve Cowan, Kelley Willis, Julianne Parker, Priscilla Miller, Dr. Therese Rowley, Susan Williams, Karis Adams, Julie Goss, Judd Walker, Lori Markman, Mary Monttein Alonso, Debbie Russell, Nancy Miller, Kimberly Wechsler, Elizabeth Conn, Michael Reisman, Mary Jo Rausch, Priscilla Miller, Kathleen Hayden, Candace Stone, Dr. Sandra Bontempts, Dr. Cynthia Champion-Olson, Harrison Evans, Chris Koustoubardis, Marilyn Flemming, Jacqueline Cornaby, Carole Friesen, Chef Terry French, Richard Graves, and so many friends who have helped me in more ways than I can list. Thank you for believing in me and for your support and continued encouragement.

Thank you to my dear friend Lisa Endicott of Lisa Endicott PR, and to your staff, for all you have done for me with your skill, expertise, thoughtfulness, and kind consideration. You have been there with me throughout all my journeys. You've enriched my life, and it has been a delight to work with you.

Thanks to all my dear friends at the National Speakers Association and the North Texas Chapter for all your help, support, kindness, and generosity.

Thanks to all my dear friends from Dallas and the Park Cities for all your help, support, kindness, and generosity.

Thank you to the Institute of Integrative Nutrition and all my friends that I met there. I have loved the journey with you.

Thank you to all my friends and associates at Allie Beth Allman and Associates, for all your kindness, generosity, and encouragement.

To all the wonderful friends and neighbors from my life who have honored me with your friendship, endless patience, cheerful words of encouragement, and constant support, I thank you all for making my life so much brighter. Bless you all.

I want to thank Nick Sakulenzki who took my photograph for this book.

Thank you, Kytka Hilmar-Jezek, for creating my cover and helping with other details associated with book publishing. I truly appreciate your faith in me and for your help. I have greatly appreciated your dedication to helping me with my book in so many ways.

Thank you to Susan Doyle, my dear friend, for all your special editing assistance with this book and other writing projects. You have helped me in so many ways that I can't even count. I am truly grateful for your input, thoughtfulness, expertise, and devotion to my mission.

Thank you, Matthew Howard, for helping me edit my book in creative, dedicated, and illuminating ways. You were amazing and went way beyond the call of duty! I am extremely grateful for all your outstanding hard work and dedication to my mission to help people with their health and lifestyle as well as your fantastic work with this project! It was an honor to work with you.

I am grateful for all of you. Bless you all. Please accept my deepest heartfelt thanks.

I thank God for the constant love, support, inspiration, knowledge, experiences, and energy that it took to put this book together.

May God bless this book and all who read it.

"If a 250 pound, obese, mildly diabetic hypertensive, patient has a heart attack and is fully compliant with plant-based nutrition treatment, profound changes occur.

By 8 months, he weighs 190 pounds and is no longer obese, his diabetes and hypertension are gone as is any risk for a future heart attack.

He will also protect himself from erectile dysfunction and dementia."

—Dr. Caldwell Esselstyn, Jr.

Director of the cardiovascular prevention and reversal program at The Cleveland Clinic Wellness Institute.

Foreword

by Gary L. Massad, MD

I have been fortunate to practice medicine in many fields and have had the opportunity to study nutrition from some of the best experts in the field. Nancy Gibbons Addison is one of those experts. Nancy promotes thoughtful discussion and improved understanding of disease processes and, most importantly, through *Diabetes and Your Diet*, she promotes an increased life span for people throughout the world. Food connects us all in some way, shape, or form. We make a powerful choice in what we choose to eat. In this book, Nancy has prepared a menu for health and a prescription for a better, healthier choice.

I've worked with patients and athletes for more than 30 years and have witnessed changes in the approach to nutrition, weight loss, and food in general. Food choices have changed because the composition of food has changed. This book is an invaluable resource that offers a comprehensive overview of protein, carbohydrates, fats, sugars, and vitamins. It includes valuable information about their role in restoring and maintaining your health. Nancy cuts through the myths and hype to present the facts as they are. The result is an overview of everything you need to know about living well every day of your life. She makes it easy to understand and even easier to put into action. With the help of this book, you can live longer and get the health results you want.

Nancy is passionate about sharing her knowledge with her loved ones, her family and friends, and, most of all, those who may benefit dramatically by increasing the quality of life through reversing disease. Her knowledge is impressive, and her approach to the selection and preparation of foods is beyond compare. There is always a place for you at her table, so sit back and enjoy the food and feeling healthier.

—**Gary L. Massad, MD**, was head physician at the 1989 World Championships for the United States Cycling Federation in France, attending physician for the United States Cycling Federation (USCF) to the Tour of Texas, attending physician for the Ironman Hawaii, and First National Corporate Medical Director and founder of Occupational Health Centers in America. He is attending physician for the United States Triathlon Association, the United States Tae Kwon Do Association, and the United States Cycling Federation.

Introduction

Diabetes: What You Need to Know
To Take Control of Your Health

D iabetes has increased by more than 700 percent in the last 50 years. About one in four people in the US have been diagnosed with diabetes or pre-diabetes. Juvenile diabetes numbers have been rising at a very rapid rate, especially for white youths ages 10–14, whose rates have risen 24 percent in the past few decades. More alarming is the 200 percent increase in diabetes among black children. Even worse, recent studies predict these numbers will double by 2020 for all youth.[2]

As I've researched health and nutrition over the past 28 years, I've seen this increase directly correlate with a number of trends:

- The increasing addition of harmful substances to our foods such as high-fructose corn syrup, artificial sweeteners, trans fats, food dyes, monosodium glutamate (MSG, which is a flavor enhancer commonly added to Chinese food, fast or processed foods, canned vegetables, soups, and processed meats), and other chemicals.
- The low exposure to, and absorption of, Vitamin D in our society.
- The decrease in exercise and fresh air as people become more sedentary, watch more television, and work more at computers.

- The growth in the genetically modified food industry, which results in food being deficient in nutrients that are necessary for health and well-being.
- The increased number and variety of unhealthy GMO and hybrid crops (example: corn, soy, and wheat) that have carcinogenic (cancer-causing) poisons built into them and/or applied to them when they are in the field. This is aided by government tax incentives that support industries growing GMO (genetically modified) and hybridized foods, and government policies encouraging cheap prices for food that can harm health.
- The increased use of microwave ovens, which destroy the nutrients and integrity of the water and food they cook.

Food is our medicine. But food and our environment have become toxic and unhealthy, and our increasingly sedentary lifestyles are not helping.

However, research has shown Type 2 diabetes is preventable and virtually 100 percent reversible, simply by implementing dietary and lifestyle changes which are easy and inexpensive. In this book, I discuss how to eat higher quality foods that will contribute to your overall health. I'll go into detail on nutrients, preparation, recipes, and lifestyle suggestions you can use to move yourself into a healthier, happier life.

Warning signs that you may be diabetic.

Frequent infections of the skin and/or urinary tract
Numbness or tingling in hands and/or feet
Hunger, even after eating
Slow wound healing
Excessive thirst
Blurred vision
Irritability

A diabetic can no longer produce sufficient insulin to process glucose (sugar) in the blood. To lower glucose levels, diabetics need to increase insulin, either by taking medication that increases their own insulin production, or by injecting insulin directly. (A diabetic can be on four or five medications to control blood glucose.) But these treatments do nothing to address the root cause of the problem.

Diabetes medications also have serious side effects. For example, Avandia was used in a two-year study published in the *New England Journal of Medicine*. This study linked Avandia to a 43 percent increased risk of heart attack, along with a 64 percent higher risk of cardiovascular death as compared to patients being treated with other methods.[3]

Even with those devastating results, the FDA voted to allow it to remain on the market. In the words of wise medical researcher Dr. Bruce Lipton, "There is no such thing as side effects. They are direct effects." I recommend being thoughtful about what you put in your body.

A more effective way to lower glucose levels is to eat fewer foods that produce high glucose levels. Glucose is the product of carbohydrates, which are found principally in wheat, corn, rice, potatoes, fruit and sugars. The refined, processed, GMO, non-organic ones are much worse than the whole, unrefined, less processed ones.

Cutting down on these foods will keep blood glucose low. Replacing those unhealthy carbohydrates with healthier varieties of plant-based protein, fats, and carbohydrates—the most naturally satisfying of foods—often eliminates hunger. People can lose weight without starving themselves, or even counting calories.

When you want to reverse disease, one of the most important dietary changes you can make is the elimination of sugar (especially fructose) and refined grains from your diet. This means eliminating processed, fast, nutrient-empty, chemically grown, chemically enhanced drinks and foods from your diet.

Diabetes is a disorder of insulin and leptin signaling, a disorder which can be caused by processed sugar and chemicals in processed food. Leptin is a hormone produced in your fat cells.

Leptin's primary functions include regulating your appetite and body weight. It tells your brain when to eat, how much to eat, and when to stop eating, which is why it's called the "satiety hormone."

Many of the chemicals and processed, refined sugars in so many of the fast and processed foods and drinks on the market today interfere with this hormone and prevent it from signaling. Therefore, eliminating those chemicals and processed sugars will help your body heal and begin to function in a healthier way.

Jeffrey M. Friedman and Douglas Coleman were two researchers who discovered the leptin hormone in 1994.[4] In the research, Friedman found that obese people have very high levels of leptin in their blood. He decided to look into that. He found that "obesity can cause a resistance to leptin—in other words, the signaling pathway for leptin becomes skewed in obese people, causing the body to over-produce leptin just as it does glucose when you are insulin-resistant."[5]

Friedman and Coleman also discovered that leptin is responsible for the accuracy of insulin signaling and for your insulin resistance. Elevated insulin levels are not only symptoms of diabetes, but also heart disease, peripheral vascular disease, stroke, high blood pressure, cancer, and obesity.

Thus, the primary role of insulin is NOT to lower your blood sugar, but to store the extra energy for future consumption (as glycogen, a starch). Insulin's ability to lower your blood sugar is merely a "side effect" of this energy storage process. Ultimately, this means diabetes is both a disease of insulin and of a malfunction in leptin signaling.

That's why "treating" diabetes by merely concentrating on lowering blood sugar can be a dangerous approach. It does not address the actual issue of metabolic miscommunication that's going on in every cell of your body when your leptin and insulin levels are disrupted and stop working together the way they should."[6]

What this research has shown is that your diet and weight can have an incredible effect on your health and be more effective than any known drug.

Dr. Richard Johnson, head of Nephrology at the University of Colorado wrote *The Fat Switch* about diet and weight loss. His research found that consuming fructose activates a powerful biological response that causes weight gain. It also causes the brain to not think it is satisfied or "full" after eating or drinking it, which leads to overeating. High rates of obesity and diabetes correlate with the overwhelming amount of fructose in processed foods and drinks today.

While glucose is designed to be used by your body for energy, high-fructose sugar breaks down into a variety of toxins that can destroy a person's health. Dr. Johnson's research found that consumption of high-fructose sugar:

- **Elevates uric acid**, which can cause inflammation, hypertension, kidney disease, and fatty liver.
- **Leads to insulin resistance**, a factor in Type 2 diabetes, heart diseases, and many cancers
- **Tricks your body into gaining weight.** Fructose doesn't appropriately stimulate insulin, which, as a result, fails to suppress ghrelin ("hunger hormone") and to stimulate leptin ("satiety hormone").
- **Rapidly leads to metabolic syndrome**, with weight gain as the result. It can also decrease HDL, increase LDL, elevate triglycerides, elevate blood sugar, and cause high blood pressure.
- **Metabolizes like ethanol,** causing toxic effects like non-alcoholic fatty liver diseases (NAFLD).[7]

In Dr. Johnson's 10-week study, 16 volunteers went on a controlled diet which included high levels of fructose. They produced new fat cells around their hearts, livers, and digestive organs. They also showed signs of abnormalities linked to diabetes and heart disease.

Another group of volunteers on the same diet, but with glucose sugar replacing fructose, did not have these problems. The study showed that fructose in any form—including high-fructose corn syrup (HFCS) and crystalline fructose—is very harmful to health.

Many people purchase inexpensive processed foods full of fructose, and they think they are getting more food for their money. Why are these processed foods so cheap, and healthy, organically grown food so expensive? Because most of the fructose is made from crops (mainly corn) that are heavily subsidized by the federal government. These subsidies make fructose a less expensive ingredient for processed food manufacturers.

Fructose can be found in diet foods, water products, infant formulas (which can contain as much as a coca cola), and even animal feed. Reading ingredient labels is vital these days! Read the ingredient labels on everything you buy. Don't go by the packaging, which can be very misleading.

According to one study, drinking just ONE soda or other sweetened drink per day—including sweetened, bottled water with vitamins in it—can raise your risk of developing diabetes by 25 percent, compared to drinking just one sugary drink per month.[8]

It's particularly important to eliminate processed meats. In a groundbreaking study comparing processed meats to unprocessed meats for the first time, researchers at Harvard School of Public Health found that eating processed meat is associated with a 42 percent higher risk of heart disease and a 19 percent higher risk of Type 2 diabetes. Interestingly, they did not find any risk of heart disease or diabetes among individuals eating unprocessed red meat such as beef, pork, or lamb.[9] (Processed meats usually have fructose and chemicals added to them.)

Eight Ways to Increase Your Insulin and Leptin Sensitivity, and to Prevent or Reverse Diabetes.

1. **Exercise.** Exercise is one of the fastest, most powerful ways to lower your insulin and leptin resistance.

2. **Eliminate grains and sugars and ALL processed foods**, especially those made with fructose and HFCS.

3. **Eliminate processed meats**.

4. **Eliminate all trans fats.**

5. **Consume healthy fats**, including **Omega 3** fatty acids.

6. **Consume probiotic-rich, fermented foods**.

7. **Get enough Vitamins B, C, and D, magnesium, zinc, and chromium**. (They are all important, but especially Vitamin D.)

8. **Eat fresh, organic, vegetables in their whole, real form every day**.

When you decide to take these steps, you will be on the road to radiant health! Everyone deserves to be radiantly healthy. When you give the body the right tools, it can do miraculous things.

So, let's get started!

Food is Our Medicine.

Dr. Max Gerson was friends with Dr. Albert Schweitzer. He cured Schweitzer's wife of lung tuberculosis after all conventional treatments had failed.

Afterward, Dr. Schweitzer followed Gerson's treatment plan of a healthy, plant-based diet containing lots of raw vegetables.

Schweitzer's own Type 2 diabetes was **cured** by this diet.[10]

1

Diet Can Be a Powerful Treatment for Diabetics

More than 100 million people today have diabetes or pre-diabetes. A recent study conducted by a team of American and Japanese researchers shows that people who have diabetes can vastly improve their health by eating an entirely plant-based diet.[11]

During my work with people who have diabetes, I have found they show remarkable improvement in their health and well-being from consuming a plant-based and almost completely raw-food diet. Dr. Gabriel Cousens promotes a mostly raw food, vegan diet in his 2008 book, *There Is a Cure for Diabetes*.[12]

Diabetics who would like to reduce their medications can now understand that the type of food they eat has a direct impact on their health. In 2014, *Cardiovascular Diagnosis and Therapy* published a study in which researchers performed a meta-analysis of six significant prior research studies. Researchers found that a plant-based diet significantly improved blood sugar control in Type 2 diabetes.

The results were that plant-based diets improved a key indicator of blood sugar control, an indicator called Hemoglobin A1c. The results improved as much as 1.2 points, which is much greater than the effect of typical oral diabetes medicines.[13] The benefits of excluding meat, cheese, and eggs from the diet was as much as 0.7 points in some of the studies, and averaged 0.4 points overall.[14]

2 | Nancy Addison

Dr. James Anderson studied 25 Type 1 and 25 Type 2 diabetics. This study involved placing the patients on a high-fiber, high-carbohydrate, low-fat diet in a hospital setting. Dr. Anderson initially put the patients on the American Diabetes Association recommended diet plan for one week. Then he switched them over to a vegetarian, plant-based diet for three weeks.

None of these patients were overweight when they started the study, but they were on insulin shots to control their blood sugar levels. All through the study, Dr. Anderson measured their blood sugar levels, their cholesterol levels, their medications, and their weight. Type 1 diabetics cannot produce insulin, and it was thought that dietary changes would not affect this situation.

But, the results showed that after three weeks on a vegetarian, whole-food, high-fiber diet, the "Type 1 diabetics were able to lower their insulin medication by an average of 40%", "their blood sugar profiles improved dramatically", and their "cholesterol levels dropped by 30%".[15]

These results were more impressive with the Type 2 diabetics who had not incurred as much damage to their pancreas. After three weeks on the high-fiber, vegetarian diet, 24 of the 25 Type 2 diabetics could discontinue their insulin medication completely.

The one Type 2 diabetic who wasn't able to get off his medication had been a 25-year diabetic taking 35 units per day. After three weeks of vegetarian food, his requirement dropped down to only eight units per day. As he continued the vegetarian eating plan at home, he was able to cut out all insulin shots after another eight weeks.[16]

Studies have shown that eating more plant-based whole food increases your dietary fiber intake. This can be extremely important to "protect from development of atherosclerotic cardiovascular disease, certain types of cancer, some gastrointestinal disorders, hypertension, obesity, and non-insulin-dependent dishes. Furthermore, increasing fiber intake provides therapeutic advantages for management of high blood lipids, certain gastrointestinal disorders, hypertension, obesity, and diabetes".[17]

Besides adopting a plant-based diet, diabetics can take six important dietary actions to regulate their blood sugar and support their health:

1. chromium,
2. cinnamon,
3. Omega 3 fatty acids,
4. Vitamin D,
5. zinc, and
6. unrefined, mineral-rich sea salt.

The mineral **chromium** helps transport glucose from the blood to the muscles. According to the National Institutes of Health, "Chromium is known to enhance the action of insulin, a hormone critical to the metabolism and storage of carbohydrates, fat, and protein in the body."[18] People who eat non-organic foods have a greater likelihood of being deficient in this important trace mineral. The chemical fertilizers used in industrial farming destroy chromium that would naturally be in the soil. This is one of many reasons organic food is always the best choice at the grocery store.

Chromium supplements should have GTF (Glucose Tolerance Factor) on the label. It should say, "Chromium GTF". Avoid synthetic supplements that don't list whole, organic foods as the ingredients.

Cinnamon is emerging as a true wonder food. Research shows that cinnamon can help lower blood sugar, cholesterol, and triglyceride levels in people with Type 2 diabetes. Cinnamon contains antioxidants that create healthier arteries and reduce the risk of cardiovascular disease. Cinnamon can also benefit us with increased alertness and energized senses. Even a teaspoon a day helps tame blood sugar levels.

Ceylon cinnamon is the best cinnamon to use. Cassia, Saigon, and Chinese cinnamon contain five percent coumarin, which is problematic for the liver. Ceylon cinnamon has only .0004 percent coumarin. Sprinkle it on your morning toast, oatmeal, or other dishes.

Omega 3 fatty acids are healthy fats our bodies cannot make and must obtain from food. Studies show that adding Omega 3 to your diet promotes healthy blood sugar levels. Try adding cold-pressed, organic flax or hemp seed oil to your smoothies and other foods, like oatmeal chia seed pudding in the morning.

Vitamin D (known as the sunshine vitamin) is a prohormone; that is, a fat-soluble vitamin. It is in a family of compounds that includes vitamins D-1, D-2, and D-3. These vitamins can affect as many as 2,000 genes in the body.

Johns Hopkins University School of Medicine studied the medical information of 124 subjects between the ages of 36 and 89 with Type 2 diabetes. Those with the lowest levels of vitamin D had the highest levels of blood sugar. Only six percent of the subjects were taking a vitamin D supplement. You may need to address a possible vitamin D deficiency. I supplement my vitamin D intake with a whole-food, organic, raw multi-vitamin.

Zinc is one of the most important minerals used by the body. It helps with the production of approximately 100 enzymes. Zinc contributes to building up the immune system. Zinc is required for protein and DNA synthesis, insulin activity, and liver function.

Zinc is not really stored in our bodies, so we need a regular supply. Men need about one-third more zinc than women, because the prostate gland and semen are highly concentrated with zinc. A zinc deficiency may appear as skin problems, impairment of taste, a poor immune system, hair loss, diarrhea, fatigue, wounds not healing properly, or a poor or slow growth rate for infants.

Even if you eat zinc-rich foods, you may need a supplement, because phytic acid and dietary fiber in certain foods can inhibit the absorption of zinc. If you take a vitamin supplement of any kind (such as a multi-vitamin, vitamin D, chromium, or zinc), make sure it is in a natural form, not a synthetic one. Synthetic forms of any nutrient can be harmful to the body[19]. Instead, buy dietary supplements that show whole, organic foods in their ingredient list.

Unrefined sea salt promotes the proper balance for the endocrine, adrenal, and thyroid glands to function properly. It supports healthy blood pressure, detoxifies the body, and—along with water—is necessary for the optimal functioning of the immune system, hormonal system, and cardiovascular health.[20]

Dr. David Brownstein says low-salt diets "promote toxicity" and have:

> ...adverse effects on numerous metabolic markers, including promoting elevated insulin levels and insulin resistance. Low-salt diets have been associated with elevating normal cholesterol and LDL cholesterol levels, which in turn, have been associated with cardiovascular disease. Finally, low-salt diets will lead to mineral deficiencies and the development of chronic disease.[21]

In conclusion, you can see diet is a huge factor in curing or managing diabetes and preventing so many diseases that diabetes often leads to: blindness, amputation, stroke, and heart disease. It can prevent having to take insulin injections for the rest of your life.

It's a personal decision that no one can make for you. I always feel it is so powerful when someone finally decides to take control of their health and well-being and choose to make the necessary changes. It all starts with making that decision and taking action to execute it.

"Eating one quarter pound of beef raises the insulin levels in diabetics as much as a quarter pound of straight sugar."

—*Diabetes Care 7, 1984; p. 465*

2

Getting Started

Choosing Plant-Based Foods for Optimum Health

The human body was not designed for consuming meat. We don't have the correct teeth for tearing. Our saliva isn't as acidic as carnivores. Our digestive juices are not acidic or strong enough to break down meat well on an ongoing basis.

Because our intestinal tract is long and curvy, undigested meat can stay in the intestine too long. It can putrefy and rot in the intestines, allowing toxins and acid to build up. This creates inflammation and disease.

Studies show that people on healthy vegetarian diets have lower risks of:

- Heart disease.
- Colorectal, ovarian, and breast cancers.
- Diabetes.
- Obesity.
- Hypertension (high blood pressure).[22]

Dr. Caldwell B. Esselstyn, Jr., former president of the medical staff at the Cleveland Clinic, writes that you can reverse heart disease with no drugs and only a plant-based diet. He bases this conclusion on the groundbreaking results of his 20-year nutritional study. Backed by solid scientific evidence, he argues that we can end the heart disease epidemic simply by changing what we eat. Dr. Esselstyn recommends a plant-based, oil-free diet that he says can prevent heart disease, stop its progress, and even reverse its effects.[23]

The late Walter Kempner, MD, founded the Rice Diet. He advocated a diet of rice, fruit, and vegetables on the basis that it has the power to do miraculous things for people and help them gain back their health. He treated hundreds of people at Duke University where he prescribed a diet of rice, vegetables, and fruit that reversed hypertension, diabetic eye changes, heart failure, kidney failure, and obesity.[24]

Dr. T. Colin Campbell, PhD, professor emeritus at Cornell University and co-author of *The China Study*, the most comprehensive human nutrition study to date, advocates a plant-based diet for optimum health. I was fortunate to be part of Dr. Campbell's class at Cornell University, where he told us:

> Plant-based eating is a superior way of eating. Benefits of eating this way: Live longer, look and feel younger, have more energy, lose weight, lower blood cholesterol, prevent and even reverse heart disease, lower your risk of prostate, breast and other cancers, preserve your eyesight in your later years, prevent and treat diabetes, avoid surgery, vastly decrease need for pharmaceutical drugs, keep bones strong, avoid impotence, avoid stroke, prevent kidney stones, keep your unborn baby from getting Type 2 diabetes, alleviate constipation, lower your blood pressure, avoid Alzheimer's, beat arthritis and more.

Dr. Campbell discussed studies he had done on the diseases that arise in populations when meat protein is introduced into the diet. He continued:

> My early research gave me the understanding that animal protein, when tested experimentally, was substantially different from plant protein in its ability to promote tumor development. It turned out that animal protein had its effect by operating through a constellation of integrative mechanisms. The division between animal and plant foods was a signpost of a division of the kinds of foods having an effect on cancer.[25]

In Dr. Campbell's class on plant-based nutrition, I learned of many studies that prove it is possible to be healthy or overcome illness on a plant-based diet. Recently, one study conducted by a team of American and Japanese researchers showed that people who have diabetes can vastly improve their health by eating an entirely plant-based diet.[26] More than 100 million people today have diabetes or pre-diabetes.

The researchers also undertook a new meta-analysis—which is considered the highest level of scientific evidence—in which they compared six significant prior research studies. The researchers found a plant-based diet significantly improved blood sugar control in Type 2 diabetes, and specifically in a key indicator of blood sugar control called hemoglobin A1c. The participants' results improved as much as 1.2 points, which was greater than the effect of typical oral diabetes medicines.[27]

The study also combined the results of all of the available studies. It indicated the benefits of excluding dairy (including cheese), eggs, and meat from the diet was as much as 0.7 points in some studies, averaging 0.4 points overall. The participants in most of these studies were not required to reduce their calorie or carbohydrate consumption.

The study's findings agree with my experience. Working with people who have diabetes, I have found they show remarkable improvement in their health and well-being from consuming a plant-based and almost completely raw food diet.

I've learned everyone needs to find the diet that works best for them, and find balance in their life. I also know that the quality of the food we eat is vital. An organic, plant-based diet can benefit your health, and even heal your body.

The 10 Keys to Healthy Eating

Now that we know a vegetarian diet can reverse diabetes, as well as heart disease and cancer, let's look at the various aspects of how to eat a healthy vegetarian diet. It can be quite easy to get all the nutrients you need if you just know what nutrients your body requires and where to get them. You can also feel full, satisfied, and more energetic on this eating plan, if you are eating the right quality foods. A healthy vegetarian diet is straightforward if you follow these 10 basic principles.

1. Eat high-quality, nutrient-dense foods. The body becomes much cleaner and more vibrant if it is getting the best variety of nutrients. The body also becomes more aware of problems. Your taste buds become cleaner and more discerning.

Many people just need to add some nutrient-dense, concentrated food to their diet to feel satisfied on a deep cellular level. The lack of nutrients in our food may be because soils have become depleted and food just isn't as nutrient-dense as it was a hundred years ago. Studies have shown a decrease of anywhere from 40–80 percent of nutrients in food today, as compared to food in 1914.[28] [29] Everyone should eat nutrient-dense foods with more minerals, and fermented probiotic-rich foods.

Nourishing our bodies should be a major reason we eat food in the first place. What we consume becomes our blood, cells, skin, and hair. Our well-being depends on the quality of our food.

2. Eat organic and non-GMO foods. Because what we eat becomes our blood and cells, I recommend buying organic whenever possible. If we eat foods that have poisons on them, or put into them by genetically modifying seeds, then we ingest poison.

Moreover, the chemical fertilizers used on GMO and non-organic foods destroy many vital nutrients in the soil which therefore do not make it into our food. These nutrients are necessary to our body's health and well-being.

3. Avoid processed foods. Choose unprocessed foods so you aren't ingesting MSG, potassium bromate, aspartame, wood pulp, artificial dyes, chemicals, and other additives the FDA allows in food. Many of us grew up thinking additives are normal to ingest, but our bodies were not made to assimilate chemicals and preservatives.

Whole, real food that has been grown, harvested, and stored in a safe and healthy way is what we are meant to have as nourishment for our body. Most processed, refined foods have had the fiber and nutrients removed, leaving these foods empty of the very elements we need for optimum health.

4. Eat more raw, whole foods. Eating organic, live, fresh, vine-ripened or tree-ripened whole food can feed the body on deeper cellular level than cooked or processed foods. Foods ripened on the vine or tree have salvestrols in them that have cancer-fighting properties.

Organic, unprocessed foods have nutrients like sulfur and chromium in them. These natural nutrients are critical to having a healthy body. Cooking, storing, or processing whole, raw foods can destroy some of the vital nutrients in them.

5. Eat a varied diet. Because our bodies can become allergic to anything we consume too frequently (no matter how healthy it is), avoid eating any ingredient every day. Avoid eating any one particular food every day on a continual basis. I recommend eating a variety of fresh seasonal vegetables and fruits regularly.

6. Eat whole, sprouted and gluten-free grains. When eating pasta, bread, crackers, and chips, consume only whole, sprouted grains. Avoid corn and wheat, especially genetically modified varieties. If you want to lose weight, cut out corn and wheat. Gluten-free and sprouted grains are preferable.

7. Cut out sugar or consume as little as possible. Do not use fake sugar substitutes in any way, shape, or form. Stevia, dates, xylitol, pure organic maple syrup, and pure unfiltered raw organic honey are my top choices for sweeteners, if you choose to use any at all.

8. Make sure you are not low in any nutrients. Be certain to get enough protein each day, and a *variety* of proteins, so you get the right amino acid complex combinations. Ensure that all of the B vitamins, especially B12, are in your diet and absorbed well. Iodine, iron, calcium, zinc, Vitamin D, sulfur, chromium, and magnesium are all important nutrients and should not be overlooked.

9. Consume only good fats like pure, organic, extra-virgin coconut oil or pure, high-quality extra-virgin olive oil. Make sure you get enough of the essential fatty acids—Omega 3, in particular, every day. Avoid all trans fats and vegetable oils with cottonseed oil or canola oil in them.

10. Chew food thoroughly to aid digestion and avoid drinking beverages, particularly cold beverages, when having your meal. Avoid drinking beverages with your meals, because they water down and dilute your digestive juices. Beverages water down digestive juices, making the digestive juices diluted. This makes it harder for the body to digest the food you are consuming.

Food List for Healing

This is my basic list for transforming your life through food and hydrating liquids. I've included brief notes about the foods, methods of preparing them, and what cookware you need.

These are the most important foods for transitioning to a healthy lifestyle or healing your body from diabetes and other diseases. When you are well and have reversed your diabetes, keep these foods and beverages as a major part of your daily eating plan to maintain your health.

Reversing disease involves eating high-quality, nutrient-dense vegetables, fruits, herbs, teas, mushrooms, roots, and salts in their whole, organic, fresh form. I will expand on these foods and beverages throughout the book with more details and delicious recipes.

Many of the foods in this list are prebiotics. Prebiotics are a type of un-digestible plant fiber. Prebiotics are food for the probiotics, which are bacteria that support the immune system. The more prebiotics the probiotics have to eat, the more efficiently these live bacteria work—and the healthier your immune system and your intestinal tract will be.

All the foods should be **organically grown**. No canned, processed, microwaved, or fast foods of any kind. All food should be fresh, whole and organic. The anti-oxidant is in the color. Eat a rainbow of colors every day!

Eighty percent of the foods should be **raw, uncooked, fresh organic foods**. All fresh, organically grown, vine-ripened vegetables are a basis for this healing diet. The antioxidant is in the color pigment; so you want to always buy the most **colorful, dark, organic food** possible.

Eat lots of **fresh, baby, leafy greens and sprouts**. The baby greens will be much easier to digest and have even more nutrients.

You can have **some raw beets and raw squash**, a time or two a week on a limited basis.

Fresh juices should optimally be consumed within 20 minutes of juicing. Note: I suggest adding some of the pulp back into the juice before drinking. This will provide some fiber to the drink. You would do this in order to slow down the sugars from going into the blood stream too quickly.

Cucumbers are especially good because they contain a "hormone needed by the beta cells of the pancreas to produce insulin. The enzyme crepsin in cucumbers is targeted toward breaking down excessive protein in the kidneys."[30] Cucumbers have an amazing amount of nutrients in them. They can be used extensively in the healing diet.

Celery has a calming effect on the nervous system. It is full of electrolytes. Celery is highly alkalizing. It is a good vegetable to use in juicing, soups or other recipes.

Dandelion greens are particularly beneficial for overall health. Dandelion greens are packed with nutrients, including Vitamin K (one-cup serving of raw dandelion greens provides you with 535 percent of your recommended daily value of Vitamin K), Vitamin A, calcium and iron. They are particularly supportive of the liver. Dandelion greens are easy to grow in your own garden or yard. Keep them organic and avoid using any weed killer on them!

Onions and garlic are natural probiotics. These two foods also contain extremely potent organosulfur compounds that offer a lot of benefit to those who eat them. An enormous amount of flavonoids (the largest nutrient family known to scientists) is concentrated in the onion's outer layers. Maximize your health benefits by peeling off as little as possible. Just remove the paper layer, if you can. As an example, a red onion can lose about 20 percent of its quercetin (a flavonoid) and almost 75 percent of its anthocyanins (a flavonoid), if it is "overpeeled".

When onions are simmered in a soup, the flavonoids (quercetin) do not degrade. It simply gets transferred into the water part of the soup. These flavonoids have high antioxidant and anti-inflammatory properties. Use onions in your recipes frequently for the health benefits.

Raw garlic is loaded with nutrients such as manganese, Vitamin B6, Vitamin C, and selenium.

Garlic may help improve your iron metabolism. That's because the diallyl sulfides in garlic can help increase production of a protein called ferroportin. (Ferroportin is a protein that runs across the cell membrane, and it forms a passageway that allows stored iron to leave the cells and become available where it is needed.)[31]

Research is showing that consuming garlic can help to regulate the number of fat cells that get formed in the body, and that it has anti-inflammatory properties.[32]

Cooking garlic is completely fine, but garlic is fragile and should only be cooked very lightly, because cooking destroys garlic's active ingredient: allicin. Allicin is one of the sulfur-containing compounds found in garlic. But, the allicin gets deactivated by heat. So, if you want the full potency of this healing food, then avoid cooking it, or add it at the end after you have removed the food from the heat.

If you want maximum healing benefits from the allicin, then crush the garlic and wait 10 minutes before consuming it. This enhances the formation of allicin, which activates the garlic's healing properties.

You can add raw garlic to your diet by putting it in hummus, vegetable stir-fries, and salsas.

High-protein beans, peas, lentils and legumes. Dark Beans and lentils: kidney beans, small French lentils, red beans, pinto, black beans, garbanzo beans, and green beans all have amazing high protein and fiber content, which is incredibly healthy, filling, and great for digestion and supporting the probiotics of the immune system.

All peas, beans, lentils, and legumes have a high phytic acid content and should be soaked overnight, or for 2-3 days if they are large, to sprout them. I put the necessary steps in the recipes in my cookbooks: *Raising Healthy Children* and *How to Be a Healthy Vegetarian*.

Raising Healthy Children:
http://myBook.to/childrenbook

How to Be a Healthy Vegetarian
http://myBook.to/vegetarianbook

Then, drain off the water they were soaking in and put them in fresh water before they are used in a recipe or cooked. This helps them become more digestible and removes the enzyme inhibitors.

Non-sweet fruits. Fruits are considered edible parts of plants that contain the seeds and pulpy surrounding tissue: **lemons, limes, grapefruit, tomatoes, red pepper, and avocado**.

Warning about Grapefruit and Medication.

Be mindful that some medications are affected by grapefruit and can be deadly, so make sure you know what interactions your medications may have, if you are taking any pharmaceutical drugs.

Some **unsweetened, organic berries** are good to eat. Blueberries, raspberries, tart cherries, cranberries, pomegranate, huckleberry, and goji berries in their whole form (not processed or juiced) are very healing foods.

Fats and oils. The essential fatty acids in flax, hemp, and chia seed oils support brain health and give you energy. They need to be a part of the healthy diet, because our body doesn't make them. We need to get them from a food source.

Omega 3 fatty acids are anti-inflammatory and protect against heart disease, strokes, and clots in the lungs. They provide anti-carcinogenic activity against tumors.

Oils (except coconut oil) should be kept refrigerated, because they are fragile and can become rancid if not stored properly.

If using an oil for sautéing or cooking, only use coconut oil that is meant to handle heat. Use coconut oil for greasing pans and coating parchment paper for lining pans.

Sprouted, organic, raw nuts and seeds. Pine nuts (from Europe only, not from China, Mexico, etc.), walnuts, sunflower seeds, pecans, pumpkin seeds, sesame seeds, hemp seeds, and chia seeds are all good choices.

Super algae foods. Klamath Lake blue-green algae, spirulina, chlorella, and raw, organic, green food powder. Spirulina is a super food. It contains "gamma linolenic acid (GLA)".[33]

Chlorella and spirulina are "two of the most nutrient dense foods known and easily qualify as whole, perfect super foods. They have a balanced complement of protein (60 percent), carbohydrate (19 percent), fat (6 percent) bio available minerals (8 percent) and moisture (7 Percent)."[34] They are an excellent source of high-protein vegan food.

Sweeteners. Stevia, cardamom, raw unrefined, unprocessed honey (limited basis) and cinnamon.

Milks. Non-dairy milks are recommended. Unsweetened, vanilla hemp, sprouted seed or nut or coconut milk. You can sweeten non-dairy milks with stevia, but only on a limited basis. Stevia is a plant from South America. This sweetener comes in an array of choices. Make sure to read the ingredients. Some have preservatives in them. One of them has grapefruit seed extract in it. Make sure it doesn't have anything in it that does not go well with medications.

Electrolytes/Unrefined Sea Salt. Electrolyte is simply a fancy medical term for "salt." We cannot be healthy or even survive without the minerals in unrefined sea salt.

Whole, unrefined, mineral-rich sea salt is very different from white, refined salt which has had the minerals taken out of it. **White, refined, processed salt is NOT a part of this healthy eating plan. Avoid it completely.** Processed, fast, and low-fat foods are usually loaded with the salt you want to avoid.

I recommend mined salts because they come from old, mineral-rich oceans that were around before pollution and before the world became so depleted in nutrients. Here are some brands of mined salts I like: Bolivian Rose Salt (has some natural iodine content), Real Salt (mined in Utah), and Himalayan Salt. Always look for the mineral content on the label. *See the section on Salt in Chapter 7 for more information.*

Spices. Ceylon cinnamon, mesquite, and turmeric.

Condiments. Cacao and carob.

Spreads. Organic ghee, raw, organic sprouted nut or seed butter, avocado, and organic hummus.

Sprouted grains or seeds once or twice a week on a limited basis. Quinoa, oats, buckwheat, millet, spelt and amaranth.

Raw, sprouted, organic, unsweetened **granola** is fine once in a while. Some whole grain, sprouted, unsweetened **rice** is alright once a week.

Fermented and cultured food. Organic apple cider vinegar, organic miso, raw, organic, pure sauerkraut and probiotic drinks like low sugar kombucha.

Hydration is important for optimum health. Drink room-temperature, purified, well, spring, or mineral water with a pinch of sea salt. Green teas, tulsi tea, ginger tea, herb or approved fruit or vegetable-infused waters, and pure organic coconut water are all good beverages. If you must sweeten, use the approved sweeteners from this list.

Protein powders. Organic, raw, hemp; organic, raw, sprouted grains, lentils, peas, beans, and legumes. (Garden of Life is a plant-based protein powder I use.) I discuss this subject in greater depth in the chapter on protein.

Raw, organic green food (baby leafy greens, sprouts, and grasses) powder supplements. Raw (living) and organic are your best choices.

Take **digestive enzymes** that are organic and raw.

Make sure to have a whole-food, organic, raw **vitamin** which includes Vitamin A, B complex, C, D, E, magnesium, iodine, chromium GTF, and zinc.

Cookware. Do not use aluminum cookware or foil. Do not use non-stick cookware. Use only glass; steel or non-lead ceramic cookware.

No-Nos!

Never use a microwave. It destroys the cellular nature of the food, water, and nutrients.

Do not use anything from a can. Most cans are lined with hormone-disrupting plastic. Glass is a better choice.

Avoid processed meats completely. Along with added refined salt (high-concentrated sodium), they have added sugar (usually in the form of fructose or high-fructose corn syrup) to make them palatable. Researchers at Harvard found that consuming processed meat is associated with a 42 percent higher risk of heart disease and a 19 percent higher risk of Type 2 diabetes as compared to people consuming unprocessed meats.[35]

Do not eat anything with "natural flavorings", soy, whey, corn, wheat, dairy, peas, potatoes, beef, meats, chicken, fish, fructose of any kind, artificial sweeteners of any kind, and sugar.

No soda, coffee, alcohol, hydrogenated oil, white refined flour, white refined sugar, and white refined table salt of any kind.

The human body is approximately 2/3 water.

The brain is about 85 percent water.

About 75 percent of Americans are chronically dehydrated.

Water

Water is the elixir of life! It is a key ingredient to our health and well-being because our bodies are 66–72% water. Blood uses water to transport oxygen, nutrients, and antibodies to all parts of the body. Many illnesses are actually a result of dehydration, so it is important to maintain an adequate intake of water throughout the day. By the time you feel thirsty, you are already dehydrated.

I always drink a glass of pure mineralized water as soon as I wake in the morning. When you wake up, your body is empty, so it will absorb whatever you ingest like a sponge. Therefore, a glass of high-quality, mineral-rich water will be utilized most efficiently upon awakening. Avoid drinking water with meals because it can dilute the digestive enzyme juices, making it harder to digest food. It is best to drink water between meals, not during meals.

Dr. Fereydoon Batmanghelidj, MD, studied water while he was a prisoner in an Iranian jail. Using water and a little sea salt, he treated and cured approximately 3,000 prisoners suffering from what he called chronic intracellular dehydration. He found that most people are sick because of dehydration. He wrote many books on the subject after his release. The "water cure" he prescribed is:

1. **Sufficient water.** Drink an ounce of water for every two pounds of body weight daily. This means that someone weighing 200 pounds should drink 100 ounces of water a day. This is in addition to any other beverages. Consume water the first thing upon getting up in the morning, and then drink it all day long on a continual basis every two hours.

2. Sea salt. Put 1/8 teaspoon of sea salt on the tongue with every 16 ounces of water.

The unrefined sea salt is a key component in the "water cure." This is really important for people suffering from allergies or asthma; the salt acts like an antihistamine.

The Dangers of Chemical Contaminants.

Be mindful of the source of the water you drink, bathe, and swim in. Almost all public water supplies have chemicals added, including chlorine and sodium fluoride—both of which are poisons.

Chlorine was the first poison developed for warfare. It destroys Vitamin E in the body and the good probiotics in the intestines. "Industrial chemist J.P. Bercz, PhD, showed in 1992 that chlorinated water alters and destroys unsaturated essential fatty acids (EFAs), the building blocks of people's brains and central nervous systems."[36]

Our skin is our largest organ. While showering or swimming in chlorinated water, chlorine is absorbed directly into the skin and enters the blood stream in the same way we absorb medication delivered by a skin patch. Research that links swimming in chlorinated pools to medical conditions continues to make headlines. Studies indicate, among other things, that swimming in chlorinated water may increase the risk of developing cancer and may damage the lungs.[37]

Sodium fluoride is a byproduct of the manufacture of aluminum and fertilizers, and can be contaminated with lead and arsenic. It is commonly added by governments to our municipal water supply on the pretext that it is good for our teeth and health, but the dental studies upon which this practice is based were done using calcium fluoride, not sodium fluoride.

Fluoride has been used in Chinese medicine as a tranquilizer, and also in many places as a rat poison. The chemically derived fluorides added to our water are completely different from naturally occurring fluoride. According to Dr. Paul Connett, PhD:

> Fluoride is a cumulative poison. On average, only 50 percent of the fluoride we ingest each day is excreted through the kidneys. The remainder accumulates in our bones, pineal gland, and other tissues. If the kidney is damaged, fluoride accumulation will increase, and with it, the likelihood of harm.[38]

Fluoride affects the thyroid gland and all of our enzymatic systems. Side effects from fluoride ingestion include weight problems, damage to the immune system, and other serious disorders. Fluoride affects people of different ages differently. According to Dr. Connett:

> The level of fluoride put into water (1 ppm) is up to 200 times higher than normally found in mothers' milk (0.005–0.01 ppm) (Ekstrand, 1981; Institute of Medicine, 1997). There are no benefits, only risks, for infants ingesting this heightened level of fluoride at such an early age. (This is an age where susceptibility to environmental toxins is particularly high.)[39]

I learned recently about a study from 2001 on fluoride and osteosarcoma, which was a critical study in the form of Dr. Elise Bassin's PhD dissertation at Harvard University. It found a strong, statistically significant relationship between "fluoride exposure during the sixth through eighth years of life (the 'mid-childhood growth spurt') and the later development of osteosarcoma among young males."[40]

Dr. Bassin's thesis was extremely well-researched and detailed, with accurate assessments of her subjects and the content of their drinking water. Her work detected a direct association with fluoride and osteosarcoma. Her work and her findings show:

> Bone is the principal site for fluoride accumulation within the body, and the rate of accumulation is elevated during the periods of bone development. Thus, the cells in the bone, particularly during the growth spurts, may be exposed to some of the highest fluoride concentrations in the body.[41]

Her study shows that fluoride is toxic and carcinogenic. Osteosarcoma, a rare form of cancer, appears in young men in their late teens and early twenties. Her research and her findings have never been disproven.

I then looked back at where fluoride was first introduced as the way to prevent tooth decay, and at the study used to promote it. It was a study done in the cities of Newburgh and Kingston, NY, which are 40 miles apart. However, a 1995 review of tooth decay in these communities found:

> After 10 years of the trial (which was methodologically flawed), it looked as if there was a large decrease in dental cavities in the fluoridated community, compared to the non-fluoridated community. However, when children were re-examined in these two cities in 1995 (50 years after the trial began), there was practically no difference in the dental decay in the two communities. If anything, the teeth in the non-fluoridated Kingston were slightly *better*.[42]

It looks like to me like there was a study, with no long-term effect yet in place, promoting the use of fluoride in our water to provide better dental health. Yet as long-term studies were done, they found that was actually not the case. It did not help with dental health; in fact, adding this toxic chemical to the water supply was found to cause many other health problems. It was added in a way that was not regulated in dosage or concentration, thus causing a cumulative effect in people's bodies.

Then, consider the numerous studies done by leading dental researchers showing results that the mechanisms of fluoride's benefits were mainly "topical not systemic," meaning that fluoride worked some when they put it on teeth topically. It didn't work when ingested.[43]

Studies show that dental decay has been *declining* in every country at about the same rate, even since before fluoride was introduced. Decay rates are still declining, whether the countries have fluoride or not. [44, 45] Is it because the toothbrush was introduced? Maybe our hygiene has just improved over the last decade.

What I realize from my research is that ingested fluoride can cause severe health problems, including and not limited to thyroid health problems,[46 , 47,48] brittle bones,[49] and cancer.[50,51] Sweden, Denmark, Holland, Germany, Belgium, Norway, and France do not put fluoride in their water. Some of these countries have made it illegal to add it to the water supply.

Huge numbers of Safe Drinking Water Act violations are reported each year by water treatment facilities. Many areas have old, dirty water pipes, and some even have really old lead pipes. *New Scientist* reported that a comprehensive survey of US drinking water showed it contained an array of hormonally active chemicals like MTBE (methyl tertiary butyl ether)—a chemical found in fuel, and a potential human carcinogen in high doses—and atrazine, a US pesticide that was banned in the European Union. Atrazine has been linked to reproductive problems in lab animals and is also linked to both breast cancer and prostate cancer.

In 2010, *National Geographic* reported that drinking water in schools in 27 states was contaminated with toxic substances, including lead.[52] In 2009, the Associated Press analyzed data from the EPA and found the public water for approximately 100 school districts contained lead, pesticides, and other toxins.[53] If they are being pumped into schools, then they are probably being pumped into homes and businesses as well.

So, what do we do? We need to drink water. What is the best choice? Reverse osmosis is a very good method for filtering water, but it takes everything out—even the good minerals you need—and it makes the water very acidic. Your body will pull minerals from your bones, muscles, and body fluids to combat the buildup of these waste acids and to process the water if the water is void of minerals.

Natural spring water, well water, or fresh water sources contain minerals and nutrients, so they are good options. When drinking purified bottled water, you can add some minerals, like a pinch of sea salt. When you do this, your body won't need to pull minerals from itself to process the water.

The Problems with Plastic.

Bottled water is what most people choose a good deal of the time, but is that a great choice? Here are eight things you should know about bottled water.

1. The EPA standards of the Clean Water Act do not apply to bottled water. There is very little regulation on bottled water, which is why I recommend having your own filter. The labels on bottled water often show springs with clear fresh water. But 25–45% of the bottled water is actually just TAP WATER! Not only that, but tap water is at least regulated and tested hundreds of times a month. The bottled water is only required to be tested once a week.

Some independent tests by the EWG (Environmental Working Group, a non-profit independent analysis company) of 10 major brands of bottled water have shown 38 pollutants, including disinfection byproducts, fertilizer residue, and pain medication.[54]

Two of the 10 brands tested, Walmart's and Giant's store brands, bore the chemical signature of standard municipal water treatment—a cocktail of chlorine disinfection byproducts, and for Giant water, even fluoride. In other words, this bottled water was chemically indistinguishable from tap water.[55]

2. Bottled water is environmentally harmful from a community standpoint and a landfill standpoint. I'm from Texas, and Ozarka is draining many of the underground aquifers that the communities and farmers depend on for their water. Another major brand, FIJI Water, is draining the Fiji Islands' aquifer. The company has a 99-year lease and almost exclusive access to a major 17-mile aquifer on the island.

The Fiji citizens are deprived of access to this aquifer. Today they suffer from drought, crumbling pipes, and antiquated water treatment plants, but access to what should really be *their* water is denied them. Ironically, tests conducted by the Cleveland water department on FIJI water found that it contained much more arsenic and other contaminants than Cleveland tap water.[56]

3. Store water in glass or stainless steel containers, not plastic.
The potentially hazardous chemical BPA is found in many plastic
containers. BPA is a hormone disrupter. Studies have concluded
that hormone-altering chemicals are damaging, even in very small
doses. Scientific studies have linked BPA to asthma, cancer,
infertility, low sperm count, heart disease, liver problems, early-
onset diabetes, early puberty, and ADHD.[57] It can leach into water
for various reasons, including when a water-filled plastic container
heats up—especially if it is left sitting in a hot car.

Some would say to only use plastic containers marked with #2,
#4, or #5 on the bottom, because they are supposedly safer. But
really, thousands of chemical additives are added to plastics.
Additives called "plasticizers" are used to soften plastic. PVC, one
of the "plasticizers," contains phthalates, which are known to
disrupt the endocrine system.[58] Phthalate chemicals have also
been found to be carcinogenic.[59]

Studies have found that when plastics are heated, by leaving
them in a hot car or washing them in a dishwasher, this increases
the leaching of chemicals. Bottled water often travels many miles
and through many climates, so the chance of it getting heated up
at some point in its journey is very real.

4. Plastic pollution is a worldwide crisis. It's a problem
worldwide, but the plastic pollution in oceans is massive. I was
secretary of the Earth Society affiliated with the UN, and I
volunteer with a non-profit trying to restore life and natural
balance to the sea grasses and sea life off the Texas coast. What
I've learned is really shocking.

New research published in *PLOS One* estimates "more than five
trillion pieces of plastic, collectively weighing nearly 269,000
tonnes, are floating in the world's oceans, causing damage
throughout the food chain".[60] There is an island of plastic in the
Pacific Ocean that is as large as the state of Texas.[61] Water bottles
are a large part of the plastic pollution. The US alone will discard,
on average, 38 billion water bottles a year.

5. More than a million marine species are killed every year due to plastic pollution. Getting caught in plastic litter is a major cause of death of seabirds, sea turtles, seals and other marine mammals. Plastic ingested by sea life cause excruciating deaths. We all suffer as a result of this. And if you eat fish because you think it will be good for your health, remember you are ingesting whatever the fish have ingested as well.

6. Plastic manufacturing, which uses petroleum or natural gas, requires a huge amount of energy and resources. More than 17 million barrels of oil are required to produce the water bottles in the US alone.

7. Manufacturing water bottles causes air pollution. Phthalates, the chemicals used to make some plastics soft, are toxic and are constantly releasing their toxicity into our air and environment, everywhere they are.

8. 80% of water bottles are not recycled. Most of them end up on beaches and roadways, and in streams.

Reverse Osmosis for Your Home.

If you want to continue to drink water, but you don't want to use plastic water bottles, what do you do? You can't drink the tap water. We've already become aware of the pollutants in that. So, I recommend using a water filter in your home, and filling your own glass or steel water bottle. This will cut down on the plastic-infused water and the huge amount of pollution the plastic water bottles cause.

There are many options for home water filters, ranging from carbon to reverse osmosis to home distillers. People ask me about the less expensive pitchers with the carbon filters. Many don't remove enough of the contaminants, and most are unable to remove fluoride.

Reverse osmosis systems produce extremely pure water, and they can be an excellent solution. But, they have always needed to be installed under the sink, and they can cost hundreds or thousands of dollars depending on the size you want. Then, buying new filters for them can be a major cost each year as well.

I've been researching water filtration systems for the home for over 30 years. But recently, I learned about a brand new countertop reverse osmosis unit that is very affordable, requires no installation fees, and has minimal maintenance costs. This unit is called the AquaTru. It is a high-quality, affordable filter that can be a fantastic solution for someone who wants safe, delicious, environmentally conscious water for their family.

The AquaTru is a countertop unit that takes only a few minutes to set up. It's easily movable, and it doesn't require any plumbing. It utilizes a patented four-stage process that removes chlorine, salt and metal ions (including fluorides), VOC gasses, and many other contaminants. In fact, tests showed the AquaTru removed 128 contaminants.

The best part of all is probably the price. A quality reverse osmosis system can easily cost $650 or more, plus installation, and hundreds of dollars per year in maintenance costs. But this one sells for $349. Get yours today for your home and your family, at: https://www.aquatruwater.com?src=affiliate&aid=20873

A Unique Element.

Water is unique, and its quality and structure can directly influence our health and well-being. For example, Dr. Pollack at the University of Washington has been studying water for more than 10 years. He reported that when muscles are not functioning properly, it is the protein and water that are not functioning properly.[62]

According to Dr. Martin Chaplin of London South Bank University, "Water is not just H2O molecules. It contains a number of molecular species, including ortho and para water molecules, and water molecules with different isotopic compositions such as HDO and $H_2^{18}O$." Chaplin explains that these molecules are "part of weakly-bound but partially covalently linked molecular clusters containing one, two, three, or four hydrogen bonds, and hydrogen ion and hydrogen ion species".[63]

Because 66 percent or more of our body is made of water, it is a critical component of our health and well-being. Through the years, I have become fascinated with water and with attempting to make it as healthy and absorbable as possible.

Here are a few things I do to my water:

1. Add electrolytes (a medical term for salts) to purified water. Add 1/8 tsp. unrefined, mineral-rich sea salt to every 16 ounces of purified water.

2. Stir water in a circular motion with a spoon to create a vortex. Dr. Pollack's research showed this increased water structure. (I stir mine in a counter clockwise direction.)

3. Drink spring or well water containing natural minerals, especially naturally occurring sulfur.

4. Use drops of Crystal Energy to add patented mineral combinations to water, increasing the "wetness" of the water. Patrick Flanagan, MD, PhD developed them. You can order them at phisciences.com.

I recommend drinking electrolyte-rich, structured water for great health. If the study of water molecules and structure interests you, watch the movie *Water, the Great Mystery* and see Masaru Emoto's information and photographs at
http://www.masaru-emoto.net/english/water-crystal.html.

Masaru Emoto, who was born in Japan, is known for his studies showing that the environment of water directly affects its molecular structure. He exposed water to various words, pictures, or music, then froze it and photographed the molecular structure of the water crystals with microscopic photography.

Mr. Emoto claims the crystalline structure of water differs depending on the source of the water.[64] For instance, the crystals in a water sample taken from a pristine mountain spring are a different shape than those taken from polluted or tap water.

In one of his first experiments, he put water from the same exact source in identical plastic jugs, placed labels on them bearing positive and negative words and sayings, and left them overnight. The next morning, the molecular structure of the water in the jugs with negative sayings looked like pus.

On the other hand, the molecular structure of the water in the jugs with positive words attached—words like "love" and "gratitude"—looked absolutely beautiful, like snowflakes. The comparison was startling.

If positive and negative words are able to affect the molecular structure of water, what are the physical effects of positive and negative self-talk on people? How do the words we tell ourselves affect us due to the water in our body and the water around us in our life? Food for thought? Water for thought?

"Nothing will benefit human health and increase the chances for survival of life on Earth as much as the evolution to a vegetarian diet."

—Albert Einstein

3

Raw and Living Foods

W hen I was a child and I was eating food right off the tree, I just thought that was fresh food. But today that kind of fresh, whole food is called raw or living food. Raw and living food, has become quite a movement for many who want to heal their body and get away from the processed, unhealthy fast foods that are so prevalent in our society today.

What is raw and living food? Raw and living foods are foods that have not been heated over 105–118°F. It's basically eating food in its whole real form, without damaging the true nature and nutrition of the food. The enzymes in the food retain much higher nutrient levels in this form.

We need enzymes for digestion and nutrient absorption. Live enzymes in foods help us digest efficiently and completely. Remember, the key to health is a clean and nutrient-rich body.

Raw and living foods are the best form of foods for optimum health and wellness. These foods will feed the body on a deep, cellular level without stressing it as much as cooked food does. Cooked foods are dead. They don't supply any live enzymes.

When foods are devoid of living enzymes, it means the body has to work much harder and supply more of its own enzyme store to digest the foods. Pulling enzymes from storage and using them to digest enzyme-empty food makes the body work harder compared to eating foods that supply their own enzymes ready for digestion.

In addition, raw and living foods have more nutrients available for the body during digestion. One of the most vital nutrients is sulfur, which is often overlooked. Sulfur is critical to our body's metabolism, specifically the catalytic function of large numbers of enzymes. Without the proper levels of sulfur, our bodies aren't able to build good healthy cells, and this leads to illness.

Although sulfur is present in most organically grown fresh food, it is mostly found in fruits, vegetables, and some grains. Due to its unstable nature, the sulfur is quickly lost from food when it is processed, cooked, or stored. That's another reason having a diet high in freshly picked, raw, unprocessed, whole, organic food is vitally important.

Raw, living, unprocessed foods are also highly alkalizing. The body's pH (acidic balance) should ideally be 7.2–7.3. However, most people with chronic or acute diseases usually have overly acidic bodies with a pH well below 7.3. Eating foods that are highly alkalizing can help the body maintain a healthier pH.

What kinds of foods are found in a raw and living food diet? Uncooked (not heated over 105°F) and unprocessed fruits, vegetables, nuts, seeds, and grains make up this diet. Fruit is a pure form of food that digests quickly compared to other foods.

Many people have started eating raw foods to heal their bodies and be healthier. But be careful. If eating raw is taken to extremes, it can create an imbalance in the body and cause stress on the thyroid, spleen, and pancreas. Watch for foods such as spinach and Swiss chard that have oxalic acid. Oxalic acid can be hard on the body if taken in large amounts. More than that, it can prevent the body from absorbing other nutrients, like calcium. Consuming these types of greens in a micro greens or baby greens form will give you more nutrients and less or no oxalic acid.

What else can bring more balance to your body? Three things:
1. Eating a diet which varies the amount of raw food intake.
2. Eating with the seasons.
3. Eating lighter raw foods in the warmer months.

If you add warm foods to your diet in the cool months, this can be supportive to certain parts of the body. For instance, the thyroid is better supported when cruciferous vegetables such as broccoli and cauliflower are lightly steamed or sautéed instead of eaten raw. This is because these foods—as well as yams, Brussels sprouts, and cabbage—contain natural chemicals called goitrogens that can interfere with thyroid hormone synthesis. Lightly steaming or cooking these vegetables deactivates these chemicals. Adding foods like cooked whole, sprouted grain rice can work as a tonic for the spleen and pancreas.

A diet with a ratio of about 80 percent raw to 20 percent cooked food will work for most people throughout most of the year.

When I was breastfeeding, I noticed I made more milk when I was eating a lot of fresh greens. All the animals that make large amounts of milk eat fresh greens daily. So, it made sense to me to be a "grazer" if you are breastfeeding.

Enjoy your raw foods, but listen to your own body and be mindful of how they affect it. Your goal is to create balance in your health, your diet, and your life, too.

Enzymes in Living Foods

According to Merriam-Webster, an enzyme is "a chemical substance in animals and plants that helps to cause natural processes (such as digestion)."

Live enzymes, such as those in raw and living foods, regenerate our cells and feed our bodies. In *The Status of Food Enzymes in Digestion and Metabolism*, Dr. Edward Howell wrote:

Enzymes emerge as the true yardstick of vitality. Enzymes offer an important means of calculating the vital energy of an organism. That which has been referred to as vitality, vital force...probably is synonymous with that which has been known as enzyme activity.[65]

This opinion is equally shared by other prominent scholars, like Professor Moore of the University of Oxford in England, Professor Willstatter of Munich in Germany, and Dr. Northrop of the Rockefeller Institute for Medical Research.[66]

The more organic, living, whole foods we eat, the more ammunition and fuel our bodies have to nourish, heal, and purge ourselves of toxins we accumulate throughout the day. Food that hasn't been heated or processed over 105°F is living food. Heating and processing food destroys the live enzymes in it.

A Limited Supply.

Live enzymes in food play a crucial role in our health because we have a limited supply of digestive enzymes in our system. When we are young, we have a natural abundance of enzymes. By the time we are elderly, we have lost over half of our enzymes. Making new ones becomes more and more difficult, if not impossible.

Eating certain foods like meats, not properly chewing our food, exposure to pathogenic microbes, and **chewing gum** all make our body utilize more of our digestive enzymes and deplete the amount we have to use. Yes, **chewing gum** can make the body waste the precious digestive enzymes. So, my advice is to stop chewing gum or chewing on things that trick your body into making precious enzymes for digestion that you are not going to use.

According to Dr. Howell, our digestive system is only able to digest about half of the food we eat.[67] A raw apple that has not been irradiated (which destroys the enzymes) contains enough live enzymes to break down about 40–60 percent of the apple when it is consumed. Our body has to produce the enzymes or acid to complete the digestion process.

Cooked food, on the other hand, has no living enzymes in it to help the body digest it. Therefore, the body is forced to use its precious supply of digestive enzymes to break down the food and utilize the nutrients. This causes stress on the digestive system, the pancreas, and the immune system.

In his book *Enzyme Nutrition,* Dr. Howell said, "We know that decreased enzyme levels are found in a number of chronic ailments, such as allergies, skin disease, and even serious diseases like diabetes and other severe diseases."[68]

In his studies, Dr. Howell found that rats fed a raw, living food diet lived about 50 percent longer than rats that ate cooked food. His studies with people in a sanitarium led him to conclude it was "impossible to get people fat on raw foods... regardless of the calorie intake."[69] Along with that conclusion, Dr. Anthony Cheung, FRCP, noted:

Dr. Howell's use of food enzymes suggests that the supply of human enzymes is limited at birth. The faster we consume our enzymes, the shorter our life span will be. Raw food is a good source of food enzymes. Ingestion of raw food or enzyme supplements will lessen the work of our digestive system, so that more energy is reserved for other metabolic activities.[70]

In addition to Dr. Howell's studies, Dr. William S. Peavy, who has an MA in horticulture from the University of California and a PhD from Kansas State University, said:

"All of us have a limited capacity to produce enzymes, like the engine of a car that has a limited capacity to produce horsepower. And this capacity declines with age. It is this capacity which we are born with that determines our maximum potential life span. Some are born with a greater potential life span, and others less.

In any case, as we age, in general, our body is able to produce less and less enzymes. It is this general decline in enzyme activity in our body that is a fundamental cause of aging. When enzyme activity gets too low, the process of death occurs..."

Both doctors concur that we have limited enzymes; and when we use them up, we die. So, preserving them, supplementing them, and utilizing them in the best way possible is important for good health—especially as we age.

The Pottinger Cat Study.

Dr. Francis Pottinger performed an extensive, 10-year study of approximately 900 cats. He examined the effects of raw food versus cooked food on the health and well-being of two groups of cats. One group was fed a diet of raw meat and milk (which naturally contained live enzymes and probiotics), and the other group was given cooked meat and pasteurized milk (whose enzymes and probiotic nature had been destroyed with heat).

Dr. Pottinger found the cats eating raw food remained healthy and disease-free for generation after generation. But the cats on the cooked food diet started to get lazy and have degenerative diseases. The second generation of cats on the cooked food diet developed mid-life degenerative diseases. Cats in the third generation of the cooked-food diet developed diseases, blindness, shorter lifespans, and infertility.

Take a Good Digestive Enzyme Supplement.

Digestive enzymes are critical to our health because they enable us to digest our food more efficiently. If you take a digestive enzyme a few minutes before each meal and/or eat lots of fresh sprouts with every meal, it will help your body break down your food. Digestive enzymes are critical to our health because they

...help the digestive process to assimilate proteins, carbohydrates and fat... If we do not get enzymes with our daily food to aid our digestion, our body's digestive enzymes will carry the complete load, depleting the limited resources. Enzymes have a vital activity factor that is exhaustible, and our capacity to make enzymes is limited. It appears that the safest answer is to sprout all your intake of seeds and grains. In this process, the inhibitors are neutralized, and the life process commences with enzymes that are alive and active.[71]

Sprouts have large amounts of enzymes, which can contribute to the amount of enzymes in the stomach that can aid in the digestion process. Digestive enzyme supplements from whole food, (non-synthetic) ingredients can help as well.[72]

Slow Down and Chew Your Food.

The brain knows what enzymes to use in the stomach by what it detects being chewed in the mouth. This is why chewing gum is not a good idea. It tricks the mind into thinking we will be digesting food soon. It calls out the enzymes, and the precious supply of digestive enzymes is wasted. We will use up our enzymes this way. Slow down and really chew food. It will help your body produce the enzymes needed to digest it much more thoroughly.

Live enzymes are a key to staying healthy and youthful. We want to do everything we can to protect the ones we have, and supplement them when we can by eating foods with live enzymes and/or taking additional live enzyme supplements.

Probiotics and Our Immune System

More than 70 percent of our immune system is located in our digestive tract in the form of micro flora, or beneficial bacteria, which we now call **probiotics**. *Pro*biotics are mostly bacteria, which assist in the maintenance of the natural balance of microorganisms (micro flora) in the intestines. A normal, healthy human digestive tract has approximately 400 types of probiotic bacteria.

Friendly bacteria (micro flora) are paramount to the proper development of the immune system, for protection against microorganisms that can cause disease, and for the digestion and absorption of food and nutrients. [73] By contrast, unhealthy or imbalanced intestinal microorganisms (micro flora) are implicated in chronic diseases such as heart disease, some cancers, allergies, asthma, obesity, IBS, and digestive problems.

When we are healthy, it is in large part due to the fact that these probiotics (beneficial bacteria) are healthy. The probiotics help us digest and absorb our food, boost our immune systems, and even contribute to the manufacturing of certain vitamins that are necessary for our overall health and well-being.

These beneficial bacteria in our digestive system can be supported by eating food rich in **prebiotics**.

*Pre*biotics are the non-digestible plant foods that are rich with fiber that are resistant to our digestive enzymes. This fiber passes through the stomach undigested and ends up in the lower colon, where it ferments and produces short-chain fatty acids that nourish the probiotic bacteria.

Prebiotics stimulate growth, health and activity of the probiotics in our digestive systems. They are found naturally in cruciferous vegetables such as broccoli, cabbage, cauliflower, kale, radish, asparagus, and whole grains.

Creating a thriving immune system rich with healthy, well-fed probiotics is just one additional reason that eating more vegetables on a daily basis can support strong overall health.

Why does consuming and supporting probiotics seem more important today? With the widespread use of antibiotics, the beneficial bacteria in our digestive system have become compromised because antibiotics wipe out all bacteria—good *and* bad. Good bacteria keep bad bacteria in balance. If we don't have enough good bacteria in our system to support our immune system, then our immune system is compromised. So, the inclusion of probiotic food in our diet is vital to the health and strength of the immune system.

Our lives have become saturated with antibiotics, even if we don't take them. They are in our water supply because of people disposing of medicines and using the restroom, as well as run-off from farms. Farms are the number one purchaser of antibiotics because many farm animals are given antibiotics on a regular basis.

Any time you use an antibacterial hand sanitizer gel or soap, it is like taking an antibiotic. The antibacterial agent is absorbed right into the skin, like the medicine on a skin patch, and goes into the blood stream. This can kill the beneficial bacteria in the body, just like taking an antibiotic capsule or pill.

Because of the widespread saturation of antibiotics in our lives, it is important to replenish our beneficial bacteria on a regular, ongoing basis. In addition, researchers have found that bacterial populations in the gut of diabetics differ from non-diabetics, and that modifying your gut microflora with probiotics can help improve the health of diabetics.[74]

Try making some form of these probiotic foods a part of your daily diet: garlic, raw unprocessed apple cider vinegar, raw unprocessed soy sauce, unpasteurized coconut yogurts, unpasteurized kefir, rejuvelac, kombucha, some cottage cheese, miso, tempeh, some coconut products, and fermented foods.

Sprouts and Sprouting

According to Merriam-Webster, *sprout* means:
  1. to grow, spring up, or come forth as or as if a sprout.
  2. to send out new growth.

Examples of *sprout* in a sentence
  1. Seeds *sprout* in the spring.

Sprouts are the ultimate superfood—incredibly nutritious and packed with power. Sprouts are the basis of life because they rejuvenate, re-energize, and heal. Sprouts are one of the most nutritionally-rich foods. A complete food, they contain protein, carbohydrates, and good fat. They are rich in vitamins, minerals, and natural enzymes. Sprouts can contain all the nutritional value of the whole plant in one little sprout!

Studies have shown that when seeds and grains are germinated, they show an increase in "activities of hydrolytic enzymes, improvement in the contents of certain essential amino acids, total sugars, and B-group vitamins, and a decrease in dry matter, starch, and anti-nutrients."[75]

Because of the protein shortage during World War II, Dr. Clive M. McKay promoted sprouted soybeans as a wartime food source. The Chinese have included sprouts as a nutritional part of their diet for thousands of years. Adding sprouts is an easy way to add a wealth of nutrition to your diet.

The mung bean is one of my favorite sprouts. A sprouted mung bean has the carbohydrate content of a melon, Vitamin A of a lemon, thiamin of an avocado, riboflavin of a dry apple, niacin of a banana, and ascorbic acid of a loganberry—in one sprout! Dr. Paul Talalay of the American Cancer Society said that "broccoli sprouts are better for you than full-grown broccoli and contain more of the enzyme sulforaphane, which helps protect cells and prevents their genes from turning into cancer."[76]

Growing your own sprouts is easy. Anyone can do it, and the sprouts are ready to harvest in four days to a week. All you need are seeds, clean water, and a sieve or sprouting bag or jar. (If you are growing something like wheat or barley grass or sunflower seed sprouts, you'll also need some trays and nutrient-rich soil.)

The FDA said contaminated food plant seeds can cause food-borne illness, so cleaning seeds first is recommended. Clean seeds with a mixture of lime juice and vinegar or a tiny bit of food-grade hydrogen peroxide.

After this, soak them with EM, an effective microbial inoculant, which is a probiotic blend. Microbial inoculant products include three groups of naturally occurring beneficial bacteria: yeast, photosynthetic bacteria, and lactic acid bacteria. The probiotic "works together with microbes in the area to which it is added, to promote a healthy environment for beneficial microorganisms and larger forms of life, including insects, worms, pets, livestock and people."[77]

Make a mild mixture of one drop of EM in one cup of pure water, add the seeds, and let them sit for 10 minutes. The seeds and the earth benefit from probiotics, which boost their ability to fight off harmful bacteria, just as our body benefits from probiotics which keep bad bacteria in check. In a sense, we are boosting the earth's immune system.

Then, put the seeds in pure water and soak them overnight. Drain the water. Put them in a sieve or a sprouting bag or jar, and then put it in a dark, cool place. If you are growing wheat or barley grass or sunflower seeds, put them in a flat sprouting tray with some organic soil and sprinkle a bit more soil over them.

The ideal temperature is 70°F. I simply lay a dish towel over my sprouts or put them in a dark room. Rinse the seeds (or water the sprouting tray and soil) one to three times a day with pure water until they start to sprout. When they start to sprout, they will grow quickly.

After a full day or two sprouting, you can move them to the sunlight. There they will develop chlorophyll, the green pigment found in plants. Chlorophyll has anti-inflammatory and antioxidant properties. Antioxidants prevent or slow oxidation. (Oxidation leads to cell damage, production of abnormal cells, and disease.) Antioxidants also stop the damage caused by free radicals.

Plus, chlorophyll gives sprouts high levels of oxygen. Nobel Prize winner Dr. Otto Warburg found that cancer cells, bacteria, and viruses could not survive in a body with high amounts of oxygen.[78] He also determined the ideal pH of the human body is approximately 7.

Processed foods are acidic and can make the body acidic. Sprouts are a great source of oxygen, and are also an alkaline food. Leave the sprouts in the sunlight for a day or more to get as much chlorophyll as you can into your sprouts.

Add sprouts to salads, sandwiches, dips, smoothies, green drinks, and juices!

"The food you eat can either be the safest and most powerful form of medicine… or the slowest form of poison."

—Ann Wigmore

4

What's the Skinny on Fats?

W hen people tell me they feel they need more protein in their diet, I think what their bodies really crave is good fat. When I refer to good fats, I am talking about raw, unprocessed, organic, pure fats in their natural form.

The advertising industry would have us believe that all fat is bad or fattening. This may be because, in the 1960s, the sugar industry funded research that downplayed the risks of sugar and highlighted the hazards of fat. This was reported in September, 2016, in the *JAMA Internal Medicine*.[79]

The SRF had sponsored scientific research by Harvard scientists that was then published in the *New England Journal of Medicine* in 1967, with no mention of the sugar industry funding. The truth that good fat can be critical to maintaining our health and controlling our weight was not disclosed. This study may be the main reason so many products started marketing low-fat foods.

Fat tells the body how to utilize protein and carbohydrates. Fat can make our food taste more rich and satisfying, and good fats are vital for good brain health. They give us energy.

In contrast, many low-fat or fat-free products are filled with salt (probably white, refined, and lacking necessary minerals that are provided in unrefined sea salt), sugar, chemical additives, and MSG to make up for the lack of flavorful fat.

Trans fats should always be avoided completely. Trans fats are hydrogenated fats that have been chemically changed to stay solid at room temperature and have an extremely long shelf life, which is not their natural state. This type of fat is unhealthy even in tiny amounts.

Canola is a type of oil that was developed in Canada from the rapeseed plant, which is a member of the mustard family. It is used in many products and foods because it is low in saturated fats and has a high proportion of **monounsaturated** fats.

Many foods that are prepared at restaurants, stores, and bakeries have canola oil as an ingredient. Rapeseed oil is said to contain 30-60 percent erucic acid, which is a toxic level. Canola oil has been developed to contain between 0.3 and 1.2 percent erucic acid.

I have seen advertisements that say it is all right to use canola oil when cooking with heat. Canola oil is fairly new, however. It hasn't been around long enough for its effects on humans and animals to be studied and understood completely, and it has been subject to much controversy. It is up to you to decide if canola oil is right for you. I never use canola oil and avoid purchasing products that contain it.

Essential Fatty Acids

Essential fatty acids are called essential because they are not made by our body and must be obtained through the diet. Omega 3s and 6s are the specific essential fatty acids I'll address in this book.

We should all try to have a balance of Omega 3 and Omega 6 fats in our diet every day. Many doctors recommend a ratio of three to one of Omega 6 to Omega 3. However, doctors teaching at the Institute of Integrative Nutrition said the ratio really should be closer to one to one. Most Americans get much more Omega 6 than Omega 3, so it may be important for you to work on getting the proper amount of Omega 3 essential fatty acids into your diet.

Because Omega 3s have anti-inflammatory properties, they help with the prevention of many health problems: heart disease, rheumatoid arthritis, macular degeneration, asthma, eczema, other immune dysfunctions, and cancer. Omega 3s also improve memory and mood. A deficiency may appear as inflammation, water retention, and high blood pressure.

Chia seeds, ground flax seeds, or ground hemp seeds can provide Omega 3s. A good coffee bean grinder is a great way to add some of these nuts and seeds easily to foods. These grinders are about $25 and are well worth the investment. Mine is about 20 years old, and I use it constantly. Just grind the fresh nuts or seeds in the grinder and sprinkle them on dishes the way you would a seasoning.

My favorite way to add them to my recipes/food is to add my freshly ground flax seeds or hemp seeds to salads, smoothies, casseroles, and soups. I also sprinkle chia seeds on many of my dishes. They don't have a flavor, so they don't change the taste of the food, but they do add wonderful health benefits.

Avoid buying already-ground flax or hemp seeds because they will have lost some of the nutrients from exposure to oxygen. You always want to have them freshly ground. Add the freshly ground flax or hemp seeds to food after it is cool. You can also buy Omega 3 flax seed oil at the grocery store.

Omega 6 essential fatty acids need to be balanced with Omega 3 essential fatty acids because an excess of Omega 6 can cause water retention, raised blood pressure, and increased blood clotting. I've heard some doctors say they think diabetics have an overload of Omega 6s and hardly or possibly no Omega 3s in their system.

Almonds are extremely high in Omega 6 (a ratio of 1,800 Omega 6 fatty acids to 1 Omega 3), so make sure to balance almonds with a high source of Omega 3.

Make essential fatty acids a regular part of your diet, but always use fresh, cold-pressed oils and refrigerate them. This is crucial because essential fatty acids can become rancid and create free radicals in the body, which will foster aging and a weakened immune system.

I like raw, cold-pressed nut and seed oils. Pumpkin, walnut, flax, sesame, hemp, and macadamia nut are some of my favorites. I only use them in recipes where they are not being heated, or I add them after the other ingredients have been cooked and cooled down. This is because very few oils handle heat well. Never heat any oil over its smoking point because the smoke can be toxic.

Keep all nut, seed, and vegetable oils refrigerated and away from light.

The foods you make and eat will be more satisfying and delicious with an added health benefit if you use good fats. If you are worried about weight gain, good fats can actually help with weight loss. The bad fats and other additives in processed foods are what can cause ill health and weight problems. Choose organic, whole-food, cold-pressed, unprocessed good fats and enjoy your food.

Don't feel guilty about adding healthy fat to recipes. Your body and your brain will be glad you did!

Types of Healthy Oils

Coconut oil, a type of "nut" fat, is highly effective as an antioxidant. In most parts of the world, it is seen as the superfood of fats. It is a unique saturated fat and a medium-chain fatty acid, which means that pancreatic enzymes or bile are not required for the body to process it. This also means it is easily absorbed by the body.

Coconut oil nourishes the body, and the medium-chained fatty acids provide a good source of energy. Also, the lauric acid in coconut oil is a natural immune system booster. [80] For years, many people thought coconut oil was bad for your health because it raised cholesterol. But in actuality, it provides good cholesterol (HDL).

In fact, the top nutrition advisory panel in the US is planning to drop its caution about eating cholesterol rich food. They are no longer considering it a "nutrient of concern." They have found that rich foods heavy with saturated **animal fats** are the biggest danger to people's health. Rich fatty meats and dairy contribute to a risk of heart disease. [81]

Pure coconut oil has many benefits, including:
- promoting heart health.
- supporting immune system health.
- supporting a healthy metabolism.
- providing an immediate energy source.
- keeping skin healthy and youthful-looking.
- supporting the proper functioning of the thyroid gland. [82]

Coconut oil also appears to be unique in its ability to help with brain function. Dr. Mary T. Newport, who cured her husband of

Alzheimer's disease, began by adding coconut oil to his diet, asserting this to be one of the main components of his cure.[83] So, what is Alzheimer's disease, and why would coconut oil help? Alzheimer's disease, according to Dr. Joseph Mercola,

> appears to be a type of diabetes of the brain, and it's a process that starts happening at least 10 or 20 years before you start having symptoms. It's very similar to Type 1 or Type 2 diabetes in that you develop a problem with insulin. In this case, insulin problems prevent brain cells from accepting glucose, their primary fuel. Without it, they eventually die.
>
> But there is an alternative fuel: ketones, which cells easily accept. Ketones are metabolized in the liver after you eat medium-chain triglycerides, like those found in coconut oil."[84]

Throughout this book, I have used coconut oil in many of my recipes because I have found it to be a healthy and safe oil for any recipe. A highly chemically stable fat, it is resistant to peroxidation and rancidity.

The Natural Gourmet Institute for Food and Health always uses coconut oil whenever cooking with heat because certain coconut oils handle high heat very well. Read labels and make certain you are purchasing the type that is meant to handle whichever cooking method you are using. Some coconut oils that are more refined will say whether they are meant for cooking with high heat.

Make sure you purchase organic, extra virgin, pure coconut oil. You do not want to purchase or confuse pure coconut oil with a hydrogenated or trans-fat variety.

Olive oil is a wonderful, unique ingredient. It is an Omega 9, monounsaturated, long-chained fatty acid, and the only vegetable oil that can be pressed and used in its pure form. The key ingredient found in olive oil is oleic acid.

Extra virgin olive oil has more Vitamin E in it than other types of olive oil. According to Dr. Joseph Mercola, it "contains major health benefits because of its vitamin E and A, chlorophyll, magnesium, squalene, and a host of other cardio-protective nutrients. It has also been shown to reduce some cancers, as well as rheumatoid arthritis."[85] It is a good fat and a staple in a healthy Mediterranean diet.

Olive oil can become rancid if heated or stored improperly. It needs to be kept refrigerated and away from light. It should be used only with recipes and food preparation that don't require it to be heated, unless it says on the label it is meant to handle high heat. More refined varieties of olive oils can handle certain high temperatures.

George Mateljan—biologist, businessman, and nutritionist who is best known for his book *The World's Healthiest Foods*—says that extra-virgin olive oil should never be heated above 200–250°F, otherwise toxic fumes can be created from the overheated oil. [86] Heating extra-virgin olive oil destroys its nutrients, turns the oil rancid, and releases dangerous free radicals in its smoke.

According to the National Consumers League, you need to be aware of products labeled as extra-virgin olive oil.

NCL purchased 11 different varieties of olive oil, all labeled extra-virgin, each bought in January, 2015, from four major Washington, DC-area retailers (Whole Foods Market, Trader Joe's, Safeway, and Giant). One bottle of each product was tested, so this was not meant to be a "study" or a "buyer's guide," but rather off-the-shelf testing as to what a consumer might buy within a year.

This was an independent sampling, which NCL paid out-of-pocket, that included a battery of chemical and sensory tests that are not inexpensive. Bottles were selected from the back of lower shelves to ensure they were not damaged by exposure to natural or artificial lighting. US and European brands and oils were tested, including private label oils. NCL did not test all brands that a consumer might buy.

Of the eleven products tested, six failed to meet extra-virgin olive oil standards as set by the International Olive Council (IOC). Five were found to be extra-virgin olive oils. These are:
- California Olive Ranch "Extra-Virgin Olive Oil"
- Colavita "Extra-Virgin Olive Oil"

- Trader Joe's "Extra-Virgin California Estate Olive Oil"
- Trader Joe's "100% Italian Organic Extra-Virgin Olive Oil"
- Lucini "Premium Select Extra-Virgin Olive Oil"

According to NCL, consumers should:
- Choose brands that consistently pass testing. Research prior testing and articles on authenticity, determine which producers are transparent in their processing, and judge for themselves which oils work well with their food and cooking and which don't.
- Check for "best by" dates, or—even better—harvest dates.
- Avoid buying oils in clear glass bottles or from the top shelf, which could be more likely to be degraded. But, warned the NCL, even that is not foolproof, and buying oil in tins or dark bottles does not mean that there is extra-virgin oil in there.

Remember that the USDA Organic label is also no indication of authenticity, and the fact that an oil is from Italy or another producing country is likewise not a good indicator.[87]

In conclusion, extra-virgin olive oil is a very healthy oil. But to be on the safe side, avoid cooking with olive oil above 200°F. For recipes that don't require heating, choose organic, extra-virgin olive oil, which is from the first press of the olive, and purchase brands known to be labeled properly.

Hemp oil contains significant amounts of Omega 3s and Omega 6s. Hemp oil also contains significant amounts of Vitamin E, which is important for the thyroid gland. One easy thing you can do for your diet is to freshly grind hemp or flax seeds and add them to recipes for an extra benefit of Omega oils, as well as protein and fiber.

Flax seeds are one of the best sources of Omega 3 essential fatty acids. They are rich in alpha-linolenic acid, fiber, and lignans. Lignans are phytoestrogens, or plant compounds that have an estrogen-like effect, with antioxidant properties. These lignans can help stabilize hormone levels and reduce PMS and menopause symptoms. They can also potentially help reduce the risk of developing prostate or breast cancer. Alpha-linolenic acid is anti-inflammatory. It promotes the lowering of C-reactive protein in the blood, which is a biomarker of inflammation.

To get the full benefit, freshly grind flax seeds when using them. Do not buy flax seeds that are already ground. Store flax seeds in a dry, waterproof container. Always store ground seeds in the refrigerator.

Chia seeds have been cultivated for thousands of years in Mexico. The word "chia" means "strength." Unlike flax seeds and hemp seeds, chia seeds do not have to be ground for the body to utilize the nutrients and oils, making them much easier for the body to use. Chia seeds have more Omega 3 fatty acids than Atlantic salmon. But, unlike salmon, chia seeds are about 10 percent Omega 6 oil. They are a more perfect balance of Omega fats, with a ratio of three Omega 3s to one Omega 6.

Along with the rich Omega oils, chia seeds have almost five times more calcium than milk (one ounce of chia has 179 mg calcium and one ounce of whole milk has 36 mg calcium); more antioxidants than fresh blueberries; and more protein, calcium, and fiber than flax seeds. Chia seeds are one of the best nutrient-dense superfoods around.

Clarified butter (ghee) is butter that has had the milk solids removed from it. It has been used for centuries in Ayurvedic medicine. It is said to enhance the essence that governs the tissues of the body, balance hormones, assist in healing injuries and gastro-intestinal problems, and help the body resist disease.

Dr. Rudolph Ballentine, MD, did some studies and found it contains butyric acid, which has anti-viral and anti-cancer properties, and can also help in the prevention of Alzheimer's disease.

Clarified butter is usually sold in the Asian/Indian food area or in the baking goods area of stores. I love the buttery flavor of ghee and use it at the end of many recipes, in small amounts, just to add that touch of butter flavor to the coconut oil or other fat I used.

5

Protein

P rotein is made up of amino acids, which are crucial for building and maintaining cells and tissues. The body uses amino acids to make hemoglobin and insulin. Protein is also essential for maintaining healthy sugar levels in the blood, especially when eating carbohydrates.

Yet ideas about how much and what type of protein we need have changed over time. Even today, experts' opinions vary. What is important is that you make the right diet choices for your individual needs. Let's look at all the research to date.

At the beginning of the twentieth century, Russell Henry Chittenden, the father of biochemistry, was disturbed that physicians were recommending high-protein diets of 135 grams a day. He thought this was wrong and set out to test this dietary theory. Chittenden began by doing a study on himself using a low-protein diet. He lost weight, had more energy, got rid of his arthritic joint pain, and was, in his opinion, healthier than he had been on a high-protein diet.

He began testing colleagues, students, and athletes at Yale. On the low-protein diet, they all had more energy, felt better, and increased their performance ability by more than 35 percent. In 1904, Chittenden concluded that "35–50 grams of protein a day was adequate for adults, and individuals could maintain their health and fitness on this amount."

Studies over the past century have consistently confirmed Professor Chittenden's findings." [88] The current recommended daily allowance of protein for adults is 46–56 grams per day.[89]

Many vegetarian proteins are a combination of carbohydrates and protein. I like to use ones that are a high combination of pure, raw, organic, non-GMO, sprouted, seeds, nuts, lentils, peas and beans. It you find one that is a combination of a couple of them, you are more likely to get a combination of nutrients and avoid becoming allergic to one, which can happen if you just have one type of protein every day. Eat seasonally and change it up now and then, so you don't become allergic to anything from eating it too frequently.

Blood Types. Some studies say that the amount and type of protein a person should eat depends on his or her blood type. Dr. Peter J. D'Adamo and Catherine Whitney's book *Eat Right 4 Your Type* looks at the connection between blood type, diet, and health.

I haven't seen any in-depth research to support this theory, so I look at it with some skepticism. But since so many people ask me about it, I decided to address it in this book.

My blood type is O, as is my daughter's. *Eat Right 4 Your Type* says "O blood types are meant to thrive best on a high protein (red meat) and low carbohydrate diet."[90]

I have been vegetarian for 29 years, and so has my daughter. We seem to do quite well on a vegetarian diet, but we do make sure we consume enough protein-rich plant foods like beans, lentils, nuts, seeds (quinoa is a seed), and whole-grain rice. We also have a good amount of healthy fats in our diet.

I suspect that consuming foods high in phytic acid (like beans, lentils, nuts, seeds, and grains) may be one of the reasons they came up with this theory. These foods need to be properly prepared to remove the phytic acid. In the recipes in this book, I show you how to easily remove the phytic acid to make these foods healthier and easier to digest.

The authors say that A blood types are supposed to be vegetarian (high carbohydrate and low fat); B blood types should eat dairy, meat, fish, grains, vegetables, and fruit; and AB blood types should consume mostly vegetarian food, with moderate meat and dairy. In the book, the authors list various foods that are good, better, best, or worse for each blood type.[91]

I haven't seen in-depth studies to back up these theories, and they don't seem to apply to me and my family. So, in my opinion, it is up to you to decide if this theory is right for you.

Protein and Athletic Performance. Many athletes today are filling their bodies with protein-rich food, thinking it will make them stronger and their muscles bigger. According to the Vegetarian Resource Group:

> Athletes used to eat thick steaks before competition because they thought it would improve their performance. Protein supplements are sold at health food stores. This concern about protein is misplaced.
>
> Although protein is certainly an essential nutrient which plays many key roles in the way our bodies function, we do not need huge quantities of it. In reality, we need small amounts of protein. Only one calorie out of every ten we take in needs to come from protein. Athletes do not need much more protein than the general public.[92]

This is backed up in an *AARP* article by tennis athlete Martina Navratilova, who says:

> On days that I work out, I'll have a little protein with some carbs after exercising. This combo speeds up the manufacture of new glycogen (the carbohydrate that is stored in muscle and supplies energy) and elevates key hormones in the body that are involved in muscle repair and growth. In addition, the snack amplifies the fuel I get from carbs.[93]

Martina Navratilova is one of the best professional women's tennis players ever. She was the number one player in the world for a total of 332 weeks, in women's singles. She says her plant-based diet is one of the reasons that she was able to play professionally into her 40s.

This fits in with what I have read from other top athletes like Brendan Brazier, two-time Canadian 50K ultramarathon champion. He thinks recovery time from working out is really the most critical factor for success as an athlete, rather than protein intake. He lives and thrives on a 100 percent plant-based diet.

Carl Lewis earned ten Olympic medals in track and field in his lifetime, nine of which were gold. He became a vegetarian in 1990. By 1991, Carl Lewis had become completely vegan—after which he claimed he had the best athletic year of this career.

Carl wrote in the introduction to Jannequin Bennett's book *Very Vegetarian*, "It's a myth that muscles, strength, and endurance require the consumption of large quantities of animal-based foods. This myth began before anyone even talked about protein... Your body is your temple. If you nourish it properly, it will be good to you and you will increase its longevity."[94]

Protein Myths. There are several myths about protein. For instance, in the 1971 book *Diet for a Small Planet*, Frances Moore Lappé wrote that plants contained "incomplete proteins" with inadequate amounts of specific essential amino acids for them to meet the dietary needs of people.

She emphasized the need to combine vegetable-based foods to obtain the complete amino acid complexes needed for optimum health when choosing not to consume animal protein.

However, according to Dr. John McDougall, Lappé did not understand the scientific research on human protein needs and the sufficiency of plant-based foods. Dr. McDougall says that plant combining "is unnecessary and implies that it is difficult to obtain 'complete' proteins from vegetables without detailed nutritional knowledge. Because of her complicated and incorrect ideas, people are frightened away from vegetable-based diets."[95]

Thankfully, such myths are slowly but surely being dismissed as untrue. The American Dietetic Association (ADA) revised its position statement on vegetarian diets and now agrees that well-planned vegetarian diets are "a healthy, nutritionally adequate dietary practice for all stages of life."

In addition to this, according to Mladen Golubic, MD, PhD of The Cleveland Heart Clinic:

The more protein—especially animal protein—one eats, the higher the risk of different chronic diseases. For example, in a recent study of more than 6,000 people in the best nationally representative dietary survey in the United States, those between 50 and 65 years old who reported high protein intake had a 75 percent increase in dying from any cause, a four-fold increase in cancer death risk during the following 18 years, and a five-fold increase in death from diabetes. Those with moderate intake had increased cancer death risk three-fold when compared with the low protein intake group!

It is important to note that these associations were either abolished or attenuated if the proteins were plant derived. The composition of amino acids, building blocks of protein, derived from animals is different than from plant proteins. What we need are amino acids, not the proteins themselves.

As for the amount of protein we eat, it is not practical or very accurate to measure that on a daily basis. 0.8 g/kg is generous. According to the World Health Organization, 0.5 g/kg is adequate for good health. Make sure you get enough calories from unprocessed whole foods of plant origin, and you will get enough protein.

...You should eat a variety of legumes (beans of any type, shape, or color, including soybeans, lentils, and peas), and 100 percent whole-grain products and vegetables. Do not worry about getting enough proteins. If you get enough calories from these whole foods, you are getting enough protein.

As for other nutrition, there is not a single nutrient (with the possible exception of vitamin B12) that you cannot get from plants. In fact, meat or fish do not have any dietary fiber, and only minuscule amounts of beneficial compounds that are not technically essential nutrients. However, these essential nutrients are richly present in plants and seem quite beneficial for human health.[96]

Dr. Andrew Weil, a prominent expert in the health field, also addressed this subject:

You may have heard that vegetable sources of protein are incomplete and become complete only when correctly combined. Research has discredited that notion, so you don't have to worry that you won't get enough usable protein if you don't put together some magical combination of foods at each meal.[97]

Whether or not you're a vegetarian, I recommend that you divide your daily calories as follows: 40–50 percent from carbohydrates (including vegetables, fruit, whole grains, starchy roots and tubers, and legumes), 30 percent from fat, and 20–30 percent from protein, which amounts to between 100 and 150 grams on a 2,000 calorie-a-day diet.[98]

Dr. Weil, then, actually recommends more protein than Dr. Chittenden. Take into account that Dr. Chittenden was probably using "meat" protein as a good portion of his diet study. So, the type of protein may vary from person to person. In my opinion, you have to decide what type and amount of protein works best for you.

Dennis Gordon, MEd, RD, voices the same opinion as Dr. Weil and Dr. McDougall. In the article "Vegetable Proteins Can Stand Alone," Gordon wrote:

Complementing proteins is not necessary with vegetable proteins. The myth that vegetable source proteins need to be complemented is similar to the myths that persist about sugar making one's blood glucose go up faster than starch does. These myths have great staying power, despite there being no evidence to support them and plenty to refute them.[99]

Dietitian Dr. Reed Mangels, PhD, RD, also has spoken about protein combining:

It is very easy for a vegan diet to meet the recommendations for protein, as long as calorie intake is adequate. Strict protein combining is not necessary. It is more important to eat a varied diet throughout the day... The RDA recommends that we take in 0.8 grams of protein for every kilogram that we weigh (or about 0.36 grams of protein per pound that we weigh).

This recommendation includes a generous safety factor for most people... To meet protein recommendations, the typical adult male vegan needs only 2.5 to 2.9 grams of protein per 100 calories and the typical adult female vegan needs only 2.1 to 2.4 grams of protein per 100 calories. These recommendations can be easily met from vegan sources.[100]

Even major medical groups are recognizing the fact that a vegetarian diet is what truly heals the body. Kaiser Permanente, the largest managed healthcare organization in the United States, has published a remarkable nutritional update for physicians. Kaiser is now telling doctors that healthy eating may best be achieved with a plant-based diet:

Research shows that plant-based diets are cost-effective, low-risk interventions that may lower body mass index, blood pressure, HbA1C, and cholesterol levels.

They may also reduce the number of medications needed to treat chronic diseases and lower ischemic heart disease mortality rates.

Physicians should consider recommending a plant-based diet to all their patients, especially those with high blood pressure, diabetes, cardiovascular disease, cancer, or obesity.[101]

Protein myths have been around for almost a century, but sprouted beans, sprouted seeds, leafy greens (45 percent of spinach is protein), sprouted legumes, algae (spirulina and chlorella), mushrooms, and sprouted grains are all healthy sources of protein. Quality of course is very important. But the fact is that vegetarian foods are among the best sources of protein.

Nuts and Seeds

Nuts and seeds are perfect foods because they are a combination of protein, fat, and carbohydrate.

They contain delicate polyunsaturated fatty acids that can become rancid shortly after being shelled, so store them in a tightly sealed container (preferably glass) in the refrigerator. Nuts that come from tropical climates can contain high levels of fungal mycotoxins, which result from improper storage.

Almost all nuts and seeds also contain certain compounds that include enzyme inhibitors and phytic acid, which can prevent the body from absorbing some nutrients. To help diminish the phytic acid and enzyme inhibitors, and to make them more digestible, place them in a glass or steel bowl and soak them for 12–18 hours in non-chlorinated water and a little bit of whole sea salt.

You can dehydrate or roast them in the oven at a low temperature. Eat them within a few days. When buying nuts and seeds, look for products that are sprouted or have been soaked.

Have your physician check your mineral levels if you have a diet high in nuts and seeds.

Pine nuts (pignoli) can be expensive, but they are nature's only source of pinolenic acid, which helps diminish your appetite. They have the highest concentration of oleic acid, a monounsaturated fat that aids the liver in eliminating harmful triglycerides from our body, which helps protect our heart. Pine nuts are also packed with 3 mg of iron per one-ounce serving and are rich in Vitamin B1 and Vitamin B3, manganese, copper, magnesium, molybdenum, and zinc. They are a source of Vitamin B2, Vitamin E, and potassium.

There are more than 29 varieties of pine nuts. Most of the pine nuts in US grocery stores are from trees grown in China, Mexico, and Korea. All pine nuts are nutritious, but the most nutrient-dense are Mediterranean pine nuts, which come from the Stone Pine (*pinus pinea*, or Umbrella Pine) native to Portugal, Spain, and Italy. Mediterranean pine nuts are lower in calories; have a great ratio of Omega 3 to Omega 6 essential fatty acids; have a higher level of phytosterols, which are known to lower cholesterol; and have a greater protein content than other varieties of pine nut.

Pine nuts are wonderful to have as a snack or add to a meat substitute, protein drink, or smoothie.

Hemp seeds are actually nuts. They contain significant amounts of Omega 3 and Omega 6 fatty acids, as well as protein. They also contain significant amounts of Vitamin E, which is important for the thyroid gland.

Hemp seeds are seen as an excellent food because of their great combination of high-quality oil, or good fat (44 percent), protein (33 percent), and fiber (12 percent). Hemp protein contains all the complex amino acid proteins, and it is extremely similar to the type of protein in animal foods. It has a wonderful digestibility and appears to be free of the anti-nutrients found in soy. Hemp seeds deliver a good source of readily absorbable, nutrient-dense protein that can be readily utilized by the body.[102]

Almonds are actually seeds. They are a powerhouse of nutrients, including manganese, magnesium, copper, Vitamin B2, and phosphorus, and are a great source of protein and fiber. One quarter cup of almonds has 12 grams of protein. That is more than twice the amount of protein in one egg. However, almonds contain 1,800 more Omega 6 fatty acids than Omega 3 fatty acids. This can seriously throw off the balance of Omega 3 to Omega 6 fatty acids in the body. For that reason, I use more whole, sprouted quinoa or coconut milk these days than almond milk.

Walnuts are especially good for the vegetarian diet. They are high in protein; are a very good source of manganese, copper, tryptophan, and Omega 3 and Omega 6 fatty acids; and have a fairly good ratio of Omega 3 to Omega 6 fatty acids (four Omega 6s to one Omega 3) with only eight percent saturated fat.

Cashews are a very good source of copper, magnesium, tryptophan, and phosphorus. Copper is necessary to maintain healthy bones and connective tissues. Cashews have 117 Omega 6 fatty acids to one Omega 3, and have 12.5 percent saturated fat. I love cashews, but I try to combine them with other nuts and seeds when I eat them to help balance out the Omegas and saturated fats.

Pumpkin seeds are a good source of protein and fiber, as well as minerals, including zinc, iron, magnesium, phosphorus, potassium, copper, and manganese. Pumpkin seeds have 117 Omega 6 fatty acids to one Omega 3 and have a saturated fat content of 14 percent.

Interestingly, pumpkin seeds are terrific at helping the body get rid of parasites. I am a certified wildlife rehabilitator, and I use pumpkin seeds on a regular basis when feeding the wild animals I rehabilitate. I grind the seeds and immediately add them to the animals' food, and it is amazing to me how many tapeworms and other types of parasites come out in their bowel movements. Because of this, I use pumpkin seeds frequently, in a freshly ground form, in my own and my pets' foods.

Protein Supplements

Sometimes people eating a plant based diet feel they are just not getting enough food, protein, or sustenance. They probably need concentrated nutrients from protein and carbohydrates, along with some good fat. When the body is getting a combination of protein, carbohydrates, and fat from nutrient-dense, whole food full of live enzymes, the body can feel nutritionally satisfied.

Studies have shown that after an intense workout, it is helpful to replenish your glycogen by having carbohydrates combined with protein, which supports muscle. The fat tells the body how to use the protein and carbohydrates. When I use a meal replacement or protein powder, I add a tablespoon of good fat to the mixture—usually coconut oil or flax seed oil, or a combination of both.

If you choose to use a protein supplement, I recommend using one that contains protein that is organic, vegan, gluten-free, raw, and whole, sprouted seed or grain. Protein supplements made from whole, sprouted seeds, nuts, grains, rice, legumes, peas, and beans are some of my favorites.

When buying protein supplements, make sure they aren't mystery protein by reading the ingredient list very carefully. Anything that simply says "protein" could be ground leftovers from meat packing plants. Those leftovers can include hair, nails, hooves, and other animal parts.

Be careful which protein powders or supplements you buy. *Consumer Reports* tested 15 high-protein drinks and found that many contained levels of toxic heavy metals. Here is an excerpt from the report:

> Our investigation, including tests at an outside laboratory of 15 protein drinks, a review of government documents, and

interviews with health and fitness experts and consumers, found most people already get enough protein, and there are far better and cheaper ways to add more if it's needed.

Some protein drinks can even pose health risks, including exposure to potentially harmful heavy metals, if consumed frequently. All drinks in our tests had at least one sample containing one or more of the following contaminants: arsenic, cadmium, lead, and mercury. Those metals can have toxic effects on several organs in the body.[103]

Again, read the ingredients carefully and buy ones that contain only organic, whole, vegetarian food.

Marketing for high-protein drinks is sharp, savvy, and targeted to bodybuilders, athletes, baby boomers, and pregnant women. The advertising can say that the drinks build muscle or help shed unwanted pounds. People have the idea that if they consume more protein, their bodies will build more muscle, but lifting weights and exercising are what builds muscle.

Whey

I do not recommend whey protein for a healing diet. It is animal-based, and can contribute to excessive protein consumption which has several negative effects on your health.

Whey protein, a naturally occurring substance derived from milk, is considered vegetarian. Whey protein is separated from the curds in milk during the cheese-making process. It is usually refined into a powder that is commonly added to protein powders or bodybuilder protein drinks. Protein powder can be mixed with beverages such as juice.

Since whey is derived from milk and has some lactose in it, people who cannot digest lactose can have allergic reactions such as sneezing, itching, and rashes after ingesting it.

Whey protein is in many products that are widely marketed to athletes, seniors, and teenagers for meal replacement, weight loss, and body building. Many people consume these whey drinks or supplements without being aware they are ingesting excessive amounts of whey protein and accumulating too much protein.

Excess protein damages the body. High amounts of protein, specifically whey protein "can cause some side effects such as increased bowel movements, nausea, thirst, bloating, cramps, reduced appetite, tiredness (fatigue), and headache." [104] The American Council on Exercise reported that large amounts of whey protein can be stored as a form of fat.

Studies have shown that whey protein can also stress the liver and kidneys, because they break down the majority of protein. Excessive whey protein intake can result in kidney stones or calcium deposits in the kidney, which can be very harmful if untreated.

According to a study in the *International Journal of Sport Nutrition and Exercise Metabolism*, daily protein ingestion of less than 2.8 grams per kilogram of body weight does not harm renal function in athletes. The American Diabetes Association says that diabetics should consume only the recommended daily amount or less than that. Liver and kidney disease patients should ensure that their whey protein intake is closely monitored to avoid complications.

The National Institutes of Health recommend a moderate protein diet. Be very cautious about using whey protein powders on a regular basis and monitor how much is being ingested, so you aren't getting too much. Remember: this is animal protein. "The more protein—especially animal protein—one eats, the higher the risk of different chronic diseases. ...According to the World Health Organization, 0.5 g/kg is adequate for good health."[105]

Soy

I do not recommend soy protein for a healing diet. It has many negative effects on health because it is difficult to digest, affects your hormones, and is closely linked to GMOs, pesticides, and harmful processing chemicals.

Soy protein is a complete protein but can be very hard to digest. The Chinese did not eat unfermented soybeans, because they contain quantities of natural toxins or "anti-nutrients" and are high in phytic acid. This means ingesting unfermented soy can prevent the body from absorbing other nutrients like calcium, magnesium, copper, iron, zinc, and particularly protein. In China, soy was not used as a food until fermentation techniques were discovered in the Zhou Dynasty (1046–256 BC). When soy is fermented—as in miso, tempeh, or soy sauce—the soy nutrients are more digestible and easier to absorb.

Soy has been linked to gastric distress and pancreatic problems, including cancer, and it can impair our body's uptake of amino acids.[106] It also contains goitrogens, which are known to suppress the functioning of the thyroid.[107]

Most soy on the market today is from genetically modified (GM) seed. 91 percent of soybeans planted in the United States are GM, and the rate is rapidly growing throughout the world, according to *Natural News* newsletter.[108] Dr. Gregory Damato points out that "more than 95 percent of GM soy (and 75 percent of other GM crops) is engineered to tolerate glyphosate herbicide, the most common formulation of which is Roundup."[109]

Recent studies by French scientists on the Toxicity of Roundup and Glyphosate found this herbicide carcinogenic.[110] They found it:

1. Causes cell cycle dysregulation, which is a hallmark of tumor cells and human cancers.

2. Inhibits DNA synthesis in certain parts of the cell cycle—the cells' reproductive process, which underlies the growth and development of all living organisms.

3. Impedes the hatchings of sea urchins. (Sea urchins were used because they constitute an appropriate model for the identification of undesirable cellular and molecular targets of pollutants.) The delay was found to be dose dependent on the concentration of Roundup. The surfactant polyoxyethylene amine (POEA), another major component of Roundup, was also found to be highly toxic to the embryos when tested alone, and could therefore be a contributing factor.[111]

These reasons are why I don't eat soy if I can avoid it, or any other genetically modified food or non-organically grown food. I recommend reading more about glyphosate herbicide if you are eating non-certified organic foods.

Be aware that soy is added to tortillas, breads, fake meats, and many other foods, supposedly for the "health" benefit. In my opinion, it is really used as cheap filler.

Health and nutrition expert Dr. Joseph Mercola writes that the advertising industry has misled the public about the safety and health benefits of soy, as well as the widespread use of it in the Asian diet. He states, "A study of the history of soy use in Asia shows that the poor used it during times of extreme food shortage, and only when the soybeans were carefully prepared (e.g. by lengthy fermentation) to destroy the soy toxins."[112] He goes on to say that, contrary to some reports in the West, it is not the usual practice in Asian countries to feed soy milk to infants.[113]

Be aware of this when you read food labels that refer to soy's health benefits, even those that display an FDA statement that soy can help lower the risk of heart disease. In 2000, two FDA employees, Daniel Doerge and Daniel Sheehan, were so worried about the danger of soy that they wrote a controversial letter to their employer, protesting the positive health claims for soy that the FDA was approving at the time. They wrote:

> There is abundant evidence that some of the isoflavones found in soy—including genistein and equol, a metabolite of daidzen—demonstrate toxicity in estrogen sensitive tissues and in the thyroid. This is true for a number of species, including humans.
>
> Additionally, isoflavones are inhibitors of the thyroid peroxidase which makes T3 and T4. Inhibition can be expected to generate thyroid abnormalities, including goiter and autoimmune thyroiditis. There exists a significant body of animal data that demonstrates goitrogenic and even carcinogenic effects of soy products.
>
> Moreover, there are significant reports of goitrogenic effects from soy consumption in human infants.[114]

Think carefully about the effects that soy can have on the thyroid (our master gland which affects almost all aspects of our health) and estrogen. Many doctors and nutritionists are soy proponents. Be careful and research this yourself if you are concerned.

A billion-dollar industry advertises soy as the answer to many health issues, from heart disease to weight problems. Soy is frequently touted as the answer to women's menopause hormone imbalances. This is one of the reasons why so many doctors and older women were happy to embrace it.

Soy and soy-based products contain isoflavones or phytoestrogens, which are plant-based estrogens. Soy is not the only food that contains phytoestrogens. There are other less controversial and more digestible foods with phytoestrogens you can include in your diet.

For men, eating soy isoflavones can significantly reduce testicular function and lower luteinizing hormone (LH) production, which is what signals the testicles to work. A high soy intake which potentially lowers level of LH increases the probability of estrogen dominance in men, contributing to hair loss, swollen and cancerous prostates, and insulin resistance. Dr. Doris Rapp, MD, a leading pediatric allergist, asserts that environmental and food estrogens are responsible for the worldwide reduction in male fertility.[115]

Soy consumption has been linked with cancer in adults, notably breast cancer, as I read in an article by Jim Rutz. He went on to say:

> That's why the governments of Israel, the UK, France, and New Zealand are already cracking down hard on soy... In sad contrast, 60 percent of the refined foods in US supermarkets now contain soy. Worse, soy use may double in the next few years because (last I heard) the out-of-touch medicrats in the FDA hierarchy are considering allowing manufacturers of cereal, energy bars, fake milk, fake yogurt, etc., to claim that "soy prevents cancer." It doesn't...

P.S.: Soy sauce is fine. Unlike soy milk, it's perfectly safe because it's fermented, which changes its molecular structure. Miso, natto, and tempeh are also okay, but avoid tofu.[116]

Soy can create allergic reactions. In 1986, Dr. Stuart Berger, MD, placed soy among the top seven allergens, one of the "sinister seven."

Finally, completely avoid soy protein isolate. It is a byproduct of soybean oil processing that is found in a huge number of vegan foods. A standard soybean contains 40 percent protein, while soy protein isolate is usually about 95 percent protein. But it poses serious health risks.

The processing of soy protein isolate is done mostly in aluminum tanks that leach high levels of aluminum into the product. Then MSG, flavorings, preservatives, sweeteners, and synthetic chemicals are frequently added to help get rid of the "beany" taste and add more "meaty" flavor. In animal experiments, the test animals fed soy isolate developed enlarged organs, particularly the thyroid and the pancreas.

After the soybeans—which are mostly GMO varieties—are crushed to extract the oil, the leftover soy "chunks" (which still contain fiber, water, some fat, and other carbohydrates) then undergo another extraction process that involves hexane—a neurotoxin that is also a substantial component in gasoline. The next step involves soaking these chunks in a chemical mixture (which commonly contains ammonia and hydrochloric acid) to help concentrate protein levels and achieve a sponge-like texture. Finally, the mixture is spray-dried.[117]

Soy protein isolate can only be made in factories. Healthy, whole foods should be possible to make in a kitchen. You can grind your own almond flour at home from almonds. You can make your own seitan (wheat meat) at home. You can make your own rice milk or hemp milk at home with a blender and some whole-food ingredients. The only way to make soy protein isolate is by using extremely flammable and hazardous chemicals, like hexane, and extreme temperatures that you could not possibly obtain in a kitchen setting.

Hexane is not used in the production of organic soy protein isolate. For a list of which protein bars and soy burgers are made using hexane-extracted soy protein isolates and which aren't, go to: www.cornucopia.org/hexane-guides/hexane_guide_bars.html.

As I researched soy, I came to seriously reconsider its use. When I first became a vegetarian, I used soy for many things. I used to feel that soy milk, soy beans, and other soy products were foods I should use. I learn something new every day. No one knows everything, so be open to new information.

I found some soy vegetarian alternative meats worked really well as transition foods from a meat-based diet. Some of them didn't taste very good and were a huge waste of money, but a few were pretty good. I always looked for organic ones, but those were rare. I slowly weaned myself off them. There are many more choices today that are organic and taste much better than what was available in 1988.

But as I have learned more about soy, I avoid it. I do, however, use organic fermented soy sauce. I also use organic miso and tempeh occasionally. There are alternative organic misos now that are made with brown rice, garbanzo beans, and barley—and they taste terrific. I buy these instead of the soy variety.

In conclusion, if you are going to buy soy, buy certified organic soy because it won't be from genetically modified seeds. Buy sprouted and/or fermented soy for a more digestible and less harmful soy protein, and avoid soy protein isolates.

Beans

Beans—including black beans, garbanzo beans (also known as chickpeas), pinto beans, and kidney beans—are a great source of protein, fiber, and antioxidants. Beans are relatively inexpensive and easy to store in a dry, cool place for a fairly long time.

The fiber in beans has been shown to help lower cholesterol by binding with bile acids, which are used in making cholesterol. Fiber isn't absorbed into the body. It passes out of the body, taking the bile with it.

Beans also help prevent blood sugar levels from rising too quickly after a meal, making beans a good food choice for people with diabetes or hypoglycemia. Combining beans with whole-grain rice gives you all the essential amino acids.

A little-known and beneficial attribute of beans is that they contain the enzyme sulfite oxidase, which can detoxify sulfites. Sulfites are a common preservative used in many foods today. Many people are sensitive to sulfites, resulting in weight gain, headaches, and rapid heartbeat.

Eating one cup of black beans can give you 172 percent of the daily value of the trace mineral molybdenum, which is the key component of sulfite oxidase.

The *Journal of Agriculture and Food Chemistry* researched beans and found they are as rich in anthocyanin—an antioxidant compound—as cranberries, oranges, and grapes. In fact, black beans had approximately 10 times the amount found in oranges. The darker the bean, the higher the antioxidant properties were. Gram for gram, black beans had the highest levels of antioxidants. They descended in order of black, red, brown, yellow, and white.

Vegetarian Protein Sources

Almonds (¼ cup) 12 grams
Amaranth (3½ oz.) 16 grams
Baked beans (8 oz.) 11.5 grams
Broccoli (3½ oz.) 3.1 grams
Brown rice (7 oz.) 4.4 grams
Buckwheat (3½ oz.) 12 grams
Bulgur (1 c. cooked) 6 grams
Cashews (¼ c.) 5 grams
Chlorella (3 oz.) 48 grams
Cow's milk (½ pint) 9.2 grams
Egg (boiled) 7.5 grams
Garbanzo beans (chickpeas) (7 oz.) 16 grams
Hard cheese (1 oz.) 6.8 grams
Hemp seeds (1 oz.) 11 grams
Lentils (4½ oz.) 9.1 grams
Mediterranean pine nuts (1 oz.) 10 grams
Muesli (2½ oz.) 7.7 grams
Nori seaweed (3½ oz. dried) 35 grams
Nutritional yeast (3½ oz.) 50 grams
Oatmeal (1 c.) 6 grams
Peanuts (1 oz.) 7.3 grams
Pine nuts (1 oz.) 6.8 grams
Porridge (6 oz.) 2.4 grams
Potatoes (7 oz.) 2.8 grams
Pumpkin seeds (raw) (1 oz.) 7 grams
Sesame seeds (3½ oz.) 19 grams
Spinach (fresh) (1 c.) 1 gram
Spirulina (3½ oz.) 68 grams
Sunflower seeds (3½ oz.) 24 grams
Tofu (5 oz.) 10.3 grams
Walnuts (¼ cup) 25 grams
Whole-grain bread (2 slices) 7 grams

"The number one cause of death among diabetics is heart disease."

—Dr. Caldwell Esselstyn, Jr.

6

Sugar and Alternative Sweeteners

S ugar consumption is out of control. According to the US government, the average American consumes half a cup of caloric sweeteners per day, or 152 pounds per year.[118] Sugar has a reputation as the "white poison" because of the harmful effects it has on health. Although fat has been made out to be the cause of many diseases or problems, sugar is one of the most harmful ingredients in our diet.

In fact, early warning signs that one of the main causes of coronary heart disease was a result of sugar (sucrose) consumption emerged in the 1950s.[119] The Sugar Research Foundation (SRF) quietly paid for a study by Harvard scientists. They asked the scientists to point blame at fat for the main cause of coronary heart disease and leave out or minimize the blame on sugar.

This research study was published in the *New England Journal of Medicine* in 1967, with no mention of the sugar industry funding.[120] When they did this, food manufacturers responded by making more and more foods with low or no fat. They now believed that fat was the cause of coronary heart disease.

But when they took the fat out of foods, they lost the savory flavor. Thinking that sugar was not as bad for us, they would add sugar (frequently in the form of high fructose corn syrup or fructose crystals) and refined salt to foods to make them taste better and make up for the lack of flavor that fat had provided.

Sugar (including high fructose corn syrup or fructose crystals) is an ingredient in almost all processed foods, fast foods, and dairy products, but it can be hiding in many products you would not normally expect. I even see it added to dried fruits, trail mixes, and granolas in healthy grocery stores. When food companies started making low-fat products, many added additional sugar to help the food taste more appealing.

Studies conducted by the *American Journal of Clinical Nutrition* found that diabetes and obesity are directly linked to eating refined sugar and high-fructose corn syrup—the cheapest form of sugar and the choice of many food manufacturing companies.[121]

Along with diabetes and obesity, sugar intake can contribute to hypoglycemia, cardiovascular disease, kidney disease, high blood pressure, tooth decay, systemic infections, memory disorders, allergies, upset hormonal imbalances, and autoimmune and immune deficiency disorders. It supports the growth of cancer cells.

The list of health problems goes on to include adrenal gland exhaustion, anxiety, bloating, bone loss, eczema, cataracts, candidiasis, insomnia, ulcers, psoriasis, over-acidity, gout, gallstones, fatigue, acne, menstrual difficulties, indigestion, high triglyceride levels, and more. These are all good reasons to limit the amount of sugar in one's diet—especially high-fructose corn syrup or fructose, or fructose crystals.

Dr. Richard Johnson, head of Nephrology at the University of Colorado has studied fat, fructose, and diabetes. He wrote a book about his findings: *The Fat Switch*. "Dr. Johnson's book makes the case that the fructose/uric acid switch is probably the underlying major mechanism for the obesity epidemic."[122]

In *The Fat Switch*, Dr. Johnson documents many of the adverse effects of fructose. His list includes:

- **Elevates uric acid**, which can lead to inflammation and other diseases that include high blood pressure, kidney disease, and fatty liver.
- **Leads to insulin resistance**, an underlying factor in Type 2 diabetes, heart diseases, and many cancers

- **Tricks your body into gaining weight.** Fructose doesn't appropriately stimulate insulin, which, as a result, fails to suppress ghrelin ("hunger hormone") and to stimulate leptin ("satiety hormone").
- **Rapidly leads to metabolic syndrome**, or weight gain and abdominal obesity (beer belly), decreased HDL, increased LDL, elevated triglycerides, elevated blood sugar, and high blood pressure.
- **Metabolizes like ethanol**, causing toxic effects like non-alcoholic fatty liver diseases (NAFLD).[123]

Digestion breaks down the food we eat into components the body can absorb, including glucose, which powers every cell in the body. After glucose enters the blood stream, the pancreas secretes insulin, which enables glucose to enter cells and be used for fuel.

Sugar is about 50 percent glucose and 50 percent fructose. Glucose is the body's preferred form of fuel to use for energy. On the other hand, fructose breaks down into a variety of toxins, including the elevated levels of uric acid.

Plus, fructose doesn't appropriately stimulate insulin, which, as a result, fails to suppress the "satiety hormone" leptin, which makes us feel satisfied. In this way, consumption of fructose contributes to weight gain, abdominal obesity (a beer belly), decreased HDL, increased LDL, elevated triglycerides, elevated blood sugar, and high blood pressure. Fructose also "metabolizes like ethanol, causing toxic effects like non-alcoholic fatty liver diseases."[124]

When glucose gets into your bloodstream too quickly—usually because of lack of fiber in the food to slow it down—your blood sugar level spikes. This puts pressure on your pancreas to make more of the hormone insulin to regulate your blood sugar level. Insulin is important for maintaining healthy glucose levels in blood.

Fructose, particularly as high-fructose corn syrup and fructose crystals, is very hard on the body and the digestive system. These sugars are read by the body as nutrient-empty. When the body consumes them, it has to pull stored nutrients out of itself to process them. This depletes the body of stored nutrients and can result in extreme cravings for nutrients. That is why feeding the body empty calories of refined carbohydrates, such as white sugar, can result in hunger pangs.

Many people today who have extreme obesity or weight problems are actually starving to death. Their bodies are not getting the nutrients they need, and fructose is suppressing the hormones that make them feel satisfied. As a result, they feel very hungry and eat more of the same nutrient-empty (possibly fructose-containing) food.

The sugars, particularly fructose, do not appropriately stimulate insulin, so digesting these foods overworks the pancreas. Then, the body has an increasingly difficult time creating insulin to restore normal, healthy glucose levels. The constant roller coaster of blood sugar spiking can wear out the pancreas, which may then create less insulin or none at all.

Also, an excess of glucose in the system can be stored in the liver as glycogen. When the liver can't hold any more, it will return it to the blood stream as fatty acids. This can create insulin resistance, which can lead to diabetes. A diet of too much empty sugar (particularly in the form of fructose) on a continual basis can result in disease and obesity.

Sugar can affect our mental health, too. A study conducted by British psychiatric researcher Malcolm Peet showed that a diet high in sugar is strongly linked to depression and schizophrenia because it suppresses a key growth hormone in the brain called BDNF.[125] This hormone plays a vital role in memory function.

Sugar is like an addictive drug. It gives the body an artificial energy surge, and the body begins to crave that energy. Dr. Francis Stern states, "A characteristic of sugar 'binges' is that the taste for sweets, for some reason, leads to a craving for more of the same, just the way other drugs create cravings."[126]

FDA Consumer reported in February 1988, "Drugs upset the body's homeostasis (balance) mechanism so completely that, in a struggle to get back to normal, the addict can only take another dose of the same drug. Heroin, cigarettes, coffee, sugar—it's the same kind of addiction."[127] Stimulants like caffeine or alcohol can cause sugar cravings.

Today, large amounts of sugar (usually in the form of fructose or high fructose corn syrup) are added to almost all packaged foods, including canned foods, jams, jellies, dry cereals, baked goods, breading, and dairy products. It is a hidden ingredient in many foods. In addition to the obvious reason—that it makes the food taste sweeter—sugar is also added to processed foods because it reduces shrinkage, keeps their texture smoother, and keeps them from drying out.

Here are just a few examples of foods in which you will find added sugar: seafood breading, canned salmon, hamburgers in restaurants, processed lunch meats, bouillon cubes, dry-roasted nuts, peanut butter, canned tomatoes, and canned vegetables. Although they aren't a dessert, Nabisco Ritz Crackers contain six percent sucrose because "sugar is unmatched when it comes to making products tender and appetizing," according to the International Sugar Research Foundation (ISRF).[128]

It is very important to eat whole, unrefined foods that contain little or no white, refined, processed sugar, high-fructose corn syrup, fructose, fructose crystals, agave nectar, dextrose, glucose, fructose, maltose, barley malt, and sorbitol. Sugars are not all created equally, and some are far worse than others.

I recommend avoiding fake sugars and sugar substitutes altogether. Chemically-derived sweeteners can have many harmful effects on health. Artificial sweeteners are never a healthy sugar alternative. All artificial chemical sweeteners are toxic and can indirectly lead to weight gain.

They are addictive and amplify the craving for sugar, which is the opposite reason why many people consume them. In fact, given a choice between high-fructose corn syrup and artificial sweeteners, high-fructose corn syrup is recommended by far—though it's essentially asking if you should consume poison or worse poison. [129] Stick with real, whole, unrefined, and unprocessed sugars.

Check ingredient labels carefully for any sugar or sugar substitute. Or, simply make your own food. Then you will know exactly what is in it. Be knowledgeable about what you are eating.

Here are a few types of sweeteners that are alternatives to white, refined sugar. Some are good, and some aren't so good. Become sugar savvy!

Agave Syrup

Agave syrup is frequently used in many vegan foods because, unlike honey, it is not taken from an animal. Agave actually has more calories than table sugar (20 calories per teaspoon compared to 16 calories per teaspoon).

Agave is 90 percent fructose, which is actually more fructose than high-fructose corn syrup contains. In fact, agave syrup is made very much like high-fructose corn syrup.

Agave is marketed as "diabetic friendly," because it doesn't have as much glucose in it as other sweeteners. However, some studies suggest that large amounts of fructose can promote insulin resistance, and thus increase diabetes risk, boost triglycerides (fats in the blood), lower HDL ("good") cholesterol, and have other harmful effects on the heart, and possibly the liver, too. "The American Diabetes Association lists agave as a sweetener to limit, along with regular table sugar, brown sugar, honey, maple syrup, and all other sugars."[130]

You may think, "But fructose is in fruit." But whole fruit contains added nutrients, fiber, and natural electrolytes, and affects the body in a different way than refined agave syrup does.

A recent study showed agave has "minimal antioxidant activity." It is "just another form of processed (and concentrated) sugar," according to *Berkeley Wellness Alerts*.[131]

Aspartame

Aspartame is the chemical in the artificial sweeteners NutraSweet, Equal, Spoonful, and Equal-Measure, and it is found in more than 6,000 products. It is composed of three chemicals: aspartic acid, phenylalanine, and methanol. It gets converted to formaldehyde in the body.

According to the federal Occupational Safety and Health Administration (OSHA), formaldehyde is a carcinogen that can seriously harm your "liver, kidney, spleen, pancreas, brain, and central nervous systems. The occupational health hazards of formaldehyde are primarily due to its toxic effects after inhalation, after direct contact with the skin or eyes in liquid or vapor form, and after ingestion." [132] Formaldehyde can also cause allergic sensitization.

Aspartame can cause many problems, including neurological ones. According to one study:

When the temperature of aspartame exceeds 86°F, the wood alcohol in aspartame converts to formaldehyde and then to formic acid, which in turn causes metabolic acidosis. The methanol toxicity mimics multiple sclerosis; thus, people may be misdiagnosed with having multiple sclerosis. Multiple sclerosis does not lead to death, whereas methanol toxicity does.[133]

According to a report from the National Institutes of Health:
Methanol is extremely poisonous. As little as two tablespoons can be deadly to a child. About 2–8 ounces can be deadly for an adult. Blindness is common and often permanent, despite medical care. How well the person recovers depends on how much poison is swallowed and how soon treatment is received.[134]

Mark Gold of the Aspartame Toxicity Information Center writes:
Both the US Air Force's magazine *Flying Safety* and the US Navy's magazine *Navy Physiology* published articles warning

about the many dangers of aspartame. They included the cumulative, deleterious effects of methanol, and the greater likelihood of birth defects.

The articles note that the ingestion of aspartame may make pilots more susceptible to seizures and vertigo (US Air Force 1992). Countless other toxicity effects have been reported to the FDA (DHHS 1995), other independent organizations (Mission Possible 1996, Stoddard 1995), and independent scientists (e.g., 80 cases of seizures were reported to Dr. Richard Wurtman, Food in 1986).

Frequently, aspartame toxicity is misdiagnosed as a specific disease. This hasn't been reported in scientific literature, yet it has been reported countless times to independent organizations and scientists. In other cases, it has been reported that chronic aspartame ingestion has triggered or worsened certain chronic illnesses.

Nearly 100 percent of the time, the patient and physician assume these worsening conditions are a normal progression of the illness. Sometimes that may be true, but many times it is chronic aspartame poisoning.[135]

The following is a list of chronic illnesses that may be caused or worsened by the long-term ingestion of aspartame, according to researchers studying its adverse effects. In some cases, such as MS, the symptoms mimic or worsen the disease, but do not cause it. This list shouldn't be considered definitive, because regular intake of a poison is bad for any chronic illness.

- Brain tumors
- Multiple sclerosis
- Epilepsy
- Chronic fatigue syndrome
- Parkinson's disease
- Alzheimer's
- Mental retardation
- Lymphoma
- Birth defects

- Fibromyalgia
- Diabetes
- Arthritis (including rheumatoid)
- Chemical sensitivities
- Attention Deficit Disorder [136]

Stevia

> "Stevia is the only sweetener recommended. Several modern studies suggest that stevia may have the ability to lower and balance blood sugar levels, support the pancreas and digestive system, protect the liver, and combat infectious microorganisms."
>
> —Dr. Gabriel Cousens, author of *There Is a Cure for Diabetes*.

Stevia is a sweetener derived from *Stevia rebaudiana Bertoni*, a South American plant that is a member of the aster family. Japanese food manufacturers developed this sweetener in the 1970s as a zero-calorie sugar. The Japanese have done extensive research on stevia and found it extremely safe.

The stevia plant has been commonly used in Paraguay to treat diabetes, and by indigenous populations for the control of fertility. Keep this in mind if you are trying to get pregnant. Some researchers have expressed concern that stevia might have an antifertility effect in men or women. However, evidence from most (though not all) animal studies suggests that this is not a concern at normal doses.

That being said, steviol glycosides are the natural chemicals that give stevia a sweet taste. Steviol glycosides are structurally similar to the plant hormones gibberellin and kaurene, which means that stevia has a hormone structure. Anyone with a hormone imbalance or a dysfunctional immune system should be aware of the possible effect of stevia on hormones.

Stevia comes in powder and liquid form. I have been using this sweetener for years, but I use it sparingly and maybe once a week at most.

I like the liquid form best because I think it has a better flavor, while the powder form can be a bit bitter.

Make sure to read the ingredient label. Companies use different ingredients to preserve stevia or prepare it to be packaged. One company, for example, uses grapefruit seed extract, which can interact very badly with some medications. Be aware of this, and read all of the ingredients carefully before using.

The WebMD website includes this information for drug interactions:

Lithium interacts with stevia. Stevia might have an effect like a water pill or "diuretic." Taking stevia might decrease how well the body gets rid of lithium. This could increase how much lithium is in the body and result in serious side effects. Talk with your healthcare provider before using this product if you are taking lithium. Your lithium dose might need to be changed.

Medications for diabetes (antidiabetic drugs) interact with stevia. Stevia might decrease blood sugar in people with Type 2 diabetes. Diabetes medications are also used to lower blood sugar. Taking stevia along with diabetes medications might cause your blood sugar to go too low. Monitor your blood sugar closely. The dose of your diabetes medication might need to be changed.

Some medications used for diabetes include glimepiride (Amaryl), glyburide (DiaBeta, Glynase PresTab, Micronase), insulin, pioglitazone (Actos), rosiglitazone (Avandia), chlorpropamide (Diabinese), glipizide (Glucotrol), tolbutamide (Orinase), and others.

Medications for high blood pressure (Antihypertensive drugs) interact with stevia. Stevia might decrease blood pressure in some people. Taking stevia along with medications used for lowering high blood pressure might cause your blood pressure to go too low. However, it's not known if this is a big concern. Do not take too much stevia if you are taking medications for high blood pressure.

Some medications for high blood pressure include captopril (Capoten), enalapril (Vasotec), losartan (Cozaar), valsartan (Diovan), diltiazem (Cardizem), amlodipine (Norvasc), hydrochlorothiazide (HydroDIURIL), furosemide (Lasix), and many others.[137]

From what I gather, this plant can help people who are trying to lower their blood pressure or blood sugar levels. If you have any concerns, talk to your physician.

Xylitol

Xylitol: One sugar I've used over the years is xylitol, especially if a recipe calls for granulated sugar. Xylitol is a sugar alcohol naturally found in fruits and vegetables. It's usually made from birch tree bark and other hardwood trees.

Some sources say xylitol was discovered by German scientist Emil Fisher in 1891. When Finland had severe sugar shortages during World War II, people started making it commercially. After the war, Finnish dentists noticed that schoolchildren had unusually strong, cavity-free teeth. This discovery led the Finnish government to be the first to officially endorse the use of xylitol as a sweetener.

By the 1960s, Germany, Switzerland, Japan, and the Soviet Union were using xylitol as their preferred sweetener for diabetics. It was also used as an energy source for infusion therapy with patients who have impaired glucose intolerance and insulin resistance.

Xylitol is considered a five-carbon sugar, which means it has antimicrobial effects, preventing the growth of bacteria. It is also alkaline-enhancing and can replace sugar in recipes in equal substitution. Xylitol tastes and looks just like sugar with no bitter aftertaste.

Drug interactions have not been found. The only side effect is that when consumed in large doses over 30 or 40 grams at one time, it can cause gas and diarrhea. Some types of xylitol have a little bigger granule size than refined sugar. When purchasing xylitol, the smaller, finer grain variety will bake easier.

Xylitol and stevia are both sweeteners that can be used in diabetic diets. In addition to helping prevent cavities, xylitol can help repair dental enamel, regulate blood sugar for those with Type 2 diabetes, strengthen bones, decrease age-related bone loss, inhibit serious systemic yeast problems, inhibit the growth of bacteria that cause middle ear infections in young children, inhibit the growth of streptococcus pneumonia, and alleviate dry mouth. It even inhibits inner ear and other infections. Mothers love that!

In addition, xylitol has 40 percent fewer calories and 75 percent fewer carbohydrates than sugar. It's slowly absorbed and metabolized, which results in negligible changes in insulin. Its consumption can reduce sugar cravings and insulin levels, and help alkalize your body. It was approved by the FDA in 1963.[138]

Xylitol is not for pets!

Animals' systems are different from ours. Like chocolate, egg whites, and red grapes, xylitol is very toxic to dogs/animals. Please keep xylitol, and anything you use it in, away from your pet.

Purchase xylitol from US sources that use non-GMO ingredients. Here is a list of recommended brands:

1. **Smart Sweet Xylitol.** Source: Organic birch and occasionally beech trees (non-GMO). Country of origin: US and occasionally Austria in cases of limited supply. Full ingredients: Xylitol.

2. **Source Naturals Xylismart.** Source: Birch (non-GMO). Country of origin: US. (They told me it is "currently sourced" from the US.) Full ingredients: Xylitol.

3. **Health Garden Kosher Real Birch Xylitol.** Source: Birch (non-GMO). Country of origin: US. Full ingredients: Xylitol.

4. **Swanson Premium 100% Pure Xylitol Powder.** Source: Birch (non-GMO). Country of origin: US. Full ingredients: Xylitol.

5. **Xyla Xylitol Powder.** Source: Birch (non-GMO). Country of origin: US. Full ingredients: Xylitol.

Avoid the following brands due to their GMO sources:

1. **Jarrow Formulas XyliPure Xylitol Powder.** Source: Corn (non-GMO). Country of origin: China. Full ingredients: Xylitol, silicon dioxide.

2. **KAL Xylitol.** Source: Corn (could be GMO). Country of origin: China.

3. **Xlear XyloSweet All Natural Xylitol Sweetener.** Source: Both birch and corn (could be GMO). Country of origin: China and US.

Honey and Other Sweeteners

Honey is a natural sweetener that is antifungal and antibacterial. Honey can be used as a natural antiseptic. It is a natural remedy for many ailments, and it can boost energy. *Weekly World News* listed arthritis, hair loss, bladder infections, upset stomach, indigestion, influenza, heart disease, colds, and cholesterol as some of the afflictions that could be cured by honey and cinnamon.[139] Honey contains a variety of nutrients and minerals, as well as some enzymes. It is known to help the facilitation of muscle recuperation and glycogen restoration after a workout.

Honey is not for infants!

According to Ann Louise Gittleman, PhD, CNS: **Never give an infant under eighteen months of age honey or products made with honey.** This sweetener sometimes contains trace amounts of botulinum spores, which are easily denatured by the mature digestive tract of an adult, but can be harmful or even fatal to an infant, whose digestive tract is just developing.[140]

If you are concerned about the welfare of bees, then find a responsible beekeeper who doesn't take all of the bees' winter honey stores but leaves them with enough to support their hive. Such responsible beekeepers are around. We want to be conscious consumers when it comes to supporting our web of life.

Honey can be substituted for sugar in recipes. Always buy raw, unrefined honey because it will have all of the live enzymes and nutritional properties still intact.

Blackstrap molasses is the residue of beet juice or sugar cane after the sugar crystals have been removed. Blackstrap molasses contains minerals, including iron, calcium, and magnesium, even though it is still about 65 percent sucrose. Buy organic varieties.

Coconut sugar is made from boiling down the nectar of tropical coconut palm sugar blossoms. This sugar has a naturally low glycemic index. It has been used in East Asia for herbal medicine and food preparation. The glycemic index is approximately 35. It is high in potassium, magnesium, zinc, iron, and B vitamins. Buy organic, unprocessed, unbleached, and unfiltered coconut sugar with no preservatives added.

Date sugar is derived from dried dates. It has some fiber and is rich in minerals, since it is essentially dried fruit. It is a nice alternative to other sugars.

Maple syrup is a natural sugar derived from maple tree sap. It contains minerals including potassium and calcium.

7

Vitamins, Minerals, And Supplements

Chromium

The mineral chromium is important because it helps transport glucose from blood into muscles. According to the National Institutes of Health, "Chromium is known to enhance the action of insulin, a hormone critical to the metabolism and storage of carbohydrates, fat, and protein in the body."[141]

The chemical fertilizers used in industrial farming destroy the chromium that would naturally be in the soil. This means people who eat non-organic foods have a greater likelihood of being deficient in this important trace mineral. Organic is always the best choice at the grocery store.

If you take a chromium supplement, make sure it is in a natural form, not a synthetic one. It should have GTF on the label. GTF stands for "glucose tolerance factor".

Synthetic forms of any nutrient can be harmful to the body.[142] Therefore, when buying any kind of dietary supplement, look for whole, organic foods in the ingredients list.

My research has shown that non-synthetic supplements are much more effective, and that synthetic ones can cause serious health problems.[143] So, always look to see that the supplement lists whole real food (example: whole organic broccoli) in the ingredients on the label.

Fulvic Acid

Fulvic acid is the end product of decomposition of organic matter, which is nutrient dense. It is something like compost, but the smallest concentrated particle of compost. It's a micro nanomolecule, which means it is incredibly small and able to cross all blood-brain barriers and carry nutrients to the cells.

Its antioxidant capacity is enormous. One molecule of fulvic acid has 14 tetratrillion electrons that it can donate to help eliminate free radicals. It is an antioxidant agent that can act as an electrolyte in the cell.

It's been used by Dr. Daniel Nuzum, D.O., N.M.D. (Toxicologist, professor, scientist and researcher) for cancer therapy. He says that fulvic acid has the "electrolyte capacity to raise the electrical capacity in the cells and it destroys cancer cells that way."[144] If it can do this, then it is an important nutrient we should all take for optimum health.

Dr. Nuzum said he has been researching fulvic acid since 1996 and has only had good results. He went on to say that he has his whole family (including his children) take it daily.[145]

It comes in a liquid with a dropper. You take it in small doses. It doesn't taste very good, so I add it to my smoothies in the morning so I don't taste it.

Magnesium

Magnesium is a trace mineral necessary for hundreds of bodily functions. Magnesium deficiency has been linked to diabetes, migraines, allergies, anxiety, asthma, attention deficit disorder, calcification of soft tissue (including the heart valve), muscle cramps, osteoporosis, fibromyalgia, hearing loss, menstrual cramps, insomnia, irritability, trembling, twitching, and more. Magnesium deficiency can cause increased levels of adrenaline, which can cause feelings of anxiety.

A Brown University study found magnesium extremely beneficial for children with acute asthma. Additionally, children with sensitive hearing may have low magnesium levels. Two separate research teams comprised of researchers at the Harvard School of Public Health and Harvard Medical School found a link between magnesium and reduced Type 2 diabetes risk, findings published in the January, 2004 issue of the journal *Diabetes Care.*

Yet 56 percent of Americans do not get enough magnesium from their diet.[146] Another reason so many people are deficient in magnesium may be the use of calcium supplements that don't include magnesium. "High calcium intakes can make magnesium deficiency worse," according to Forrest Nielsen. [147] He says consuming additional magnesium can help. In an article on the USDA Agriculture Research Service website, Mr. Nielsen goes on to say: "The diets of many people do not contain enough magnesium for good health and sleep."[148]

Foods containing magnesium are whole grains, nuts, and vegetables, especially green, leafy vegetables. Beans contain magnesium, too—even cacao, which is where chocolate comes from. Cacao is a little bitter, which is why chocolatiers add sugar. But in its raw, unsweetened form, it is actually very healthy!

Some tasty magnesium-rich food choices for children are baked potatoes, bananas, coconut milk, peas, peanut butter, bean burritos, cacao, and cashews. Caffeine and alcohol can cause a magnesium loss. Foods and drinks that are high in caffeine include: coffee, tea, some energy drinks and bars, and various types of soda.

In addition to these reasons to add more magnesium-rich foods to your diet, Reuters, has connected higher magnesium levels with a lower risk of diabetes.[149]

An easy way to add magnesium to your body is to take an Epsom salts bath. Epsom salt baths can help prevent a magnesium deficiency. Epsom salts are formed from a pure mineral compound containing magnesium and sulfate. Both magnesium and sulfate stimulate detoxification in the body. Magnesium and sulfate are both minerals that can be absorbed through our skin and taken up into the bloodstream in a bath.

So, at the end of the day, when you are ready for bed, take an Epsom salt bath, relax, and supplement your body's magnesium levels. It helps you sleep better and helps your health in so many ways.

Salt

When I ask people if they use salt, they frequently tell me, "No, I eat a low-salt diet for health reasons." In fact, it is not salt that is bad for us, it is the *type* of salt we eat that is either "good" or "bad" for us.

The word "electrolyte" is a chemical term for salt. We need electrolytes to be healthy. As Dr. David Brownstein says, "Without salt, life itself would not be possible.[150] The misconception about salt stems from the fact that conventional medical doctors make no differentiation between white, refined salt and unrefined, mineral-rich sea salt.

Unrefined mineral-rich sea salt is natural and has not been processed. It is important for life because it: promotes the proper balance for the endocrine, adrenal, and thyroid gland to function properly; supports healthy blood pressure; detoxifies the body; and, along with water, is necessary for the optimal functioning of the immune system, hormonal system, and cardiovascular health.[151]

When we sweat, our body can lose many minerals, and these minerals need to be replenished. Unrefined whole sea salt contains these minerals. Sea salt can also help balance the body by alkalizing it. Maintaining a slightly alkaline pH is important to our health.

The white, refined table salt most of us grew up using lacks numerous minerals that are present in whole, natural sea salt. Refined table salt is 98 percent sodium chloride with added bicarbonates, chemicals, sugar, and preservatives.

Iodine, the main nutrient that supports our thyroid gland, is added to many refined salts, but in insufficient quantities "to prevent thyroid illnesses or to provide for the body's iodine needs."[152] Given that iodine dissipates after being exposed to oxygen, table salt could never be a reliable source of iodine anyway.

Many food sources today lack vital minerals and nutrients. Soils are depleted, and refining and processing take out many or all of the nutrients in foods. Salt cravings are actually a signal you may be depleted in nutrients, minerals, and electrolytes.

Salt cravings can also be a signal that your thyroid and adrenal glands need minerals. If you have been craving salt or have been under a good deal of stress, have your thyroid checked to make sure you are getting enough iodine in your diet. We don't have many food sources for iodine, and it can be extremely important to our health.

Dr. Brownstein says low-salt diets "promote toxicity" and have:

...adverse effects on numerous metabolic markers, including promoting elevated insulin levels and insulin resistance. Low-salt diets have been associated with elevating normal cholesterol and LDL cholesterol levels, which in turn, have been associated with cardiovascular disease. Finally, low-salt diets will lead to mineral deficiencies and the development of chronic disease.[153]

In 1994, The *British Medical Journal* published a study conducted in the Netherlands. The study examined 100 men and women between the ages of 55 and 75 who had mild to moderate hypertension. When refined table salt was replaced with mineral salt high in magnesium and potassium, the study showed a reduction in blood pressure equivalent to that produced by drugs which lower blood pressure.[154]

There are various types of sea salt with different mineral contents. Try a few different ones and see which you like the best. Real Salt is a mineral-rich sea salt mined in Utah. Celtic sea salt is supposed to be high in minerals, but it's taken from present-day oceans that are highly polluted. I like Bolivian Rose salt, because it has some natural iodine in it as well as iron.

Try to buy a solar-dried salt or a mined salt. Mined salt may be cleaner and more nutrient-dense because it was formed when oceans were less polluted, and during a more nutrient-dense time.

Exchanging this one refined, unhealthy ingredient in your diet for the healthier unrefined, mineral rich sea salt will help you hydrate more effectively. It helps your immune system and adrenal glands function better. You will absorb more nutrients from your food more effectively, and your food may taste richer.

As Dr. Brownstein's book says: *Salt your way to health!*

Sulfur

Sulfur is an extremely important nutrient, yet it is highly overlooked. Because chemical fertilizers destroy the natural sulfur in the soil, non-organic foods don't contain this nutrient. People who eat non-organically grown types of foods are more likely to have an insufficient amount of sulfur in their body.

Sulfur is a major nutrient we need to get oxygen into our cells, and it is the third most prevalent element in the body. With sulfur being one of our body's main nutrients, this is absolutely critical to our health. Without the proper levels of sulfur, our bodies aren't able to build good healthy cells, and this leads to illness.

Sulfur is found in all organically grown foods. But, due to its unstable nature, sulfur is quickly lost from food when it is processed, cooked, or stored. That is why a diet high in freshly picked, raw, unprocessed, whole, organic food is so vitally important.

The powdered variety of sulfur (methylsulfonylmethane, known as MSM) has limited effectiveness as a dietary supplement. Powdering it or combining it with magnesium stearate, which is used as filler in many supplements, can render the sulfur in MSM fairly useless.

Dr. Johanna Budwig, a German biochemist and author, lived from 1908–2003. She worked as a pharmacist and held doctorate degrees in physics and chemistry. She researched fatty acids, and she developed a diet she thought important in the treatment of cancer She was nominated seven times for the Nobel Prize.

Dr. Budwig was considered an expert in several fields such as pharmacology, physics, and chemistry; specifically the chemistry of fats. Dr. Budwig contributed to the Federal Research Institute of Fats and Oils. Today, her discoveries are still held in high regard.

She discovered that when she combined flax seed oil with organic cottage cheese or kefir, which contains sulfurated proteins, there was a chemical reaction which made the fat compounds water-soluble and absorbable by the cell membrane.

You can get more natural sulfur into your body by swimming, bathing, or drinking water from a natural spring or well that contains natural, organic sulfur. This type of water has been known for its healing qualities for centuries.

Vitamin B Complex

Although all nutrients and minerals are important for optimum health, there are a few nutrients that are *critical* to health. One of those nutrients is the Vitamin B complex, so make certain you are getting an adequate amount of all the B vitamins.

Thiamine (Vitamin B1), riboflavin (Vitamin B2), and niacin (Vitamin B3) are necessary for energy production.

Vitamin B5, or pantothenic acid, helps the body use fats and proteins in food and turn carbohydrates into blood sugar for energy. Foods that contain Vitamin B5 are whole grains, legumes, eggs, nuts, avocados, spinach, kale, broccoli, cauliflower, corn, and tomatoes.

Vitamin B6 helps your body process protein, as well as supporting the nervous system and immune system. Vitamin B6 is in avocados, bananas, and eggs.

Biotin (Vitamin B7) helps the body produce hormones and aids in converting food into energy.

Folate (Vitamin B9) is found in citrus fruits, peanuts, and some mushrooms. Along with Vitamin A, it is concentrated in green vegetables like romaine lettuce, spinach, turnip greens, mustard greens, parsley, collard greens, broccoli, cauliflower, beets, and lentils. The Centers for Disease Control and Prevention say expectant mothers need 400 mcg of folate daily before and during pregnancy to prevent birth defects in their babies' brain and spine.[155]

The synthetic form of folate is folic acid. High intakes of folic acid have been associated with higher risks of cancer, as well as masking B12 deficiencies. So, if you use a B vitamin supplement, make sure it contains folate in a whole-food form of Vitamin B9.

Look for 5-methyltetrahydrofolate or 5-MTHF as the folate, and avoid supplements that contain folic acid.

Vitamin B12, or cobalamin, is unique in that it is almost exclusively found in animal sources such as meat, fish, dairy, and eggs. It is the B vitamin I have found to be vitally important for vegetarians in particular. As Dr. Joseph Mercola notes, "microorganisms, primarily bacteria, are the only known organisms that manufacture B12. These bacteria often live in bodies of water and soil.

Animals get B12 by eating food and soil contaminated with these microorganisms."[156] The bacteria require cobalt to produce B12, which is why it is also known as cobalamin. Plant food can provide Vitamin B12 if it is taken from soil containing cobalt and is not cleaned, leaving the bacteria on it.

People eating a mostly plant based diet should have their blood checked by a doctor to make certain they are getting enough B12 and other B vitamins, including folate. Vegans, who eat no animal products at all, should consistently eat foods fortified with Vitamin B12—such as breakfast cereals—two or three times each day to get at least 3 mcg of B12 daily.

For example, if a fortified plant milk contains 1 mcg of Vitamin B12 per serving, then consuming three servings a day will provide adequate Vitamin B12. Other vegans may find the use of Vitamin B12 supplements more convenient and economical.

The less frequently you obtain Vitamin B12, the more you need to take, as Vitamin B12 is best absorbed in small amounts. A daily supplement of 10 mcg is required. But, the body's ability to absorb vitamin B12 from dietary supplements is limited. "For example, only about 10 mcg of a 500 mcg oral supplement is actually absorbed in healthy people."[157]

I have been using a new type of vitamin B12 called Methylcobalamin. You take it by spraying it under your tongue. This type of sprayable vitamin supplement is more absorbable.

Methylcobalamin "is the most active form of B12 in the human body. It converts homocysteine into methionine, which helps protect the cardiovascular system. Methylcobalamin also offers overall protection to the nervous system.

This Methylcobalamin B12 form can also cross the blood-brain barrier–without assistance–to protect brain cells. It contributes essential methyl groups needed for detoxification and to start the body's biochemical reactions."[158]

Look for this type of supplement. When taking vitamins, you want to thrive, not just survive.

Symptoms of deficiency include energy loss, tingling, numbness, reduced sensitivity to pain or pressure, blurred vision, abnormal gait, sore tongue, poor memory, confusion, hallucinations, and personality changes. Often these symptoms develop gradually over several months to a year before they are recognized as being due to a B12 deficiency, and they are usually reversible upon the administration of B12.[159]

When I read this list of symptoms, I was really surprised. Lack of Vitamin B could have been one of the contributing factors to vision problems I had battled all of my life. I read this, too:

According to Optometrist Ben C. Lane of the Optical Society, there is a link between nearsightedness and chromium and calcium levels, which are lowered by sugar and protein consumption. The excessive intake of sugar and overcooked proteins exhaust the body's supplies of chromium and B vitamins. Fluid pressure in the eye, a contributing factor of nearsightedness, is regulated by the B vitamins.[160]

Make certain you are getting adequate amounts of all of the B vitamins.

Vitamin D

Vitamin D is essential because it influences your entire body. Receptors that respond to the vitamin have been found in almost every type of human cell, from your brain to your bones. It is also involved in multiple repair and maintenance functions. It touches thousands of different genes. It regulates your immune system, and much, much more. Vitamin D regulates your ability to fight infections and chronic inflammation. It produces over 200 antimicrobial peptides.[161]

Vitamin D is a prohormone, which means the body converts it into an active form; in this case, calcitriol. A deficiency of calcitriol may be responsible for more than 17 cancers, diabetes, autoimmune disease, multiple sclerosis, osteoarthritis, hypertension/high blood pressure, depression, and genetic disorders, and it may increase the risk of cardiovascular disease.[162]

Rickets (bone softening) is a disease caused by Vitamin D deficiency. Sounds a lot like osteoporosis, doesn't it? If you have a bone problem, have your Vitamin D checked. Vitamin D deficiency has also been linked to cancer. Check with your physician to make certain the level of Vitamin D in your blood is optimal.

The body makes its own vitamin D from cholesterol when skin is exposed to sunlight. Vitamin D is essential for everyone. Studies show approximately 85 percent of the US population is critically low in Vitamin D.[163] It may be the use of sunscreen or working and staying indoors most of the day which prevents people from getting enough direct sunlight.

Get some sunshine! Get out in the sun every day for at least 20 minutes without sunscreen. The more skin is exposed, the more sunlight you can absorb. During the winter months, it may be harder or even impossible to get the necessary amount of Vitamin D from the sun. Full-spectrum lighting indoors can significantly help with depression, mood, and health, but it is not a reliable source of Vitamin D.

Very few foods contain good levels of Vitamin D. Parsley, mushrooms that have been exposed to ultraviolet light, and cod liver oil have Vitamin D in them, but a supplement is still needed.

Recently, UC San Diego and Creighton University have researched vitamin D extensively and come to the conclusion that vitamin D recommended intake needs to be addressed.

Researchers are challenging the intake of vitamin D recommended by the National Academy of Sciences Institute of Medicine saying their Recommended Dietary Allowance for vitamin D underestimates the need by a factor of ten. They argue that a miscalculation lead to low recommendations for Vitamin D.

Robert Heaney, M.D., of Creighton University wrote: "We call for the NAS-IOM and all public health authorities concerned with transmitting accurate nutritional information to the public to designate, as the RDA, a value of approximately 7,000 IU/day from all sources."[164]

I get a good deal of sunlight every day, and I live in Texas, so I thought I had an optimum level of Vitamin D in my body. I had my doctor test me, only to find out I was on the low end of optimum. This was even during the summer, so I was quite surprised! Since then, I have been taking about 5,000–6,000 IU's of Vitamin D a day—and I'm 61, and I feel great. But given the new study by Creighton, I am going to increase it to 7,000 a day.

I prefer to take supplements that are created with organic, whole-food ingredients. I avoid synthetic varieties, because research has shown that some synthetic varieties of vitamins may increase chances of cancer.[165] I've been using vitamins that you spray under your tongue for maximum absorption. These vitamins are organic, whole food, raw and non-GMO.

In conclusion, keep an eye on your Vitamin D, and remember that as we age, we need more of it.

Zinc

Zinc is one of the most important minerals used by the body. It helps with the production of approximately 100 enzymes. Zinc contributes to building up the immune system. Zinc is required for protein and DNA synthesis, insulin activity, and liver function.

Zinc is not really stored in our body, so we need a regular supply. Men need one-third more zinc than women because the prostate gland and semen are highly concentrated with zinc. Sexually active men need a good supply of zinc consistently. A zinc deficiency may appear as skin problems, impairment of taste, a poor immune system, hair loss, diarrhea, fatigue, wounds not healing properly, or a poor or slow growth rate for infants.

Good sources of zinc are lentils, peas (chickpeas are good), seeds (sesame tahini paste is good, and so are pumpkin seeds), whole-grain cereals or breads, beans, cheddar cheese, yogurt, and wheat germ. Some fair sources are peanut butter, figs, Brazil nuts, oranges, and almonds.

Even if you eat zinc-rich foods, you may need a supplement, because phytic acid and dietary fiber in certain foods can inhibit the absorption of zinc. Also, if the body has high levels of cadmium, the cadmium will compete with the zinc to be absorbed. We can get cadmium from sources such as secondhand cigarette smoke.

Chemicals added to processed foods also impair the body's absorption of zinc. If you do take a zinc supplement, take a high-quality, whole-food supplement.

8

Super Foods for Super Health

Chia Seeds

Because the seeds of the chia plant, a member of the mint family, are so nutrient-dense, they were one of the main survival foods used by Aztec and Mayan people. They also had many medicinal uses. The Spanish banned the use of chia seeds after their conquest of Mexico because the Aztecs, whom the Spanish considered pagan, used them in their religious ceremonies. Chia seeds disappeared for a while, but they are making a comeback.

Chia seeds don't have much flavor, so they can easily be added to many dishes. I soak them in water or coconut water overnight in the refrigerator because they swell and become gelatinous with the consistency of pudding. I add these soaked seeds to my smoothies, peanut butter, cottage cheese, yogurt, salads, pancake mix, cookie mix, and breakfast dishes like oatmeal. I make cashew crème and add it to the gelatinous chia mixture with a little fresh fruit for a wonderful breakfast dish or dessert.

Chia seeds help you feel full because they are full of highly soluble fiber that is easily used by the body, and they slowly release unrefined carbohydrates into your blood stream for natural energy. They are also a good source of Omega 3 fatty acids, which have anti-inflammatory properties. Both of these characteristics make them a great food for dieters, diabetics, or anyone who wants to reduce food cravings.

Cinnamon

Researchers have investigated the "insulin-like" effects of cinnamon for years now, and recent research on diabetes shows, cinnamon is an amazing food in the fight against diabetes.

A 12-week London study was recently conducted on 58 Type 2 diabetics with hemoglobin A1c (HbA1c) levels over 7 percent. Hemoglobin A1c is a marker for long-term glycemic control in diabetics.

After 12 weeks on 2 grams of cinnamon per day, the subjects had significantly lower HbA1c levels, as well as significantly reduced blood pressures (systolic, SBP and diastolic, DBP).

The researchers' conclusion: "Intake of 2g of cinnamon for 12 weeks significantly reduces the HbA1c, SBP and DBP among poorly controlled Type 2 diabetes patients. Cinnamon supplementation could be considered as an additional dietary supplement option to regulate blood glucose and blood pressure levels along with conventional medications to treat Type 2 diabetes mellitus." [166]

Ceylon cinnamon is the best variety of cinnamon to use because it has the lowest amount of coumarin, a substance which can be problematic for your liver.

Ceylon cinnamon has many health benefits for you. It:
- significantly reduces blood sugar levels, triglycerides, and LDL (bad) cholesterol in people with Type 2 diabetes.
- improves the effectiveness, or sensitivity, of insulin.
- supports the digestive function.
- relieves congestion.
- relieves pain and stiffness of muscles and joints.
- contains anti-inflammatory compounds that relieve arthritis.
- helps prevent urinary tract infections, tooth decay, and gum disease.
- relieves menstrual discomfort.
- contains blood-thinning compounds that stimulate circulation.

Add some cinnamon to your diet! It's an incredibly inexpensive, great-tasting spice you can add to a diet for diabetes.

Mushrooms

According to a study conducted by The University of Western Australia in Perth, eating mushrooms daily may reduce breast cancer risk by nearly two thirds. The study, conducted in China, looked at more than 2000 women, half of whom had suffered from breast cancer. Researchers found the women who ate a third of an ounce of fresh mushrooms every day had lowered their risk of developing a tumor by 64 percent.

Dried mushrooms didn't have quite the same benefit, but still reduced the risk "by around half." The study also found that the women who regularly drank green tea, combined with their daily serving of fresh mushrooms, reduced their risk by 90 percent.

When reporting this study in 2009, *The Telegraph* went on to say that animal tests show mushrooms have "anti-tumor properties and can stimulate the immune system's defenses." Mushrooms might accomplish this by blocking "the body's production of the hormone oestrogen, which can encourage the development of cancer."[167]

As the author of *How to Be a Healthy Vegetarian*, I promote a plant-based diet. A vegetarian diet "provides a variety of cancer-protective dietary factors," according to a study published in *The American Journal of Clinical Nutrition*. A vegetarian diet reduces obesity. This study's author notes that obesity increases cancer risk, and that because the Body Mass Index (BMI) "of vegans is considerably lower than that of non-vegetarians," a plant-based diet "may be an important protective factor for lowering cancer risk."[168] Mushrooms are low in calories and are 80–90 percent water, which makes them a great substitute for meat when you want to cut calories.

Mushrooms have been studied extensively for their health benefits because they have been found to aid the immune system. These dense, smooth, earthy fungi grow in thousands of varieties, and most of them are rich in potassium, selenium, copper, riboflavin, niacin, pantothenic acid, and B-complex vitamins. One medium Portobello mushroom has more potassium than a small banana. Five medium cremini mushrooms have more selenium than a large egg or three ounces of lean beef.

Plus, the copper in mushrooms helps you make red blood cells, which carry oxygen throughout your body. Mushrooms are an excellent source of the antioxidants known as polyphenols, selenium, and ergothioneine. Ergothioneine is a master antioxidant, an amino acid containing sulfur. Sulfur is an extremely important nutrient, yet it is often overlooked.

There are many varieties of mushrooms, thousands of which are poisonous, so do *not* pick them in the wild. Always buy them from a reliable and reputable supplier. Look for mushrooms that are smooth, clean, and fresh in appearance. To clean them, use a soft mushroom brush or wet paper towel to remove any parts that look dirty or mushy. You can rinse them, but do not soak them.

Keep them refrigerated in the original container until you're ready to use them. They can keep up to a week in the refrigerator in a porous paper bag, but never put mushrooms in an airtight container and never freeze them. Always trim the end of the stem before you use mushrooms. If the stems are too tough, just use the caps.

Adding mushrooms to dishes is easy. Thinly slice them for salads, pasta dishes, and sandwiches—or serve them as a side dish. Grilling them is always great, and mushrooms make a tasty and healthy alternative to a burger. I love to sauté them with onions and butter to bring out the rich flavor of savory mushrooms. Each mushroom has a different flavor, so experiment by trying different varieties.

Reishi mushrooms, the "Mushrooms of Immortality", have been used to treat countless ailments in the Far East for over 2,000 years because of their extraordinary medicinal properties. They have been found to decrease inflammation, increase energy levels, repair damaged blood vessels, and relieve hormonal imbalances. Studies have repeatedly shown that reishi mushrooms have antioxidant abilities that strengthen the body's defenses against cancer, diabetes, autoimmune diseases, heart disease, allergies, and infections.[169]

A study conducted by the Department of Pharmacology of Peking University in Beijing and published December, 2006 in the *Journal of Asian Natural Products Research* looked into the reishi mushroom's effects on diabetic kidney disease. After the eight-week trial period, the diabetic subjects showed noticeable reduction of markers in kidney stress, and a considerable reduction of triglyceride and blood sugar levels. The researchers concluded that reishi mushrooms could prevent or halt the progression of diabetic kidney complications.[170]

The mushroom is tough and woody, so you need it in a powder or extract when using it as a supplement. The reishi mushroom supplement is effective in reducing blood sugar level and the amounts of insulin required for diabetic patients. For non-insulin dependent patients, it is possible to have a better result. Diabetics should see significant effects within 1 or 2 months. The usual dose recommended is 3 or 4 capsules, 3 times daily.[171]

Turmeric

Turmeric is one of the most potent healing herbs on earth. It contains a compound called curcumin.

Curcumin is a substance that attributes to turmeric's powerful antioxidant and anti-inflammatory properties. It has been found to help decrease chronic inflammation, boosts the immune system, help with irritable bowel syndrome, just to name a few.[172]

Turmeric has been studied extensively, but recent research has shown that curcumin dramatically decreased brain tumors by 81 percent in 9 out of the 11 studies examined.[173]

Turmeric can be taken in capsule form or simply added to recipes like curry. Spice up your meals and create healthier foods!

"Children with diabetic genetic tendencies who drink cow's milk have an 11–13 times higher rate of juvenile diabetes than children who are breastfed by their own mothers for at least three months."

—Dr. Gabriel Cousens

9

Elements of Nutrition for Optimum Health

Gluten, GMOs, and Why They Matter

People ask me often what gluten is or what GMOs are and why they matter. Part of the problem with foods that contain gluten is that most of them are GMO or hybridized grains.

Gluten is a protein found in wheat, rye, spelt, and barley. More and more people are being diagnosed with gluten intolerance or celiac disease. An estimated 20 million Americans have gluten sensitivities. Because of hybridization, many gluten-containing grains today have 50–80 percent more gluten in them than they did 100 years ago.

The word "gluten" comes from the Latin word for glue. If you've ever made papier-mâché using glue made from wheat flour and water, you can understand how this mixture can be very hard for your body to digest. Symptoms from consuming grains containing gluten range from digestive problems to dandruff, skin disorders, kidney problems, and depression.

Celiac disease is the most well-known condition linked to gluten intolerance, and it can be quite dangerous. Many people have told me how they had been to doctors and clinics for years without being properly diagnosed. It is a commonly overlooked and misdiagnosed disorder.

Bloating and severe stomach pains after ingesting something with gluten in it are fairly good indications that gluten sensitivity might be the problem, and you may be wise to avoid eating foods that contain gluten.

Many people feel better when they eat a gluten-free diet. Those who have been diagnosed with conditions such as irritable bowel syndrome, leaky gut, eczema, and autism often find a reduction in symptoms when they consume healthier, gluten-free foods. Amaranth, buckwheat, corn, Job's tears (or Hato Mugi), millet, Montina (made from Indian ricegrass, which is native to the western United States), rice, wild rice, and sorghum are gluten-free, as are the following:

Tapioca flour is a gluten-free flour alternative. This rain-forest plant is very starchy. Adding tapioca flour to a flour mixture will give food a chewier, crustier, lighter texture.

Oat flour was once thought to contain gluten, but it was merely contaminated with gluten from being stored in the same silos or transported in the same containers as wheat. Use only oat flour that is labeled gluten-free.

Teff is a gluten-free Middle Eastern grain with high protein content.

Quinoa, a seed, is a complete protein food that is gluten-free. It contains more oil than some of the other grains, so it makes a chewier food.

Coconut flour, garbanzo bean flour, and other bean flours are also gluten-free options.

I recommend eating whole, sprouted-grain, gluten-free alternatives which are organically grown. Certain GMO crops have been modified to include genetic material from a bacterium, *Bacillus thuringiensis*, or Bt, because it acts as an insecticide. There is the possibility that these foods will contain Bt toxin, which may contribute to gluten-related health problems. Jeffrey M. Smith,

Executive Director of the Institute for Responsible Technology, writes:

A recent analysis of research shows that Bt toxin, glyphosate and other components of GMOs, are linked to five conditions that may either initiate or exacerbate gluten related disorders:
1. Intestinal permeability
2. Imbalanced gut bacteria
3. Immune activation and allergies
4. Impaired digestion
5. Damage to the intestinal wall[174]

Gluten-related disorders are commonly accompanied by, and are possibly triggered by, intestinal permeability, which is commonly referred to as "leaky gut." Leaky gut occurs when gaps form between intestinal cells and large particles from the digestive tract enter the blood stream, potentially triggering immune or allergic reactions.

The Bt toxin produced by genetically modified corn and soy kills insects by punching holes in their digestive tracts, and a 2012 study confirmed that it punctures human cells as well. Bt toxin is present in every kernel of Bt corn, survives human digestion, and has been detected in the blood of 93 percent of pregnant women tested and 80 percent of their unborn fetuses. This "hole-punching toxin" may be a critical piece of the puzzle in understanding gluten-related disorders.[175]

For the sake of your health, avoid eating food that contains Bt toxin by choosing non-GMO and organically grown food.

Phytic Acid

Everyone knows that nuts, seeds, grains, beans, and lentils are very healthy for you and are full of nutrients. But many people don't know they contain phytic acid. Phytic acid can prevent the body from absorbing important minerals such as calcium, magnesium, iron, and zinc, as well as cause acid indigestion. Studies suggest we can absorb more zinc and magnesium from foods that have had the phytic acid removed.[176] [177]

Phytic acid has powerful anti-nutritional effects because it binds to minerals in your food to form phytates, which makes those minerals unavailable to your digestive system. It also inhibits enzymes in the body that are vitally important for digesting food properly. The high level of phytic acid in nuts, seeds, grains, beans, and lentils is a serious problem in the modern diet, resulting in many health problems including tooth decay, nutrient deficiencies, lack of appetite, and digestive problems.

The phytic acid in nuts, seeds, grains, beans, and lentils can be removed by soaking and sprouting them. Historically, indigenous cultures always did this before consuming them or feeding them to their animals. This is not done in modern day society, to the detriment of human and animal health.

Because phytic acid is found in so many enjoyable foods, it is important to always prepare foods in a way that removes or neutralizes this acid as much as possible. This is why my recipes frequently include directions for soaking or sprouting nuts, seeds, grains, beans, and lentils. It makes them easier to digest and provides the maximum nutritional value.

Coconut flour does not require special preparation before cooking to reduce its phytic acid levels because the mineral-binding effect of the phytates formed by coconut is essentially nonexistent. In a study in the Philippines, researchers tested the mineral-binding capacity of various bakery ingredients, including coconut flour, and came to the conclusion that "coconut flour has little or no effect on mineral availability."[178]

In contrast, corn is high in phytic acid, which led Native Americans to "ferment cooked corn meal for two weeks, wrapped in corn husks, before preparing it as a flat bread or tortilla," according to health expert Ramiel Nagel. He notes that in Africa, corn is fermented for long periods of time using a lactobacillus culture, though "no such care is given to corn products in the western world!"

Nagel suggests soaking corn meal before use and adding a rye starter or rye flour to the soaking water, like the colonial Rye 'n' Injun bread made from rye and corn. "In one research project, soaking ground corn with 10 percent whole rye flour resulted in a complete reduction of phytate in six hours," says Nagel.[179]

Refined Carbohydrates: Beware!

I hear all the time that people are avoiding carbohydrates. Carbohydrates have a reputation for being unhealthy. However, it is only the *type* of carbohydrate that is unhealthy. Carbohydrates are actually the body's preferred fuel. Unrefined carbohydrates like legumes, whole grains, and vegetables are dense in nutrients and fiber, and they can give your body the fuel it needs. Refined carbohydrates like white, refined flour, pasta, and bakery goods have no or little fiber and are nutrient-empty.

There is a difference in the way refined carbohydrates and unrefined carbohydrates are converted into glucose by the body. Refined carbohydrates are converted to glucose quickly, which causes blood sugar to spike. This makes the body work hard to get the blood sugar level under control. It puts pressure on the pancreas to make and release insulin, which works "like a key to open the door of the cells so glucose... can come inside and be converted into energy."[180]

If too many refined carbohydrates are eaten on a continual basis, driving up blood sugar levels, this will stress the pancreas and eventually it will have trouble making insulin. This can result in diabetes.

The body will also turn the excess glucose into fat. This can result in weight gain and obesity. Carrying too much fat can lead to glucose intolerance. The body will start ignoring the signal to take glucose from the blood.

Many nutrient-empty, refined foods have fructose in them. Fructose doesn't appropriately stimulate insulin production, which means the body fails to suppress its "hunger hormone" leptin. This hormone suppression is what makes us feel satisfied, so fructose is actually making us feel hungrier instead of satisfied.

Then, to process these nutrient-empty, refined foods, the body must pull nutrients from itself. The spiking of blood sugar from refined and empty food results in cravings, because when the body is not getting the nutrients it needs, it will start begging for them. On the other hand, feeding the body with nutrient-dense food gives it what it needs, and there shouldn't be any cravings.

Because unrefined carbohydrates are fiber-rich, they take longer to digest. This means they do not put additional pressure on the pancreas to produce insulin in an unhealthy way. Unrefined carbohydrates, such as whole grains, should be a major part of a well-balanced diet.

Packaging can be very deceiving and misleading. When looking at a package that says "whole wheat" or "whole grain," read the ingredient list and make sure it says "whole" before every grain listed. If the ingredient list contains just the name of the grain, then it is *not* whole-grain.

If you are buying gluten-free products, make sure they are sprouted and whole-grain, and check the sugar content. I have found that even in the seemingly healthiest packages at the "healthy grocery stores," the gluten-free foods are alarmingly high in sugar. It is extremely important to find ones that are low in added sugar.

Sulfites

Sulfites occur naturally in many foods and have been used for centuries to preserve the color and flavor of food by inhibiting the growth of bacteria. But in modern times, these preservatives are added in greater amounts, and often in synthetic forms, to many foods, drinks, and medicines.

They can cause an allergy with symptoms including respiratory problems, weight gain, or the inability to lose weight. Many people who have been struggling with their weight find that after cutting out sulfites, they can lose weight much more easily and keep it off.

The most reliable way to test for a sulfite allergy is to go on a totally sulfite-free diet for three weeks. This requires you to eat nothing but whole organic foods that do not contain sulfite, sodium sulfite, sodium bisulfite, sodium metabisulfite, metabisulfite, potassium bisulfate, or potassium metabisulfite.

If all of your symptoms disappear, then you may be allergic to sulfites or another additive in the foods you cut out of your diet. To confirm the allergy, some doctors may want to give you a pill containing sulfites to see if the symptoms reoccur. This should be done under close supervision.

If you are allergic to sulfites, then you can simply regulate your diet to avoid them. Many foods—wine, for example—have natural sulfites, but my research has found most added sulfites are synthetic, not natural sulfur.

The USDA requires labeling any food containing sulfite levels of 10 or more parts per million. But, since labels on many foods change periodically, read the labels each time you buy processed food products.

Foods that commonly contain sulfites are soups, canned vegetables, dried fruits, bakery items, pickles, potato chips, many condiments, trail mixes, shrimp, and guacamole. The FDA passed a law in 1986 banning the use of sulfites on raw fruits and vegetables.

Vitamin C, the flavonoid quercetin, and the enzyme bromelain are commonly used to aid in the treatment of sulfite allergies. Vitamin C and quercetin are immune system boosters, and bromelain helps your body use quercetin. Quercetin is also known for its ability to block the release of histamines, so it helps with allergy symptoms.

A little-known and beneficial attribute of beans is that they contain the enzyme sulfite oxidase, which can detoxify sulfites. This is just one more reason to add sprouted beans to make it a healthier diet.

Even if you do not have a sulfite allergy, you may feel much better if you cut sulfites out of your diet. Removing the chemicals and preservatives out of the food you eat is a huge step toward getting healthier.

"In general, mankind, since the improvement in cookery, eats twice as much as nature requires."

—*Benjamin Franklin*

10

Guide to Cooking and Food Prep

H ealthy cooking doesn't have to be hard work. This is a chance to have some fun! Here are a few pointers to help get you started:

- Think of a recipe book as more of a **guidebook** than a rulebook. Once you feel comfortable in your knowledge of the healthiest foods to eat, feel free to start experimenting with your recipes.

- A dish tastes really satisfying when it has a **balance** of sweet, salty, sour (or bitter), savory, and spicy flavors. If a recipe doesn't taste quite right, see if you can add one of these flavors to make the dish taste more delicious.

- The **quality** of the ingredients you use is paramount to the quality and taste of the dish, so always choose the best, freshest ingredients you can, and opt for organic, non-GMO, and pasture-raised when possible.

- Don't forget that everyone's kitchen is **different**. Stoves and ovens cook at slightly different temperatures, so take this into account when you are cooking—especially when you are baking. Different climates and altitudes can also affect how recipes work.

Fruits and Vegetables

I consider fresh produce the ultimate meal. We all want to eat healthy, and many people tell me they have trouble putting more fresh fruits and vegetables on the table because the cost can add up. According to Dr. Timothy Jones, PhD, with the University of Arizona, people in the US throw out approximately $43 billion dollars' worth of food a year. That is an annual cost of approximately $600 dollars' worth of food per family.

We go to the store, buy delicious looking food, get home, and end up storing it improperly or getting busy and forget about it. Then, we find our refrigerator has over-ripe or rotting fruits and vegetables. One way we can save *and* eat healthier is by storing our fresh food properly.

Many times, we go to the store and see all the beautiful fresh fruits and vegetables in season and on sale, and we over-buy. So, buy only what you will eat in the next few days. Don't try to buy produce to last for a week. It may not last that long. Some root vegetables can last a month, if stored properly, but fresher, more fragile fruits and vegetables will only last 2–5 days.

If you do buy too much, think about making a pie, or canning, or freezing your more fragile fruits and vegetables before they spoil.

Always store your food in its complete wholeness. According to food scientist Barry Swanson at Washington State University, if you pull fruits and vegetables apart, you have broken the cells, and microorganisms will immediately begin to grow. So, avoid breaking the skin, and leave the stem intact.

He also says you should never place fruits and vegetables in airtight bags. That will accelerate the decay. Mold will proliferate quickly and can spoil the whole group of fruits or vegetables. So, throw out any spoiled produce immediately, or put it into your compost bin.

Next, store the various types of fruits and vegetables with the right partners. Some give off high levels of ethylene gas, a ripening agent that makes them (and everything around them) ripen or decay quickly.

You want to keep these types of foods separate from each other. Put things like kale and spinach in the same bin, and peaches and apples in another. If you put fruit with greens, the greens rot or turn yellow in a few days. Greens are very sensitive to ethylene gas.

There are some handy products that remove or absorb ethylene gas in the refrigerator. A few of those are: Berry Breeze, E. G. G. (which is shaped like an egg), and Bluapple. I put one of those in my refrigerator or bin with the fruits or greens. I also use produce bags by Bio-Fresh and Evert-Fresh. They will absorb ethylene gas and help your produce stay fresher longer.

Of course, if you need something to ripen faster, then you can use this knowledge to your advantage. You can put the food you need to ripen in a brown paper bag with a fruit that gives off a high level of ethylene gas, and it will ripen very quickly.

Keep root vegetables in a cool, dark, dry place. They can last up to a month if kept properly. Never store potatoes in the refrigerator because they will develop higher sugar content there. Here is a list of fruits and vegetables, showing the best way to store them.

These are high-ethylene producers you can refrigerate:
- Apples
- Apricots
- Cantaloupe
- Figs
- Honeydew

These are high-ethylene releasers, but should be stored in a cool dark place *outside* the refrigerator.
- Avocados
- Bananas, unripe
- Nectarines
- Peaches
- Pears
- Plums
- Tomatoes

There are very sensitive to ethylene gas. Keep them separate.

- Bananas, ripe
- Broccoli
- Brussels sprouts
- Cabbage
- Carrots
- Cauliflower
- Cucumbers
- Eggplant
- Lettuce and other leafy greens
- Parsley
- Peas
- Peppers
- Squash
- Sweet potatoes (root veggie: store outside the refrigerator)
- Watermelon

Purchase fresh fruits and vegetables that have been ripened on the vine or on the tree. Tree or vine-ripened foods contain salvestrols, which are compounds that have natural anti-cancer properties.[181] In fact, the word "salvestrol" comes from the Latin word "save."

Food that is picked green and then ripened on the way to market does not contain these salvestrols. Growing your own food or buying from a local farmer are two ways to get food that is ripened on the vine or tree.

Organic food is best because it is more nutrient-dense. Chemical fertilizers and pesticides can destroy nutrients in the soil—like sulfur and chromium, which are vital for our health. "The Organic Center study found that organic foods were more nutritionally dense in 61 percent of the cases," and they "found conventional foods to contain higher nitrates, which are widely considered a potential health hazard."[182]

When you get home, wash your fresh produce in water with a little apple cider vinegar in it, so you know your produce is clean and free of pesticides, bacteria, and other toxic residue. It is much better than plain water. I use one tablespoon of apple cider vinegar or food-grade hydrogen peroxide to each gallon of water, or ¼ cup in a full sink. If the produce looks *really* dirty, I'll use both.

I don't clean my fragile leafy greens or fresh herbs or berries until I am ready to use them. They should be stored until you are ready to wash them.

If you have fresh food from your garden that has been grown totally organically in organic soil, has already been rinsed by fresh rain, has not been handled by anyone else, and you know absolutely that this food is clean, it may be better to *not* rinse and clean it with a germ-killing rinse, because it will have some natural Vitamin B12 on it from the soil.

When I am cooking food, I save half of the raw vegetables and add them to the finished, cooked food as an additional way of adding living enzymes into the dish. I also add fresh vegetables to prepared foods.

If I'm using a tomato sauce from a jar, for example, I add freshly chopped tomatoes, onions, and herbs to the final product for a fresher meal containing living enzymes that can benefit my health. Look at the recipes you create and see where you can do this. It makes dishes taste so much fresher and more alive!

Don't waste the tops, tips, and leftovers of vegetables used in recipes. Save them and make a vegetable broth you can use later. Simply place the leftover ends and tips in a pot of water and bring it to a boil. Add a little kombu seaweed for more nutrient value. After it comes to a boil, reduce the heat and simmer for 10 minutes or more. Remove it from the heat and strain the broth.

Pour the broth into ice cube trays and freeze them. This way you can pop out a couple of cubes whenever you need some extra flavor in a dish.

Grains, Roots, and Herbs

Grains should be kept dry, cool, and in a sealed container. Bugs, mice, rats, and snakes can be found in grain storage units. So, when you're ready to cook with grains, rinse them under running water in a fine mesh colander. This also helps remove a good portion of the starch.

If you soak grains for a few hours, overnight, or a few days, they can sprout, and you will get a more digestible grain with active nutrients.

Store garlic and ginger root in a dry, cool, dark place. Fresh herbs will stay alive and fresher longer if you put them in a vase full of water, like flowers.

You can keep them out on a table. I love to put fresh mint in a vase of water and snip off little bits of it periodically for mint-infused water or tea. Add a fresh flower, and you have a beautiful arrangement for the kitchen.

Play and have some fun with your food!

Vegan Recipe Substitutions

You can use these substitutions to turn your recipes into vegan recipes. I substitute the following ingredients using the same amount called for in the recipe. It makes eating vegan healthy and easy.

Ingredient	Vegan Substitution
Honey	Organic brown rice syrup or maple syrup
Cheese	Vegan or nut cheese
Milk	A non-dairy milk, such as coconut, almond, cashew, rice, oat, or pine nut milk
Yogurt	Coconut yogurt
Butter	Coconut oil or avocado
Meat	Mushrooms, tempeh, eggplant. You may need to shorten the cooking time.
Eggs	Vegan Egg Substitute (recipe on the following page)

Vegan Egg Substitute

When a recipe calls for eggs, this is an easy vegan substitute. My daughter and I use it for breads, pancakes, and waffles. Each tablespoon of ground flax seeds and water makes the equivalent of one egg.

Ingredients
1 tbsp. freshly ground flax seeds
3 tbsp. non-chlorinated water

Directions
1. Place the flax seeds and water in a small saucepan and simmer for five minutes. Gently stir until it thickens to the consistency of an egg.
2. Remove from heat and let it cool for 8–10 minutes.

Notes: Flax Seed Egg Substitute will keep for a week in the refrigerator. Take it out of the refrigerator and allow it to come to room temperature when you use it in a recipe.

For larger recipes, use a ratio of one part flax seed to three parts water. For example, 1 cup of ground flax seeds and 3 cups of non-chlorinated water will make the equivalent of 16 eggs.

Basic Daily Menu Flow for Reversing or Preventing Disease

Meals should be vegan or vegetarian and mostly whole, raw food, all organic, GMO-free, and as gluten-free as possible.

First thing in morning, have a large glass of water.

Breakfast
One of the following:
-salad
-soup
-smoothie
-green vegetable juice

Wait 1½ hours after breakfast and drink ¼ of your body weight (in pounds) in ounces of pure water.

Snacks
1 pint of green vegetable juice and, if necessary, some raw, sprouted nuts or seeds

Wait 30 minutes after the snack and drink four ounces of rejuvelac.

Lunch
Salad or soup; Entrée; raw nut pâté or hummus with chips, made from raw, freshly cut vegetables or whole, sprouted-grain, gluten-free crackers.

Wait one and a half hours after lunch and drink at least one quarter of your weight of pure water in ounces. Wait 30 minutes more and drink four ounces rejuvelac.

Dinner
Salad and soup

11

Guide to Cleansing and Detoxing

T here are many reasons to clean out the inside of the body on a regular basis. Clean cells and a clean body, inside and out, are the secrets to having more energy, looking younger, and having a stronger immune system.

We *need* to cleanse because we acquire toxins in our bodies on a regular basis. We live in a world that is literally saturated with toxins. We can get toxins by breathing in polluted air, taking showers in chlorinated tap water, drinking tap water, eating foods when we don't know their source or preparation method, pesticides, toxic cleaning fluids, dry-cleaning fluids, and new, unwashed clothing.

Additionally, our bodies become acidic through stress and the foods we eat. These toxins and acids hurt our bodies deep within our cells. How can the body have a clean liver, blood, or lymphatic system if it is filled with toxins, acid, and waste? A clean intestinal system and frequent, thorough bowel movements are key elements of a truly healthy system.

We absorb most of our nutrients though the intestinal wall. If it is clean, we are able to absorb the nutrients. If it is not clean but is instead full of waste and rancid debris, then the body won't get the nutrients it needs. Dr. Anthony Bassler, a gastroenterologist, said, "Every physician should realize the intestinal toxemias (poisons) are the most important primary and contributing cause of many disorders and diseases of the body."[183]

We also need to cleanse because our intestines can become thick with plaque over time. This "mucoid plaque" can result from consuming foods like milk, wheat, and meat. It can be thick and rubbery. It can even look a little like a rope when it exits the body.

In the book *Tissue Cleansing through Bowel Management*, Dr. Bernard Jensen, DC, ND, PhD addresses this:

The heavy mucus coating in the colon thickens and becomes a host of putrefaction. The blood capillaries to the colon begin to pick up the toxins, poisons, and noxious debris as it seeps through the bowel wall. All tissues and organs of the body are now taking on toxic substances. Here is the beginning of true autointoxication on a physiological level.

One autopsy revealed a colon to be 9 inches in diameter with a passage through it no larger than a pencil. The rest was caked up layer upon layer of encrusted fecal material. This accumulation can have the consistency of truck tire rubber. It's that hard and black. Another autopsy revealed a stagnant colon to weigh in at an incredible 40 pounds.[184]

Dr. Richard Anderson, ND, NMD addresses the subject of plaque as well. Dr. Anderson, an expert on colon cleansing, wrote *Cleanse and Purify Thyself, Volumes 1 & 2*. In an article on colon plaque, he says:

The phrase, "mucoid plaque" is a coined term that I use to describe various conditions found throughout the body, especially in hollow organs and the alimentary canal. It is a substance that the body naturally creates under unnatural conditions, such as attacks from acids, drugs, heavy metals, and toxic chemicals.[185]

Professional cleanses, like colonics or enemas, can get this old, leftover waste and plaque out of the intestinal tract.

I recommend cleansing for a minimum of three days and as long as 21 days to detoxify the body and adjust its pH on a regular basis. This will keep the inner environment of the body's digestive system cleaner, healthier, and able to support a healthy immune system.

Along with this comes an additional benefit. A major part of the body's happiness chemical, serotonin, is synthesized in the gastrointestinal tract. It is no wonder people feel happier and better when their bowels are clean and functioning in the optimum way! I do a month-long cleanse every January to start off the New Year fresh and renewed after too much holiday party munching.

Each time you cleanse, it will get easier. Eventually, or maybe very quickly, you will see a difference in how you feel.

You will have to make a personal decision about the length of your cleanse. Many physicians think 21 days is the best length. You may want to consult your physician before starting a cleanse, or do the cleanse under his or her guidance. Many wonderful physicians and clinics have juice fasts, cleanses, and other programs you can do under their guidance.

Garden of Life makes a nice, easy cleanse. But for those who wish to create their own cleanse, here are a few I find very effective.

High-Fiber Cleanse

This is a basic cleanse I have been doing for more than 25 years. I raised my children on it. The two things I think are most lacking in the American diet are good, healthy fiber and good, healthy green foods. This cleanse has both. Quite simply, it is made up of the good, healthy food that most people lack in their normal, everyday diet.

The nutrients will feed your body, and they will flush and pull toxins and acids out of your cells. The fiber will absorb these toxins and expand like a sponge. You will then drink a lot of water, which will create a cleaning effect. Along with the sponge-like fiber, the toxic particles, plaque, and other debris that might be lodged in the intestines will be dragged out.

Each time you cleanse, it will clean out a little more. Think of the layers of an onion. When you start, you will get one layer, and the next time, you will get the next layer.

This cleanse is done morning, noon, and night for 3–14 days or more. You may eventually find this is a good part of your daily or weekly routine. I do this cleanse a few times a week, year-round, as a normal part of my diet.

You can buy the ingredients for this cleanse at most health food stores or grocery stores. It calls for raw organic green food powder. These organic green food powders can include the algae spirulina or chlorella (which are extremely high in protein and very detoxifying) as well as barley grass or other foods.

But, when possible, I use fresh, organic green barley grass or wheat grass juice instead of the powder. Fresh is always best, but the concentrated, powdered form makes this cleanse easy to use anytime and anywhere. If you have trouble drinking green, powdery, high-fiber drinks, buy the green food powder in capsule form.

This cleanse also calls for psyllium husks. They expand very quickly in water and turn into a thick clump you cannot drink. So, either take psyllium husks in capsule form, or drink them quickly once you add water to them. The psyllium husks will then expand in your stomach, which is why you are taking them.

They are a great fiber which makes you feel full as it works like a large sponge to clean out your body's organs on its way through. By absorbing toxins, the fiber is able to pull them, as well as waste, from your body.

A kalenite pill is another key ingredient of this cleanse. Kalenite is a blend of eight herbs "known for their ability to support proper elimination through the colon, liver, kidneys, and lymphatic system, as well as helping to tone these organs of elimination so they can function more efficiently."[186] It pulls toxins from your cells naturally and prevents you from feeling queasy. Pumpkin seeds are optional, but they work really well if you have parasites.

This is my favorite cleanse, but it is **only for someone who is able to have regular bowel movements**. If you are **not** having regular bowel movements, then you may need to simply consume raw fresh vegetable juice three times per day, or do colonics, until your bowel movements are regular.

Ingredients
Concentrated raw organic green food powder of barley grass, wheatgrass, spirulina, or chlorella (or capsules or fresh organic barley grass or wheatgrass juice). You can use one or a combination of the green food powders.

Organic psyllium husks

Freshly ground, fresh, organic, raw, sprouted pumpkin seeds (optional)

Kalenite pills (optional)

Probiotic capsules

Digestive enzymes

Directions
Days 1-3
For one to three full days, three or four times a day, starting first thing in the morning, drink an eight-ounce glass of mineral-rich water, coconut water, or ginger root tea or juice along with:

- 2-3 tsp. concentrated raw organic green food powder (or 8–10 capsules)
- 1 tsp. organic psyllium husks (2 capsules)

If you are using freshly juiced greens, drink 6–8 ounces of the juice with the psyllium husks.

Throughout the day, drink a couple of liters (one ounce of water for every two pounds of your body weight) of mineral-rich water, coconut water, fresh ginger root juice, and more fresh, organic, vegetable juices throughout the day.

Days 2-21
Starting on the second, third, or fourth day, depending on how long you are able to go with only liquids, mix together:

- 1 tsp. concentrated raw organic green food powder (or 8–10 capsules or 6–8 ounces of fresh organic barley grass, or wheat grass juice)
- 1 tsp. organic psyllium husks
- 2 tsp. freshly ground, fresh, organic, raw, sprouted pumpkin seeds (optional)

- 4 oz. purified water

Drink it very quickly with:
- 1 kalenite pill
- 1 probiotic capsule
- 1 digestive enzyme

Immediately afterward, drink a mixture of:
- 18 oz. pure water
- 1/8 tsp. high-quality sea salt.

Drink as much high-quality water throughout the day as you can (one ounce of water for every two pounds of your body weight). This is very important for helping flush the toxins out of the body.

Do it every day for 3–14 days minimum. If you are really serious about this, do it for 21 days. Start first thing in the morning on an empty stomach, and repeat at lunch and dinner (before 6 p.m.).

Please Note: You will go to the bathroom a few hours after you do the High-Fiber Cleanse. Feeling unwell is a symptom of a large amount of toxins being eliminated from the body. It means you need to drink a lot of water to help flush out all of the toxins and assist the fiber in continuing its journey out of your body.

All food should be efficiently digested, its nutrients absorbed, and its waste eliminated. If you are eating three times per day, then you should be having bowel movements three times per day. The more fiber you ingest, the easier and more efficiently the waste will be eliminated. There is not a set time period for this, but ideally it should be anywhere from 3–12 hours after each meal.

You can test your digestive function by eating a meal of raw or slightly steamed red beets. The deep red color in the bowel movement will allow you to see when that meal is eliminated. This is an easy way to see if your body is eliminating quickly and efficiently.

If you are not having regular bowel movements, then don't include the psyllium husks in your cleanse until you are. If you have already started the cleanse and are not having regular bowel movements, then stop the psyllium husks immediately and take only the greens until you are going regularly. If you feel uncomfortable and are not having bowel movements, you may want to get a colonic series to help get your system cleaned out and moving again.

Drink lots of water, fresh green organic vegetable juices and other liquids to keep the toxins, acid, and waste moving out of the body. This is so important! This cleanse is cleaning out the inside of your body. With the removal of the plaque, waste, and debris, you will also be alkalizing your body and helping your body maintain a healthier pH. Greens are highly alkalizing.

This may seem like a lot of work, but each time you do it, it will get easier, and you will start to feel better and have more energy! In situations where you feel you must have some food or really need something to chew, eat snacks or meals of raw or lightly steamed organic vegetables an hour before or after consuming the cleanse.

You may also chew on celery sticks or cucumber slices. You may sprinkle pure whole sea salt and chia seeds on your food. If you feel you must use some fat, then try using a little bit of coconut oil. The coconut oil can give you additional nourishment as well as energy.

Bentonite Clay

Bentonite clay is a volcanic ash containing many minerals. Historically, Native Americans used it for detoxifying and cleansing their bowels. They called it Ee-Wah-Kee, meaning "the mud that heals." Bentonite has the ability to bind with toxins, drugs, and heavy metals, and draw them out of the body.

You may wonder: If it is binding with these, does it bind with nutrients and pull them out, too? Some studies have demonstrated that for bentonite clay to be harmful, 50 percent of a person's food intake would have to be bentonite clay. [187] Nevertheless, I recommend you don't do this cleanse very often, and make sure that after the cleanse you add some extra nutrients to your body.

Some people put the liquid form of bentonite clay into their bath water (one cup in a tub of water) to help pull toxins from the body. The clay can dry out your skin, though. The most effective type of bentonite clay is a liquid colloid.

I had a cyst on my wrist, and I didn't want to have surgery to remove it. I started using bentonite clay on a daily basis with my High-Fiber Cleanse. Within three weeks, the cyst had disappeared.

Strongly polarized, bentonite clay has a powerful electromagnetic field when hydrated. It can attract and hold on to forms of radiation, and it has the ability to pick up a great deal more than its own weight in positively charged particles. Dr. Jensen, ND, DC, PhD, suggested using bentonite to absorb radiation from bones which are subjected to radiation through the use of X-rays, computers, television, and treatments for cancer.

The medical community has found clay to have amazing healing properties. One study by a research duo from Arizona State University's Biodesign Institute and College of Liberal Arts and Sciences found:

> Unlike conventional antibiotics routinely administered by injection or pills, the so-called "healing clays" could be applied as rub-on creams or ointments to keep MRSA infections from spreading... The clays also show promise against a wide range of other harmful bacteria, including those that cause skin infections and food poisoning... Their study, one of the first to explore the antimicrobial activity of natural clays in detail, was presented at the 235th national meeting of the American Chemical Society, the world's largest scientific society...
>
> Clays have been used for thousands of years as a remedy for infected wounds, indigestion, and other health problems, either by applying clay to the skin or eating it. Cleopatra's famed beauty has been credited to her use of clay facials. Today, clays are still commonly used at health spas in the form of facials and mud baths. However, armed with new investigative tools, researchers Shelley Haydel and Lynda Williams are putting the clays to the test, scientifically.

"Clays are little chemical drug stores in a packet," says study co-leader Williams, a geochemist in the School of Earth and Space Exploration.[188]

In addition to finding that MRSA (methicillin-resistant *Staphylococcus aureus*) was susceptible to bentonite clays, they found the clays exhibited antimicrobial effects against *Mycobacterium ulcerans* (which is related to tuberculosis, and results in a flesh-digesting disease) and two causes of food poisoning: E. coli and Salmonella.

However, pregnant women and seniors should avoid consuming bentonite clay, according to Dr. Akilah M. El, and everyone should "avoid taking bentonite clay within two hours of consumption of any medicine, including supplements."[189]

Bentonite clay can be used externally or internally. Arizona State University found that some bentonite clays were contaminated. So, only use food-grade bentonite clay that is specifically labeled safe for internal use. Consult your physician if you have concerns.

Psyllium Husk Cleanse

If you are extremely regular with bowel movements and feel you have a very clean system, then you can cleanse using only psyllium husks and purified water, with or without the addition of bentonite clay.

Ingredients
1 tsp. organic psyllium husks
1/8 teaspoon or less bentonite clay (optional)
8 oz. purified water

Directions: Drink lots of water or fluids when using psyllium husks and/or bentonite clay. This cleanse can remove more toxins but should not be done if you have any kind of blockage or any trouble at all moving the fiber through your body.

When using bentonite clay, *don't* take green food powder or capsules, as in the High-Fiber cleanse. Instead, use only the psyllium husks and water. When using bentonite with psyllium, the bentonite is so good at absorbing so many things that I would wait at least an hour or more before having anything of nutritional value. In this way, you would be more likely to absorb the nutrients and not have them removed from your body with the bentonite clay/psyllium cleanse.

Pumpkin Seed Cleanse for Parasites

We get parasites from many things, like ingesting dirt that was not completely washed off our food, eating meat, traveling in other countries, drinking water, and swimming in lakes or ponds. Dr. Bernard Jensen, an expert in colon research and therapy, states that "the average person over 40 years of age has between 5 and 25 pounds of buildup in their colon... Parasites of all sizes thrive in this undisposed residue of fecal matter, slowly but surely toxifying the whole body."[190]

Dr. Peter Wina, chief of patho-biology at the Walter Reed Army Institute of Research, says, "We have a tremendous parasitic problem right here in the US. It is just not being addressed."[191] Joseph Sterling wrote in his newsletter, *Secrets of Robust Health*, that parasitic infection is common:

Humans can play host to over 100 different kinds of parasites, ranging from microscopic to several-feet-long tapeworms. Contrary to popular belief, parasites are not restricted to our colon alone, but can be found in other parts of the body: the lungs, the liver, in the muscles and joints, in the esophagus, the brain, the blood, the skin, and even in the eyes.[192]

Some common symptoms of parasitic infection are: constipation; gas and bloating; diarrhea; back pain; joint and muscle pain; irritable bowel syndrome; allergies; insatiable hunger; itchy ears, nose, or anus; unpleasant sensations in the stomach; nervousness; grumpiness; chronic fatigue; lethargy or apathy; various skin problems; problems sleeping; nutritional deficiencies or anemia; problems with the immune system; teeth grinding or clenching; weight gain; forgetfulness; and blurry vision.

Those are all worth trying to fix with a simple detoxification cleanse. Bentonite clay and raw, sprouted pumpkin seeds rid your body of parasites and can be added to the Psyllium Husk Cleanse.

Ingredients
1 tsp. organic psyllium husks
1/8 teaspoon or less bentonite clay
½ tsp. freshly ground, fresh, organic, raw, sprouted pumpkin seeds
8 oz. purified water

There are also several anti-parasite cleanses on the market. The DrNatura brand has a capsule called Paranil that you take on an empty stomach in different amounts for 30 days, first thing in the morning. This allows for the parasite to be expelled in all of the different stages of life.

When doing the parasite cleanse for the first time, you need to do it for an entire three months (90 days). You want to make sure you rid your body of the parasite as it goes through all of the stages of life. You do not want it to re-emerge in the future, which can happen if it was in a stage not addressed by the cleanse.

Here are a few of the products and brands available:

- Perfect Food–Raw Greens by Garden of Life
- Raw Kombucha by Garden of Life
- Primadophilus Optima by Nature's Way
- Green Magna by Green Foods
- Whole Psyllium Husks by Yerba Prima
- Kalenite Cleansing Herbs and food-grade bentonite clay by Yerba Prima
- Essential Enzymes by Source Natura
- Paranil by DrNatura
- Liquid food-grade bentonite clay by Sonnes

Cilantro Cleanse for Metal Toxins

We get metal toxins in our bodies from a variety of places including dental fillings, aluminum deodorant, the aluminum foil we use in food preparation and storage, vaccinations, cadmium from secondhand smoke, and polluted air. Metal toxins are harder to rid our bodies of than other toxins, but my cilantro cleanse is highly effective. It is a bit of a challenge at first, but it gets easier. I know, because I have done it.

If you do this cleanse and you feel bad afterward, that is because it is pulling toxic metals from your cells and flushing them out into your blood stream. You really need to drink lots and lots of water to flush these toxins out. You may need to do this cleanse once a month until you can do it without feeling bad. Then you know you have gotten the metal toxins out of your body.

Ingredients
1 bunch fresh organic cilantro
½ tsp. organic, extra virgin olive oil

> **Note:** To make it even more effective, you can do a variation of this cleanse by adding some **spirulina** (algae) or **chlorella** (algae) powder or take it in capsule form along with the cilantro mixture. Algae are very effective in helping detox heavy metals, but, in my opinion, they don't taste very good.

Directions
1. Wash cilantro.
2. Purée cilantro in a food processor.
3. Mix the puréed cilantro with olive oil to improve the taste and make the cilantro easier to eat.
4. Put the mixture in a glass container, pour a thin layer of olive oil on top, and store it in the refrigerator. Make certain there is always a thin layer of olive oil over the top of the mixture. This seals it and keeps it fresh for a couple of days.

Every morning for a week, eat at least two or three heaping teaspoons of the cilantro mixture. Do it first thing in the morning on an empty stomach. Chew it thoroughly and take a digestive enzyme with it for a more thorough cleanse. Wait at least 20 minutes before drinking water or eating anything else.

For breakfast, drink a glass of freshly juiced organic green barley grass or wheatgrass, sprouts, ginger, and fresh vegetables. All day long, drink a lot of water with a tiny bit of whole sea salt added to it. This helps flush the toxins you have drawn out of your cells.

The key to any cleanse is getting the toxins you are pulling from the cells *completely out of your body*, and not floating around in the bloodstream.

Colonic Cleanse

If your body is not eliminating wastes efficiently after each meal, there may be some blockage in the intestinal tract. Anyone who has been a consumer of processed foods, fried foods, or trans fats, or meat may have blockages, plaque, or debris lodged in the colon. After years and years of eating meals that are not completely digested or moved out of the body, layers and layers of waste build up.

Natalia Rose, a New York clinical nutritionist, says that if you wake up in the morning, have a bowel movement, pull in your gut, and it is almost to your spine, then you have an empty and clean intestine. If you cannot do this, then your intestines are full of undigested waste stuck in the tissues like cement.

Master colon therapist Gil Jacobs explains that a laxative will do nothing for the normal person who is eating fairly well, except release the very newest waste, and then drive the older waste deeper into the tissue and make it harder to remove. The laxative will irritate the bowels.

He and Natalia Rose believe in colonic cleansing and recommend the gravity method. The client reclines in a large chair, and a small quantity of warm water is very slowly introduced into the colon by a narrow tube. Then the water runs out of the colon, being released through a tube and directly into the plumbing. The hydrotherapist answers questions, guiding or assisting whenever needed.

Having a colonic is actually very easy. The water cleanses the walls of the intestine. Each time a colonic is done, another layer of plaque or waste can be washed out of the lining of the colon.

People say, "I got a colonoscopy, and it was fine." However, a colonoscopy doesn't clean out the colon. It doesn't pull out the toxins or plaque embedded in the lining of the intestines. It is like a bullet going through the barrel of a gun. On the other hand, a colonic actually washes out the debris, plaque, and whatever else is stuck in the layers of the intestinal wall.

Colonics are recommended for people with a high degree of inflammation, constipation, and/or plaque in their colon. Some people find it so useful that they continue to do it once a month or more just to stay clean. Gil and Natalia say that a person who grew up eating a standard American diet of bread, meat, trans fats, sugar, and junk food could get a colonic every week for the rest of his or her life and still not have all of the waste completely removed from the colon.

A raw food diet will awaken the body and help get waste out. The food is more likely to be completely or close to completely digested. Your body will start to cleanse itself of toxins because of the antioxidant-rich food and fiber.

When the colon and the rest of the intestinal tract are cleaned up and running free and clear, the whole body will start to work in harmony. Many people will find their joint problems, headaches, back aches, skin problems, and hair problems simply disappear when they finally get their colon and intestines clean and oxygenated.

Natalia Rose also recommends enemas as another way to remove waste from the bowels. They can work well and get waste to come out of the tissues. Gil and Natalia also recommend putting a small step stool in front of the toilet. If you put your feet on the small stool when using the toilet, your intestinal tract has a better curve, making it much easier to move waste through the tract.

Coffee Enema

The liver and gallbladder can get overloaded with toxins. When this happens, a coffee enema can be the solution. Coffee enemas increase the liver's detoxification capacity.

The coffee enema was a staple of the Merck Manual (considered the "bible" of medical books) until it was removed fairly recently. It wasn't removed because it didn't work—because the coffee enema has been proven to work—but it was removed. Many of the extremely successful natural cancer centers use the coffee enema as a staple of their health programs. It is a required part of the Gerson Therapy program.

In an intense health program with juicing, the juices begin nourishing the body. The high antioxidant levels force cells to release toxins into the bloodstream. This can put a burden or toxin overload on the liver.

The liver alone, especially in a cancer patient, cannot handle the sudden flood of toxins being released into the bloodstream. Coffee enemas flush the toxin-saturated liver. This helps it regain the ability to flush even more toxins from the blood stream.

Coffee enemas have the same purpose as colonics, which cleanse the bowel. Coffee enemas increase the liver's detoxification volume. Substances in coffee stimulate a main detoxification enzyme in the liver and dilate the bile ducts to increase the flow of bile.

Another benefit of the coffee enema is emptying the bowel. It would be wise to make certain you are free of constipation before attempting a coffee enema. A series of colonics encourages a cleaner bowel and makes the coffee enema more effective.

But avoid doing both in the same day. This can deplete your body. You can read more about coffee enemas on the Gerson Therapy website, Gerson.org.

This enema requires a particular type of coffee. One highly recommended brand is S. A. Wilson's *Gold Roast*, from SAWilsons.com. You can order an enema kit, including instructions, from the Optimum Health Institute.

Oil Pulling

Oil pulling is an Ayurvedic Remedy used to enhance oral health and well-being. Oil pulling detoxifies the body, removes unsightly stains on teeth, and prevents illness and disease.

My daughter and I did it infrequently for a while and never noticed a difference; but when we did it on a continual basis for 15 days without interruption, the difference was noticeable. Amanda saw a huge difference in her health, gums, teeth and how she felt when she finally did it consistently. I have noticed a significant difference between when I do it and when I don't. When I do this in the morning, my mouth seems amazingly clean and fresh. So, I recommend doing it on a consistent basis, if you are going to try it.

Ingredients
Pure, organic coconut oil
Unrefined sea salt
Purified, (non-chlorinated) water

Equipment
Tongue scraper
Toothbrush

Directions
First thing in the morning, before brushing your teeth or eating anything, take 1 teaspoon of pure, organic coconut oil into your mouth and swish the oil in your mouth, tilting your head back, so that it can get to the back molars. (It may taste weird the first few days, but you will get used to it—if you stick with it.) It is very important that you keep the oil in your mouth the whole time and **Avoid Swallowing It**.

You suck and pull the oil through your teeth and chew the oil so that it activates the saliva. Do this for at least 10 -15 minutes. The oil will turn white in your mouth as you do this. The oil pulls toxins and excess mucus out of the blood through the mucus membranes in the mouth.

Spit the oil out in the toilet. Again, **Avoid Swallowing the Oil.** After spitting, swish your mouth with a pinch of unrefined, mineral rich sea salt in warm purified water.

Immediately following the sea salt-water rinse, brush your teeth thoroughly. Use a tongue scraper to clean your tongue well, and then use a toothbrush to clean the roof of the mouth too.

Next, drink 2–3 glasses of purified (non-chlorinated and non-fluoridated) water.

The result will be a fresh, relaxed feeling. Gums will bleed less and teeth will get whiter.

If you do this on a continual basis, you may notice that dark, puffy circles under your eyes will start to disappear. You may even have more energy, a better memory, and a better night's sleep.

"More than 100 studies have shown bitter melon's ability to decrease blood sugar, increase the uptake in glucose, and activate pancreatic cells that manufacture insulin.

The best way to have it is fresh, as juice. It can be found at Asian markets. It is bitter, so mix about two ounces with some cucumber, celery and lemon juice, and hold your nose and drink it."

—Dr. Gabriel Cousens

12

Juices and Juicing

J uicing is the process of taking a vegetable or fruit and running it through a machine or process that removes the fiber and simply leaves the pure liquid part of the food for consumption. When we juice fruits and vegetables, we get nutrients without the fiber, which makes the nutrients easier for the body to absorb than if we ate those fruits and vegetables whole. The body doesn't have to work hard to get the nutritional benefits of the food, and the intense nutrients and living enzymes feed us on a deep cellular level.

Fresh juice also alkalizes us, and the antioxidant-rich nutrients in juice are an amazing way to cleanse the body of toxins. A juice cleanse can boost your energy, balance your blood sugar, brighten your skin, and rejuvenate your hormones.

It is amazing how full you can feel after drinking a large glass of vegetable or fruit juice, so juicing is an excellent way to fast or diet without the intense hunger pangs. You get great nutrient density without all the calories. Just juice, juice, juice for life! When I am drinking only fresh, nutrient-dense juices, I never feel hungry or tired.

Juicing is great for everyone. For people who are trying to heal from various diseases, it can be powerful because of all of the nutrient-rich, antioxidant enzymes. Juicing is especially beneficial for those who need intense nutrition yet have trouble eating, such as people who are sick or elderly.

Juice Ingredients and Their Health Benefits

Organic foods ripened on the vine or tree are the optimum choice for juicing. The green parts of vegetables or vegetable plants are a powerhouse of nutrients. They have potassium, phosphorus, calcium, magnesium, iron, and zinc, along with vitamins A, C, E, and K, folic acid, chlorophyll, and micronutrients.

Are you thinking, "Oh, my goodness, greens for breakfast?" Yes! Greens purify the blood, strengthen the immune system, and improve liver, gall bladder, and kidney function. The nutrients in greens can fight depression, clear congestion, and improve circulation, which can keep skin clear and blemish-free. In traditional Asian medicine, the color green is related to the liver, emotional stability, and creativity.

Kale is known as the king of greens. Diane Dyer, MS, RD, says: The standouts are the high content of calcium, vitamin C, vitamin B6, folic acid, vitamin A (in the form of beta-carotene), vitamin K, potassium, manganese, copper, and even the plant form of Omega 3 fatty acids (alpha-linolenic acid).

In addition to the carotenoid beta-carotene, kale contains other very important carotenoid molecules called lutein and zeaxanthin (both necessary for eye health) and numerous others (probably too many to count, and maybe not even yet identified).[193]

Wheatgrass is a unique and beneficial food to juice. Dr. Yoshihide Hagiwara, president of the Hagiwara Institute of Health in Japan, advocates the use of grass as food and medicine because it is rich in chlorophyll. Chlorophyll is very similar to hemoglobin, a compound in blood that carries oxygen.

In *The Wheatgrass Book,* Ann Wigmore noted many benefits of regularly drinking freshly juiced wheatgrass. Wheatgrass:

- Increases red blood cell count and lowers blood pressure.
- Cleanses the blood, organs, and gastrointestinal tract of debris.
- Stimulates metabolism and the body's enzyme systems by enriching the blood.

- Aids in reducing blood pressure by dilating the blood pathways throughout the body.
- Stimulates the thyroid gland, correcting obesity, indigestion, and a host of other complaints.
- Restores alkalinity to the blood. The juice's abundance of alkaline minerals reduces over-acidity in the blood.
- Can be used to relieve many internal pains, and has been used successfully to treat peptic ulcers, ulcerative colitis, constipation, diarrhea, and other complaints of the gastrointestinal tract.
- Is a powerful detoxifier, and liver and blood protector. The enzymes and amino acids found in wheatgrass can protect us from carcinogens like no other food or medicine.
- Strengthens our cells, detoxifies the liver and bloodstream, and chemically neutralizes environmental pollutants.
- Neutralizes toxic substances like cadmium, nicotine, strontium, mercury, and polyvinyl chloride.
- Offers the benefits of a liquid oxygen transfusion, since the juice contains liquid oxygen. Oxygen is vital to many body processes. It stimulates digestion (the oxidation of food), promotes clearer thinking (the brain utilizes 25 percent of the body's oxygen supply), and protects the blood against anaerobic bacteria. Cancer cells cannot exist in the presence of oxygen.[194]

Recent studies show wheatgrass juice has a powerful ability to fight tumors without the usual toxicity of drugs, which also inhibit the body's natural cell-destroying agents. The many active compounds found in wheatgrass juice cleanse the blood and neutralize and digest toxins in our cells.

In *Health Magic through Chlorophyll from Living Plant Life*, renowned nutritionist Dr. Bernard Jensen mentions several cases in which his patient's red blood cell count doubled in a matter of days, just by soaking in a chlorophyll-rich bath.

He says that blood builds more quickly when a person drinks chlorophyll-rich fresh juices on a regular basis.[195] I love to juice green wheatgrass and barley grass, sunflower sprouts, and various other chlorophyll-rich foods.

Celery has natural electrolytes and is very hydrating. Cucumbers are full of nutrients and natural electrolytes, and they are great for nourishing the skin.

Juices made from the following ingredients can regulate blood glucose levels because they have an insulin-like effect: asparagus, avocados, bitter melon, black pepper, Brussels sprouts, carrots, cinnamon, cucumbers, fennel, garlic, ginger, grapefruit, guava, parsnips, raw green vegetables, onions, leeks, sweet potatoes, tomatoes, winter squash, wheatgrass, sprouts, and yams.

These are good choices for anyone, but especially for diabetics. Just pick a few and vary them with the seasons as often as you can. At the Tree of Life, where I studied raw food and organic gardening,

Carrots are beneficial to people with eye problems, but I learned not to put carrots in juices for diabetics, because of their higher sugar content.

Watermelon is a great, natural diuretic.

Juicing Tips

Always clean fruits and vegetables well, especially if you are juicing the skin.

Juice in the morning when your body is empty and can absorb the nutrients more readily.

Nutrients start to disperse after 20 minutes, so drink juice immediately after making it. When buying fresh juice, make sure it is made for you right then, not the night or morning before.

Large juicers usually don't juice grasses, while grass juicers don't handle large fruits and vegetables very well. You need two different types of juicers: one for the grasses, and one for large fruits and vegetables.

Hand-turned wheatgrass juicers are the best choice for juicing grasses. They are less expensive and more reliable than electric versions. Juicers are an investment, but they will give you dense nutrients that are so beneficial to health.

When I am cutting fruit and vegetables, I save the pieces I don't use for my next juicing—for example, the end of celery, the rind of watermelon, the base of lettuce, and the stalks of broccoli. The only skins I don't juice are the skins of melons like cantaloupe because they are prone to mildew.

Watermelon and citrus fruits are tremendously powerful and have a strong taste. I juice whole lemons when I am juicing a bunch of heavy greens. The lemons give a kick to fresh juices that contain lots of greens, and they take out some of the heavy green taste.

I add a little coconut water, kefir, or kombucha to my juices as an added benefit for my immune system. You can also add probiotic, fermented drinks containing beneficial flora that support the immune system.

Before You Begin Juicing!

Juicing is great for everyone, but before you start, there are a few special considerations to note.

Protein types: For people with O blood types, which are known as protein types, Dr. Mercola said:

> If you are a protein type, juicing may need to be done a little differently. Celery, spinach, asparagus, string beans and cauliflower would be your best vegetables to juice. You can add some dark leafy greens like collards, kale, and dandelion greens, but do so cautiously and pay careful attention to how you feel.
>
> You may also want to initially limit your serving size of juice to no more than 6 oz. and store it properly and drink smaller amounts throughout the day.
>
> Also, to make drinking vegetable juice compatible with protein type metabolism (which needs high amounts of fat), it is important to blend a source of raw fat into the juice. Raw cream, raw butter, raw eggs, avocado, coconut butter, or freshly ground flax seed are the sources of raw fat that we most recommend.
>
> In addition to adding a source of raw fat to your juice, you may also find that adding some, or even all, of the vegetable pulp into your juice helps to make drinking the juiced vegetables more satisfying.[196]

So, if you are an O blood type, you may want to add some of the pulp and possibly a little oil (for example: a tiny bit of cold-pressed flax or hemp seed oil) to the juice and see if it is easier on your digestive system. I am an O blood type and I add a tablespoon of pulp back into my juice. I also add a teaspoon of hemp oil, chia seeds, flax seed oil, or coconut oil to my smoothies and juices.

Oranges, sea salt, and potassium: I don't recommend having fruit juices without the fiber or pulp of the fruit to help slow down sugar as it enters the blood stream. If sugar enters your blood too quickly, it stresses your body and creates a high blood-sugar level, even with natural sugars such as fruit.

Oranges and orange juice are loaded with potassium, but if we don't have an adequate unrefined salt intake, our body's cells are unable to use the potassium as effectively as they could. Histamine is released to take care of the inadequate salt levels, resulting in symptoms such as hay fever, itching, nausea, vomiting, and sleep disorders.

However, when we have enough unrefined salt, potassium is properly absorbed, and it aids the body with a natural antihistamine effect, combating those symptoms. We need 1/8 teaspoon (3/4 gram) of unrefined salt for every eight ounces of orange juice we drink, according to Jim Bolen's paper "Histamine/Anti-histamine and the Dangers of Taking Anti-histamine."[197] I also add a little unrefined sea salt to a meal when eating oranges.

In the book *ABC of Asthma, Allergies and Lupus*, Dr. Fereydoon Batmanghelidj writes:

"It is a good policy to add some salt to orange juice to balance the actions of sodium and potassium in maintaining the required volume of water inside and outside the cells... In some cultures, salt is added to melon and other fruits to accentuate their sweetness.

"In effect, these fruits contain mostly potassium. By adding salt to them before eating, a balance between the intake of sodium and potassium results. The same should be done to other fruits."[198]

Phytic acid: In plants, phytic acid is the principal store of phosphate. Phytic acid can be found in grains, seeds, beans, blackberries, broccoli, cauliflower, carrots, figs, and strawberries.[199]

Phytic acid is anti-nutritional. Research has traditionally focused on its structure that gives it the ability to bind minerals, proteins, and starch, which results in lower absorption rates of these elements. It reduces absorption of valuable minerals such as calcium, magnesium, and zinc.

Some foods are less suitable for juicing because they need to be lightly steamed or cooked to neutralize their phytic acid before ingesting.

Oxalic acid: Spinach, beet greens, and chard are high in oxalic acid. These particular greens should be "taken in limited quantities by those with mineral deficiencies or loose stools because of the laxative effect and the calcium-depleting effect of their substantial oxalic acid content."[200]

Oxalic acid binds with calcium. When it does this, the body will pull the calcium from the bones unless the diet is high in calcium. This can be harmful to the kidneys. The oxalic acid can also affect the absorption of iron. So, when eating spinach, also eat food rich in Vitamin C to help your body absorb the iron in the spinach more efficiently.

Micro spinach greens, which are also known as baby greens, will have much less oxalic acid and can be denser in nutrients than full-grown spinach.

Thyroid, kidneys, and adrenals: There are five goitrogenous chemicals in broccoli that can disrupt the body's ability to use iodine. Other cruciferous vegetables that are members of the Brassica family of plants are: Brussels sprouts, cabbage, cauliflower, turnip, and mustard greens.

This can be a problem for someone with a thyroid deficiency or low iodine.[201] Steaming or sautéing these cruciferous vegetables can help remove the goitrogens. So, it is best to consume these foods when they have been lightly cooked, unless they are fermented.

Tomatoes are best when vine-ripened, because if they are picked green and later ripened, they "can weaken the kidney–adrenal function."[202]

Fresh Green Juice

A 2-ounce shot of this is rejuvenating.

This drink took me a little while to get used to; but once I did, I found it was truly life-enhancing, and I started to really look forward to it.

This drink requires a juicer that works on grasses. I use a hand-cranked one. To make it taste more palatable, add a dash of unrefined sea salt, Ceylon cinnamon, or lemon or lime (juiced with the peel). This may make it taste more palatable.

Ingredients
wheatgrass or barley grass

Directions
1. Juice the grass.
2. Drink within 20 minutes for maximum nutritional benefit.

Fresh Green Juice with Sprouts and Citrus

Juice wheatgrass and fresh sprouts as a regular morning juice for exceptional nutritional and health benefits.

This drink requires a juicer. You may want to add a couple tablespoons of the pulp back into the drink after juicing, before drinking. If you do this, it can be a little easier on your stomach.

Ingredients
wheatgrass
sunflower sprouts
pea sprouts
¼ lemon or lime (with skin)
1/8 tsp. unrefined, sea salt

Directions
1. Juice all fruits and vegetables.
2. Add the pinch of sea salt before drinking.
3. Drink within 20 minutes for maximum nutritional benefit.

Fresh Juice with High Electrolytes

Ingredients
sunflower seed sprouts
mixed sprouts,
½ cucumber
4-5 ribs of celery
1/8 tsp. unrefined sea salt

Directions
1. Juice all vegetables.
2. Add the pinch of sea salt before drinking.
3. Drink within 20 minutes for maximum nutritional benefit.

Fresh Juice with Calming Effects

This drink requires a juicer. You may want to add a couple tablespoons of the pulp back into the drink after juicing, before drinking, because it can be a little easier on your stomach.

Ingredients
2 cups whole kale or romaine lettuce
4 celery stalks
1 beet (cut into chunks)
½ lemon or lime with skin
1/8 tsp. unrefined sea salt

Directions
1. Juice all fruits and vegetables.
2. Add the pinch of sea salt before drinking.
3. Drink within 20 minutes for maximum nutritional benefit.

Fresh Juice with Tomatoes

This drink requires a juicer. You may want to add a couple tablespoons of the pulp back into the drink after juicing, before drinking, because it can be a little easier on your stomach.

Ingredients
1 cucumber
2 vine-ripened tomatoes
½ head of romaine lettuce
1/8 tsp. unrefined sea salt

Directions
1. Juice all vegetables.
2. Add the pinch of sea salt before drinking.
3. Drink within 20 minutes for maximum nutritional benefit.

Notes

1. Add 2 T. fresh barley grass, ginger root, parsley, or cilantro to any of these juice recipes for an extra nutrient kick!

2. If you don't like the taste of greens, add lemon to the juice mixture to help cut that "green" taste. I add a half a lemon or a lime, including the skin. It adds an extra bit of Vitamin C and is super-alkalizing.

3. The sea salt helps with the flavor, but also adds minerals. Avoid white refined table salt or any salt that does not contain natural magnesium and potassium.

Nancy's Favorite Green Juice Drink

This drink requires a juicer. You may want to add a couple tablespoons of the pulp back into the drink after juicing, before drinking, because it can be a little easier on your stomach.

Ingredients
5 stalks celery
1 cucumber
2-3 leaves of kale
½ lemon or lime with skin
1 pinch unrefined sea salt

Directions
1. Juice all fruits and vegetables.
2. Add the pinch of sea salt before drinking.
3. Drink within 20 minutes for maximum nutritional benefit.

Vegetable Juice Drink

This drink requires a juicer. You may want to add a couple tablespoons of the pulp back into the drink after juicing, before drinking, because it can be a little easier on your stomach.

Ingredients
5-6 stalks celery
½ cucumber
4 large leaves of kale or romaine lettuce
2 carrots
1 pinch of unrefined sea salt

Directions
1. Juice all vegetables.
2. Add the pinch of sea salt before drinking.
3. Drink within 20 minutes for maximum nutritional benefit.

Warm Limeade or Lemonade

Wake up with a delicious, hydrating, healthy beverage!

I drink this three or four times per week when I wake up, before I have had anything else. In nutrition school, I learned that doing this cleanses the organs and flushes out bacteria. It gives you a nice burst of Vitamin C. And, even though it may seem like a citrus fruit would be acidic, the body reads it as alkalizing.

Sometimes I use grapefruit juice, just for a change. It is really refreshing.

Ingredients
½ lime or lemon
1 cup water

Directions
1. Juice lime or lemon.
2. On the stovetop, heat water so it is lukewarm (not hot).
3. Combine fruit juice and water.
4 Drink within 20 minutes for maximum nutritional benefit.

13

Smoothies

S moothies are symphonies of nutrients and fiber! You can have smoothies as a meal or a snack, or freeze them in popsicle molds and have them as a healthy desert.

I put healthy fat in my smoothies because my research shows it gives us energy, supports our brain health, and helps us absorb nutrients in fruits and other food more easily.

Chew on a bite of celery or cucumber right before you have a smoothie, because it will help prepare your body for digestion.

Basic Green Smoothie

Ingredients
1 cup fresh leafy baby greens torn into pieces (Romaine, spinach, and kale are good choices.)
½ cucumber
juice of half a lemon (or lime)
1 or 2 dates (non-sulfured), pitted and soaked in water for an hour
½ avocado or 1 tbsp. raw organic coconut oil
2 cups non-chlorinated, high-quality water

Directions
Place all ingredients in a powerful blender and blend until smooth.

Variations
1. Substitute ½ dropper of stevia instead of the dates.
2. Add a teaspoon of spirulina, sprouts, and/or maca root for more health benefits!
3. If you love lemon or citrus, add more lemon juice.

Green Smoothie

Ingredients
½ or 1 avocado (peeled, pitted, and diced)
1 cup baby kale, baby spinach, or romaine lettuce (chopped)
½ cucumber (chopped into chunks)
½ cup sprouts (ex. broccoli, radish, pea)
1 tsp. cold-pressed flax or hemp seed oil
1 ½ cups non-chlorinated or spring water
½ tsp. unrefined whole sea salt

Directions
1. Blend all ingredients in a blender until smooth.
2. Drink within 20 minutes.

Variations: Add 1 tablespoon maca root. Maca root is excellent for boosting libido and helping the body handle stress. Add a half a dropper of liquid stevia if you want more sweetness.

Green Smoothie Enhanced!

This green smoothie is highly recommended for supreme health. It adjusts pH and is used by many doctors to help diabetics control blood sugar levels. It may sound unusual to you at first, but give it a try. You may be pleasantly surprised by the taste.

This drink is rich in phytonutrients and Vitamin C. Iron is more readily absorbed by the body when Vitamin C is present, which makes this smoothie a great way to absorb the iron in spinach. Spinach is also 45 percent protein!

In fact, leafy greens are the most protein-rich foods. The body has to work to turn animal protein into the complex amino acids that it uses as proteins. In contrast, the complex amino acid combinations (protein) in these greens are easily and directly used by the body.

Make this drink in good blenders like the Breville blender or Vitamix, because they easily turn nuts, fruit, and vegetables into liquid. But try to **keep the blending to a minimum**. Over-blending leads to oxidation that destroys the nutrients in the food.

Ingredients
1 cup leafy greens, torn into pieces (baby kale, baby spinach or beet greens, and fresh romaine, in any combination)
1 stalk celery, cut into pieces
½ cucumber, cut into chucks (with skin)
a drop or two of stevia or a raw pitted date (optional)
1–2 tbsp. lemon or lime juice, freshly squeezed (Or, half a lemon if you really love citrus. You can add the peel, too!)
2 cups coconut water or pure water (Add more for a thinner smoothie.)
dash of Ceylon cinnamon (optional)
1 tsp. spirulina or chlorella
1 tbsp. flax seed oil (cold-pressed)
1 tbsp. organic raw coconut oil

Directions: Put all ingredients in a blender and blend. Add half of an avocado or maca root for extra health benefits!

Super Chocolate Power Smoothie

Yes, you can have chocolate for breakfast—and it will be healthy! Cacao is one of the top, if not *the* top, antioxidant foods in the world. It is nutrient-dense and magnesium-rich!

Ingredients
2 ½ cups nut milk
1 banana with the skin (Clean the banana, cut off the ends, and cut it into chunks before putting it into the blender. The skin has more nutrients in it than the banana and is high in fiber. This supports the adrenal glands.)
1 tbsp. cacao powder or cacao nibs
¼ dropper of stevia
1–2 tbsp. nut butter (sunflower seed butter works well)
1 tsp. raw sprouted pumpkin seeds
1 scoop plant-based, sprouted protein powder (I use Garden of Life brand, or freshly ground, sprouted hemp seeds.)
1 tbsp. spirulina
1 tbsp. extra virgin, pure coconut oil
1 tbsp. cold-pressed, raw hemp or flax seed oil

Directions
Blend all ingredients well in a blender and enjoy!

Variation: Use ¼ tsp of xylitol as the sweetener instead of the stevia.

Note: You can buy sprouted seed and nut butters that have had the phytic acid removed at many healthy grocery stores. You can also order them online from Blue Mountain Organics.

Super Breakfast Smoothie

Serves: One.

Ingredients
½ avocado (peeled, seeded and cut into chunks)
1 tbsp. coconut oil
2 tbsp. cold-pressed hemp or flax seed oil
1 scoop Protein Powder (Garden of Life is a good choice, or freshly ground, sprouted hemp seeds.)
1 or 2 capsules of digestive enzymes (open them and use the contents)
2 tbsp. raw organic sprouted seed or nut butter (you can add more)
1 ½ cups organic vanilla non-dairy milk (coconut or hemp work well)
1 tsp. spirulina or chlorella
¼ tsp. unrefined sea salt
1-2 tsp. coconut probiotics (from refrigerated section of the grocery store)
1 banana with the skin (Clean the banana, cut off the ends, and cut it into chunks before putting it into the blender. The skin has more nutrients in it than the banana and is high in fiber.)
1 cup wild blueberries

Directions
Blend in blender until smooth and creamy.

Variations
1. Add a teaspoon of cacao powder to make it chocolate flavored.
2. If you want it sweeter, then add a little vanilla extract.
3. Add 1 tbsp. seaweed (organic dulse or sea lettuce).
4. Add 1 tbsp. of aloe vera juice.

Note: You can purchase pre-sprouted nuts, seeds and nut/seed butters at many healthy grocery stores. You can also order them online from Blue Mountain Organics.

14

Tea & Infused Water

L egend has it that tea was discovered by Chinese emperor Shen Nung in 2737 BC, when his servant was boiling water under a tree and some leaves blew into the water. Shen Nung, a renowned herbalist, decided to try the infusion, and this resulted in what we now call tea: hot water that is infused, usually with dried leaves or flowers.

Drinking tea is a great way to hydrate and get the soothing, healing benefits of herbs. Drink it plain, or add a drop or two of stevia or honey for sweetness. Add a squeeze of fresh lemon juice or a sprig of mint for added flavor.

A delicious infusion can also be made by steeping herbs or slices of fruit and vegetables in cold water.

Green tea is known for its anticancer properties. It can help dissolve the protein coating that hides cancer cells from the immune system. Green tea helps your immune system work optimally.

Tulsi Tea

Tulsi tea (also known as holy basil) is at the heart of India's Ayurvedic holistic health practice. Its use has been documented as far back as 5000 BC. In India, the tulsi plant is sacred. It is known for promoting a healthier respiratory system and healthier vision, as well as reducing stress.

Dr. Singh wrote in *Tulsi—Mother Medicines of Nature* that it is one of the best stress adaptogens, which means it can help you relax and stay calm, and it can boost your system to handle stress better.

Tulsi is supposed to balance the health of the digestive system, promote a healthy metabolism, support skeletal and joint support, help normalize cholesterol levels, boost stamina, help with mucus problems, protect against free radicals, and help prevent cancer.[203]

Tulsi has also been found to have the ability to control blood glucose levels. Several test-tube, animal experiments, and human clinical trials have shown that tulsi has anti-diabetic activity. Studies using diabetic animals showed that tulsi can reduce blood glucose, correct abnormal lipid profiles, and protect the liver and kidneys from the metabolic damage caused by high glucose levels.[204]

Tulsi has been shown to help lower cortisol levels and aid in reducing anxiety. Cortisol is commonly referred to as the stress hormone. This hormone can cause severe problems with weight gain, memory, lowering immune function, bone density, diabetes, and heart disease.[205] Tulsi kills bacteria and infections, making it a great natural home remedy for acne.[206]

Tulsi tea comes in a variety of flavors. I drink a cup of it just about every day. I served tulsi tea to a client one day and, about an hour after he left, he called me and asked, "What was that drink you gave me? I feel like Superman!" I told him it was tulsi tea. He went right out and bought two or three different varieties, and he now drinks it almost every day.

Ginger Tea

Ginger tea, one of my favorites, is great for the immune, digestive, and circulatory systems. It can be especially good for anyone having digestive problems.

You can buy ginger root at the grocery store, usually by the root vegetables or mushrooms. The skin should be smooth and tight, not wrinkly. The root should be firm. Keep it in a cool, dry, dark place.

Ingredients
1-inch piece fresh ginger root
2 cups hot water

Directions
1. Grate or thinly slice ginger root.
2. Pour warm or hot water over it and steep 5 minutes.
3. Strain.

Infused Water:
A Nice Alternative to Sodas

Infusing water with ingredients such as mint, citrus fruit, or cucumber is easy, inexpensive, nutritious, and delicious. It has very few calories and is a wonderfully health, fun way to enjoy a refreshing glass of water.

Thoroughly clean the fruit, vegetables, or herbs with food-grade hydrogen peroxide, food-grade apple cider vinegar, or a really good vegetable wash—whether they are organic or not. (Slices of fruits and vegetables added to drinks in many restaurants or bars have tested high in bacteria, including *E. coli*.)

Mint invigorates the mind, refreshes the senses, has antiseptic qualities, aids in digestion, helps with the function of the liver, and can help with fresh breath. There are quite a few different types of mint, and each has a wonderful, fresh quality.

Mint is extremely easy to grow in a pot or garden, so you can have mint inexpensively and with little work year-round.

Put mint in ice cube trays with purified water to make minty ice cubes for teas, water, or cold soups and sauces in the hot summer months. I give the ice cubes to my dog to help her have better dog breath!

Orange, lemon, lime, and grapefruit slices all add zing to water, and a bit of Vitamin C. Lemon balm and other herbs are healthful and fun to drink or use in recipes that call for water.

This recipe is easy to double or triple. It is wonderful to serve at parties, at group meetings, after a workout, or to children as an alternative to sodas.

Ingredients
4 cups high-quality water
1/8 cup fresh mint leaves, orange slices, or cucumber slices
1/8 tsp. unrefined sea salt

Directions
1. Combine all ingredients.

2. Let sit for an hour or more.
3. Strain leaves or fruit out of the water, leaving only the water.
4. Place a pretty sprig of mint in the serving glass as a garnish.
5. Consume at room temperature or refrigerate for storage.

15

Non-Dairy Probiotics

Coconut Kefir

Coconut kefir is a probiotic that you can drink easily. It's made with fermentation of coconut meat and water. Coconut kefir contains natural probiotics. It is rich in enzymes that aid in the digestion and detoxification. I like to use coconut kefir in my non-dairy cheeses, to give it a sour, cheesy flavor.

Ingredients
2 cups coconut meat
2 to 3 cups pure coconut water
1 packet of kefir starter (from the refrigerated section of the healthier grocery stores)

Equipment
1-gallon glass container
A small piece of cheesecloth
A large rubber band
1 large spoon

Directions
1. Place the coconut meat and coconut water in a blender and blend until creamy. The more coconut meat you have, the thicker the kefir will be. Add more meat and less coconut water if you want a more yogurt-type consistency.
2. Place the blended mixture into a large, clean jar. Stir in the kefir starter until blended.
3. Cover the jar top with the cheesecloth.
4. Place a rubber band around the top of the jar to hold the cheesecloth in place. Place the jar in a warm place.
5. Stir the mixture once a day with the spoon and replace the cheesecloth.
7. The kefir will ferment at room temperature of 70–80°F for about three days (It takes 5 days if the room is 60–65°F). After three days, you can drink it or use it in recipes.
8. Coconut kefir will last 2–3 weeks in the refrigerator.

Rejuvelac

Rejuvelac is a probiotic drink made with fermented seeds or grains. Probiotic means "for life". Most of the immune system is made up of probiotics. We need to replenish the probiotics in our body on a regular, ongoing basis.

This drink is just as easy to make as it is easy to drink. An adult would typically drink eight, four-ounce servings per day (32 ounces total).

You can purchase sprouted quinoa, or you can soak un-sprouted quinoa overnight in non-chlorinated water to remove the phytic acid. You do not need to soak the quinoa seeds if they are already sprouted.

Ingredients
1 cup organic, non-GMO (genetically modified) quinoa, sprouted.
1 gallon high-quality water
Optional: ¼ tsp. organic apple cider vinegar

Equipment
1-gallon glass container
1 small piece of cheesecloth
1 large rubber band
1 large spoon

Directions
1. Soak quinoa (if not already sprouted) in non-chlorinated water over night for 12–18 hours. Add ¼ tsp. of organic apple cider vinegar to the water to better remove the phytic acid.
2. After soaking the quinoa, rinse the quinoa in a fine mesh colander (sieve) with running water.
3. Put the rinsed grain in the gallon jar.
4. Fill the jar up with the non-chlorinated pure water. If using purified water that is devoid of minerals, add ¼ tsp. whole unrefined mineral rich sea salt to the water.
5. Cover the jar top with the cheesecloth.

6. Please the rubber band around the top of the jar to hold the cheesecloth in place.

7. Stir the mixture once a day with the spoon and replace the cheesecloth.

8. The rejuvelac will ferment for about 2 days.

9. After 2 days, pour the mixture out, using a sieve or colander. Save the liquid. The liquid is the rejuvelac. This is the liquid probiotic you will drink.

10. You can cook the quinoa immediately and eat it as a meal or side dish.

11. The rejuvelac will last about a week in the refrigerator. If you are drinking 32 ounces a day, this recipe will last you four days.

16

Non-Dairy Milks

C ow's milk is the number-one cause of food allergies among infants and children, according to the American Gastroenterological Association.[207]
Animal milk contains lactose, the predominant sugar of milk. For most people, lactase deficiency is a condition that develops after age two. At age two, the body begins to produce less lactase, which is the enzyme that helps digest lactose.

Lactase breaks down milk sugar into simpler forms that can be absorbed into the blood stream. Babies need lactase to digest a mother's milk, but our body is not meant to digest it for a lifetime.

Consider that a baby cow is 200 pounds at birth, then grows to 2000 pounds in two years. Cow milk probably isn't a good weight-loss food. Non-dairy milks are a better idea when you have a recipe that calls for milk.

Nearly 50 million American adults are lactose intolerant, meaning they lack the ability to digest significant amounts of lactose. According to the American Gastroenterological Association, common symptoms of lactose intolerance include

- Nausea.
- Cramps.
- Bloating.
- Gas.
- Diarrhea.

"Symptoms usually begin about 30 minutes after eating or drinking foods containing lactose. The symptoms vary depending on the amount of lactose each person can tolerate."[208]

In my research, I have found that goat milk is easier to handle for many people. If you want to make a healthy baby formula, you may look into finding a high-quality, organic, non-pasteurized goat's milk to use.

According to my research[209], goat milk contains A2 Beta-Casein, not the A1 Beta-Casein that cow's milk contains. Research published in February, 2003 implicated the protein A1 beta-casein as a trigger for Type 1 diabetes and other health issues.[210]

I say *non-pasteurized* because the probiotics are destroyed when the milk is pasteurized. So, pasteurization destroys one of the main reasons you are giving it to a baby in the first place, which is to provide the beneficial bacteria (probiotics) that make up a good part of a healthy immune system.

Pine Nut Milk

Serving Size: 2 cups, but you can double this recipe easily.

I experimented with different nut milks and found I like the creamy texture of pine nuts. Start this recipe the day before, to soak the nuts overnight in the refrigerator and remove the phytic acid.

I make a non-dairy milk fresh about every three days, so I have some in my refrigerator at all times.

Ingredients
1 cup raw, organic pine nuts
2 cup non-chlorinated water
Pinch of unrefined sea salt

Directions
1. Soak nuts in non-chlorinated water overnight to remove the phytic acid, if they haven't been sprouted already.
2. Drain the nuts and blend them with the 2 cups non-chlorinated water in a blender until smooth and creamy, gradually adding more water as needed until you reach the desired consistency. You can make it thicker like a cream, or you can make it thinner like milk, depending on how much water you use.

Variations: You can use walnuts or cashews, instead of pine nuts. For a sweet flavor, add Sweet Leaf brand stevia sweetener, which comes in many flavors. It has no calories. This is my sweetener of choice. In this cream, I love the toffee flavor. Vanilla is also really good.

Add a dash of vanilla extract for a more vanilla flavor. Use coconut water to soak the nuts and add it as the water, to make a wonderful coconut cream.

Walnut Milk

This is very much like almond milk, but it has a better combination of Omega 3s to Omega 6s. Almonds have 1800 more Omega 6s than Omega 3s, so I started using walnuts instead, because omega 3s are anti-inflammatory and omega 6s are inflammatory.

Omega 3s are missing from most people's diets. Omega 3s are essential fatty acids that are not made by our body. We need to get them from our food, and walnuts are a good way to do it.

Ingredients
1 cups raw walnuts
2 cups water
stevia to taste (optional)
dash of unrefined sea salt
1 vanilla bean (optional)

Directions
1. Soak walnuts in water for 12–18 hours to remove phytic acid, if they haven't been sprouted already, to remove the phytic acid. To more thoroughly remove the phytic acid, drain off the soaking water.
2. Split vanilla bean and use a sharp knife to scrape out the inside of the bean. Put scrapings in blender.
3. Combine all ingredients in blender and blend well.
4. Strain through a nut milk bag. You can store this milk in the refrigerator in a tightly sealed glass jar for 4–5 days.

Variation: Omit the vanilla bean or use an alternative vanilla flavor, like vanilla extract. I love a few drops of Toffee-flavored liquid stevia in this drink.

Quinoa Milk

Quinoa is a seed and a complete protein, and it is gluten-free. Quinoa milk has become one of my absolute favorites. I use sprouted quinoa that I've soaked at least 18 hours. I do this because it helps remove the phytic acid from the quinoa seed.

Ingredients
1 vanilla bean
1 cup whole-grain, sprouted quinoa
2 cup water
stevia to taste
dash of sea salt

Directions
1. Split vanilla bean and use a sharp knife to scrape out the inside of the bean. Put scrapings in a blender.
2. Add the rest of the ingredients and blend well.
3. Strain through a nut milk bag, or simply drink it as a thicker version. (The more quinoa you add, the thicker the milk will be.)

Variation: You can omit or use an alternative vanilla flavor for this milk. Toffee-flavored stevia (by Sweet Leaf) is one I sometimes use instead of the vanilla bean.

You can also use fresh-cooked sprouted quinoa for this recipe.

Vegan Egg Nog

This is an easy version of egg nog. It makes a nice holiday drink! This recipe is easy to double. You can also use other milks, like rice or quinoa.

Ingredients
1½ cups vanilla-flavored nut milk
1 banana
pinch of nutmeg
a few drops stevia (optional)

Directions
Place all ingredients in a blender and blend until creamy.

17

Non-Dairy Cheeses

Basic Cheese

Serving Size: 2 cups

Use all organic ingredients. I like to serve this cheese with sliced cucumber, celery, and red bell pepper as the "crackers."

Ingredients
1 cup sprouted, raw pine nuts
1 cup sprouted, raw macadamia nuts
1 cup sprouted, raw walnuts
1 cup chopped parsley
2 ½ tbsp. freshly squeezed lemon or lime juice
2 tbsp. unpasteurized organic soy sauce (Nama Shoyu is good) or alternative coconut aminos made from coconut.
2 garlic cloves

Directions
1. Put all ingredients in the food processor. Blend until creamy.
2. Cover and store in the refrigerator up to 4 days.

Variations: Substitute sprouted cashews or sesame seeds for the walnuts or pine nuts. Add a tablespoon. of coconut kefir or rejuvelac for a cheesier flavor.

Notes: This cheese can be dehydrated so you can use it as slices of cheese on sandwiches or crackers. Spread the cheese mixture on the dehydrator sheets of Teflex. Dehydrate 6–7 hours, then peel the cheese off the Teflex sheets and flip it over to dehydrate the other side 4–5 hours at less than 115°F.

If you are not using already-sprouted nuts, then start this recipe the day before you want to make it, because you need to soak the nuts, separately, overnight in non-chlorinated water to remove the phytic acid and sprout them. Drain off the water after the soaking.

You can purchase pre-sprouted nuts, seeds, lentils, peas, beans, nut butters, and flours at many healthy grocery stores. You can also order them online from Blue Mountain Organics.

Ricotta

Serving Size: 1 ½ cups

Use all organic ingredients. I like to serve this cheese with sliced cucumber, celery, and red bell pepper as the "crackers."

Ingredients
1 cup sprouted, raw macadamia nuts
1 cup sprouted, raw almonds
2 tbsp. fresh lemon or lime juice
¼ cup fresh orange or tangerine juice
1 cup non-chlorinated water

Directions
1. Place nuts, lemon and juices with water in a food processor. Blend well until creamy.
2. Place in glass container with lid and refrigerate for up to 4 days.

Cheddar Cheese

Serving Size: 2 cups

Use all organic ingredients. I like to serve this cheese with sliced cucumber, celery, and red bell pepper as the "crackers."

Ingredients
2 cup sprouted raw macadamia nuts
1 ½ cups of red bell pepper (cored and seeded)
1 large orange (peeled and segmented)
4 garlic cloves (minced)
3-4 tbsp. freshly squeezed lemon or lime juice
2 tbsp. unpasteurized, organic soy (or alternative soy sauce made from coconut) sauce (Nama Shoyu is good)

Directions
1. Put all ingredients in the food processor. Blend until creamy.
2. Cover and store in the refrigerator up to 4 days.

Variation: Add a tablespoon. of coconut kefir or rejuvelac for a cheesier flavor.

Notes: This cheese can be dehydrated so you can use it as slices of cheese on sandwiches or crackers. Spread the cheese mixture on the dehydrator sheets of Teflex. Dehydrate 6–7 hours, then peel the cheese off the Teflex sheets and flip it over to dehydrate the other side 4–5 hours at less than 115°F.

If you are not using already-sprouted nuts, then start this recipe the day before you want to make it, because you need to soak the nuts, separately, overnight in non-chlorinated water to remove the phytic acid and sprout them. Drain off the water after the soaking.

You can purchase pre-sprouted nuts, seeds, lentils, peas, beans, nut butters, and flours at many healthy grocery stores. You can also order them online from Blue Mountain Organics.

Dill Cheese

Serving Size: 2 cups

Use all organic ingredients. I like to serve this cheese with sliced cucumber, celery, and red bell pepper as the "crackers."

Ingredients
2 cups sprouted, raw macadamia nuts
¼ cup chopped dill
¾ cup chopped scallions
2 garlic cloves. minced
1 tsp. unrefined sea salt
1 tsp. freshly ground black pepper
1 cup rejuvelac

Directions
1. Put all ingredients in the food processor. Blend until creamy.
2. Cover and store in the refrigerator up to 4 days.

Variation: Substitute sprouted cashews for the macadamia nuts.

Notes: This cheese can be dehydrated so you can use it as slices of cheese on sandwiches or crackers. Spread the cheese mixture on the dehydrator sheets of Teflex. Dehydrate 6–7 hours, then peel the cheese off the Teflex sheets and flip it over to dehydrate the other side 4–5 hours at less than 115°F.

If you are not using already-sprouted nuts, then start this recipe the day before you want to make it, because you need to soak the nuts, separately, overnight in non-chlorinated water to remove the phytic acid and sprout them. Drain off the water after the soaking.

You can purchase pre-sprouted nuts, seeds, lentils, peas, beans, nut butters, and flours at many healthy grocery stores. You can also order them online from Blue Mountain Organics.

18

Breakfast Foods

Chia Seed Pudding with Cashew Crème

Serves: One to Two.

Start this recipe the day before you want to serve it. This recipe is for one to two servings but can easily be doubled.

Ingredients for the Pudding
1 cup chia seeds
3½ cups purified water
fresh berries or sliced bananas (optional)
pinch of unrefined sea salt

Ingredients for the Cashew Crème
½ cup cashews
2 cups purified water
a few drops stevia (plain, toffee-flavored, or vanilla-flavored)

Directions for the Pudding
1. Soak chia seeds in 3½ cups water, with the pinch of sea salt, overnight in the refrigerator in a very large bowl. The seeds will double in size when soaked, so be sure the bowl is large enough to hold them.
2. The next day, take the soaked seeds out of the refrigerator and gently mix in berries or banana slices.
3. Place chia pudding in individual serving bowls.

Directions for the Cashew Crème
1. Soak cashews in 1 cup water overnight in the refrigerator. Drain. (The soaking water contains the phytic acid we want to remove. The nuts are much more digestible when the phytic acid is removed.)
2. Blend cashews and 1 cup water with stevia, adding more water if you want it thinner. (I prefer it thick like a crème.)
3. Top each bowl of pudding with a dollop of cashew crème.

Note: Sweet Leaf brand stevia comes in flavors like vanilla, orange, and toffee. They are great for flavoring nut milks and crèmes. I usually find them at the healthy grocery store in the baking section or in the sweetener section. I like the liquid stevia better than the granular variety, which I think has a bitter aftertaste.

Raw Oatmeal Granola with Yogurt
Not a Vegan Recipe

Serves: One.

This is a softer version of granola. Start the night before, to allow time for the oat flakes and chia seeds to soften and the nuts to be soaked. Soaking them breaks down the enzyme inhibitors and makes the oats, seeds, and nuts more digestible. If you want the granola crunchier, make it fresh, do not soak the oats and seeds overnight, and use raw, unsoaked walnuts.

Ingredients
½ cup raw sprouted oat flakes
1 tbsp. chia seeds
1 cup water
1 cup organic, raw, unpasteurized, coconut yogurt or kefir. (cashew crème will work in this recipe as a good substitute.)
2 tbsp. walnuts
½ tsp. cinnamon
2–4 dried (non-sulfured) apricots, chopped
¼ cup raisins, softened by soaking in warm water at least 10 minutes and drained

Directions
1. Place oat flakes and chia seeds in non-chlorinated water for an hour. Drain whatever liquid you can. Then soak oat flakes and chia seeds overnight in yogurt, in the refrigerator, to soften.
2. Soak walnuts in water for 2-12 hours to help them become more digestible.
3. Drain and chop walnuts.
4. Combine softened oats and chia seeds with all other ingredients. Let the granola sit until it is room temperature, if you want it warm.

Variation: Add a teaspoon of pure, extra-virgin coconut oil.

Notes: If you have a dehydrator, you can put the soaked oats (with the extra liquid drained off) in a small shallow bowl in the dehydrator for a wonderful raw oatmeal. I leave the oatmeal in the dehydrator overnight on 105°F.

You can buy sprouted oats, nuts, and seeds from healthy food stores, or online from Blue Mountain Organics.

"Cheese and beef elevate insulin levels higher than the dreaded high-carbohydrate foods like pasta."

—American Journal of Clinical Nutrition 50, p. 1264. (1997)

19

Salad Dressings

S tore-bought salad dressings may be high in added sugar, and they often contain canola oil. Avoid dressings with added sugar, high sugar, fructose, agave, or canola oil.

Sometimes I simply squeeze the juice of a lemon or lime on my salad to make a delicious, easy, and healthy salad dressing. Adding sliced avocado, sliced onion, mushrooms, tomatoes, sprouted seeds and nuts, or fresh sprouts can make leafy greens more interesting and much healthier. Keep it vegan.

For something a little more complex, here are some delicious salad dressing recipes. They require a blender, make two servings, and will keep for two days if refrigerated. Serve them over a variety of greens or chopped vegetables.

Some good nutritious greens are: green lettuce, baby romaine, baby spinach, baby kale, watercress, and red leaf lettuce. Avoid iceberg lettuce, as it has very little nutritional value.

Cucumber Dressing

This is one of my favorite dressings. Add a little bit of extra-virgin olive oil if it's too thick. You can also add more vinegar, if you like it more tart.

Ingredients
1 cucumber (chopped into chunks with skin)
1 avocado (peeled, pitted, and diced)
1 tsp. unpasteurized apple cider vinegar or rice vinegar
¼ tsp. unrefined sea salt

Directions
1. Blend all ingredients in a blender until smooth.
2. Store in the refrigerator in a glass jar with a tight lid.

Bell Pepper Dressing

Ingredients
1 red or yellow bell pepper (stem and seeds removed, chopped into chunks)
1 tomato (stem removed, chopped into chunks)
¼ cup cold-pressed, unrefined flax or hemp seed oil
¼ cup extra virgin olive oil
½ cup cilantro (fresh)
¼ tsp. unrefined sea salt

Directions
1. Blend all ingredients in a blender until smooth.
2. Store in the refrigerator in a glass jar with a tight lid.

Creamy Italian Dressing

This is a very rich salad dressing, so use it lightly. Start it the day before you want to use it, because it is best to soak the nuts overnight. The soaking removes the phytic acid if you are using raw nuts.

Ingredients
⅓ cup raw Brazil nuts (Soak in pure water overnight, then pour off the soaking water.)
¾ or 1 small cucumber (chopped with skin)
⅓ cup olive oil
¼ cup fresh basil (chopped)
1 ½ tbsp. fresh oregano leaves
1 tbsp. ginger juice (fresh)
2 tbsp. lemon juice (fresh)
¼ tsp. unrefined sea salt

Directions
1. In a food processor or blender, blend cucumber with ginger and lemon juice and olive oil.
2. Add Brazil nuts and blend until smooth.
3. Remove from blender and place in a bowl.
4. Mix in chopped basil and oregano.
5. Store in refrigerator in a glass container with a tight fitting lid for up to three days.

Creamy Avocado Dressing

Ingredients

1 avocado
1 clove garlic, freshly minced
½ cucumber, chopped
¼ tsp. unrefined sea salt
½ cup extra virgin organic olive oil
1 tbsp. lime or lemon juice (fresh)

Directions

1. Combine avocado, garlic, cucumber, lime or lemon juice, and whole, sea salt.
2. Add olive oil in a slow, steady stream while blending the other ingredients together.

Variation: Substitute balsamic vinegar for lemon juice.

One and one half servings of green leafy vegetables per day lowered the risk of Type 2 diabetes by 14% and boosted metabolism.[211]

20

Soups

String Bean Soup

Serves: Two.

String beans have an insulin-type effect that regulates blood sugar, and they are a healthy protein. Green beans are a great vegetable for diabetics to add to their eating plan.

Ingredients
1 cup fresh green beans
1 avocado (pitted and peeled)
½ cup of non-chlorinated water
1 cup fresh tomato
2 tbsp. coconut oil
2 tsp. unrefined sea salt
1 tsp. cumin
¼ tsp. turmeric
1/8 tsp. cayenne pepper
1/8 tsp. freshly ground black pepper
1/8 tsp. coriander
1/8 tsp. mustard seeds or mustard

Directions
1. Blend the ingredients in a blender until creamy.
2. Add some non-chlorinated water, if it's too thick.
3. Serve at room temperature

Variation: Add ¼ to ½ cup of aloe vera, with the skin removed.

Spinach Soup

Ingredients
1 yellow bell pepper (diced)
2 ribs celery (diced)
2 cups baby spinach, minced
1 avocado, peeled, pitted, and diced
1 sundried tomato (soaked in water until soft)
1 tbsp. cold-pressed raw flax or hemp seed oil
1 tsp. pure coconut oil
1 tbsp. cumin
3 tbsp. fresh ground raw, sprouted pumpkin seeds
5 tbsp. cooked chickpeas, or cooked adzuki beans (mashed)
½ tsp. unrefined sea salt
1 tbsp. lemon juice, or ½ tbsp. unpasteurized apple cider vinegar
Water as needed for thinning

Directions
1. Blend bell pepper, celery, spinach, avocado, soft sundried tomato, cold pressed oil, cumin, lemon or vinegar, and sea salt in a blender until smooth. Add a little pure water to make it thinner if it is too thick.
2. Remove from blender, add the mashed beans, and combine well.
3. Add the freshly ground pumpkin seeds to the mixture.
4. Store in the refrigerator in a glass jar with a tight lid.

Gazpacho

Ingredients
3 large tomatoes (diced)
1 red, yellow, or orange bell pepper (seeded & diced)
½ cucumber (diced)
¼ cup raw cold-pressed flax or hemp oil
2 cloves garlic (minced)
3 sundried tomatoes (soaked in pure water until soft)
2 drops of plain liquid stevia
Pinch of black pepper
Pinch of cayenne pepper
Pinch of turmeric
Unrefined sea salt to taste

Directions
1. Blend all ingredients in a blender until creamy.
2. Serve at room temperature or slightly chilled.

Refreshing Summer Soup

Serves: Four.

This is a fresh and living raw green soup. It is one of my recipes from the book Maryann De Leo and I wrote that book for older people and people taking care of elderly parents, *Alive and Cooking*, page 209. It celebrates life!

Ingredients
½ cucumber, chopped
1½ cups fresh green beans
½ cup. romaine lettuce
½ cup fresh spinach
½ cup fresh basil
¼ cup fresh chives
1 tbsp. pure organic extra-virgin coconut oil
½ tsp. unrefined sea salt
1 tbsp. fresh lime juice

Directions
1. Blend all ingredients in a powerful blender or food processor.
2. Garnish with another tablespoon of fresh chives.

Cucumber Soup

Serves: Two.

This is a delicious, refreshing soup to serve cool on a summer day.

Ingredients
1 avocado
2 cucumber
4 tbsp. dill
2 tsp. lemon juice
½ tsp. unrefined sea salt or to taste
1 cup water (add a little more if it's too thick)

Directions
Blend in a blender until creamy.

Miso Soup with Mushrooms

This is an easy, delicious soup. I frequently make it to sip in the afternoon instead of tea. It is a high-protein, low-calorie, nutrient-rich, and probiotic-rich soup.

Ingredients
10 dried or fresh mushrooms, sliced or diced
4 ½ cups non-chlorinated water
¼ cup miso
¼ cup chopped watercress for garnish (optional)

Directions
1. Soak dried mushrooms at least 10 minutes in ½ cup warm water, until soft. You don't need to soak fresh mushrooms.
2. Simmer 4 cups water in a pan on low heat. Do not boil.
3. Add miso and stir until miso is dissolved.
4. Remove from heat.
5. Add mushrooms when miso water is just cool enough to drink.
6. Add chopped watercress as a garnish.

Variation: Add kombu seaweed for additional nutrition.

"*The doctor of the future will give no medication, but will interest his patients in the care of the human frame, diet and in the cause and prevention of disease.*"

—*Thomas A. Edison*

21

Breads and Crackers

Raw Crackers

Serving Size: 3 trays of crackers.

This recipe requires a dehydrator. Start the day before you want to make the crackers, because you need to soak the flaxseeds over night to remove the phytic acid.

I made these crackers for my family, who are not into eating "raw food." My brother still talks about how much he loved these crackers.

Ingredients
2 cups flaxseeds
1 tbsp. red onion
2/3 cup sun-dried tomatoes (chopped)
1 cup fresh tomatoes
1/3 cup chopped red or orange bell pepper
1 tsp. minced jalapeno
1 tsp. minced garlic
1/3 cup cilantro
1 tbsp. coconut oil
1 tsp. unrefined sea salt
2 tbsp. dried sea kelp
4 cups non-chlorinated water

Directions
1. Soak the flaxseeds in 4 cups of water overnight in a large bowl. They will double in size, so be sure the bowl is large enough to hold them even after they expand.
2. Drain off any leftover water in the flaxseed bowl.
3. Place onion, bell pepper, tomatoes, bell pepper, jalapeno, garlic, cilantro, sea salt, and sea kelp in a food processor. Blend until creamy.
4. Mix the processed vegetables into the flaxseeds.

5. Take the flaxseed/vegetable mixture and spread it onto coconut-oiled Teflex sheets. Spread it very thin, less than ¼ inch thick if you can.

6. Dehydrate at 90–100°F for 4–6 hours.

7. Flip the crackers over and put them on the screens to dehydrate for another couple of hours until they are crisp.

8. Store them in airtight containers in the refrigerator. They will keep for a couple days.

Notes: I love to eat them while they are really fresh, right out of the dehydrator.

You can leave out the kelp and onion; it's still very good. You can also make these without soaking the flax seeds first, but it's healthier to soak and remove the phytic acid from the seeds. Soaking them will make them more digestible.

Apple Bread

This recipe requires a dehydrator. You may want to start this recipe the day before you wish to serve it.

Ingredients
2 cups sprouted tiny, French lentils
2 cups shredded apple
¼ cup sprouted almonds
¼ cup sprouted walnuts
3 dates (pitted and soaked in non-chlorinated water for 2 hours)
¼ cup coconut oil
1 tsp. minced garlic
1 tsp. minced, fresh parsley
½ tsp. unrefined sea salt

Directions
1. Place the sprouted nuts, soaked dates, and all of the other ingredients into a food processor and make a smooth dough.
2. Spread the dough on a Teflex sheet and form a loaf about 1 ½ inches tall, 3 or 4 inches wide and about 6 inches long.
3. Dehydrate around 100°F for 15–17 hours. The loaf should be fairly crisp on the outside, but moist on the inside.
4. Cut in thin slices.
5. Refrigerate in an airtight container. It keeps for a couple of days.

Note: If you are not using already sprouted lentils, almonds and walnuts, then start this recipe the day before you want to make it, because you need to soak the lentils, almonds and walnuts, separately, overnight in non-chlorinated water to remove the phytic acid and sprout them. Drain off the water after the soaking.

You can purchase pre-sprouted nuts, seeds, lentils, peas, beans, nut butters, and flours at many healthy grocery stores. You can also order them online from Blue Mountain Organics.

Savory Snack Balls

Serves: Four.

This recipe requires a dehydrator. You will need to start this recipe at least one day before you want to serve it, because the chia seeds need to soak at least a few hours and it has to be dehydrated for a few hours.

Ingredients
1 cup sprouted walnuts
1 cup sprouted sunflower seeds
¼ cup chia seeds (soaked in 3/4 cup of non-chlorinated water for a few hours)
¼ cup fresh basil or cilantro
1 tbsp. freshly grated ginger root
½ tsp. unrefined sea salt
¼ tsp. turmeric
1/8 tsp. cayenne pepper
1/8 tsp. black pepper
¼ tsp. coconut oil

Directions
1. Place sprouted nuts and chia seed mixture in food processor and process until fairly smooth.
2. Add the remaining ingredients and process until you have a nicely textured dough.
3. Using a spoon or ice-cream scoop, form balls and place them on solid dehydrator sheets.
4. Dehydrate at 100°F for 3–4 hours.

Note: If you are not using already-sprouted walnuts or sunflower seeds, then start this recipe the day before you want to make it, because you need to soak the nuts and seeds, separately, overnight in non-chlorinated water to remove the phytic acid and sprout them. Drain off the water after the soaking.

Soak the chia seeds separately. They get gelatinous when they are soaked in water. Then just add the gelatinous chia seed mixture to the food processor.

You can purchase pre-sprouted nuts, seeds, lentils, peas, beans, nut butters, and flours at many healthy grocery stores. You can also order them online from Blue Mountain Organics.

Pizza

Serves: Two to Four.

This is a two-day recipe, so take that into account if you want to serve it on a special day.

Crust Ingredients
2 cups golden, dry flax seeds (ground)
1 cup sprouted almonds
1 carrot shredded
1 yellow bell peppers (seeded and minced)
½ tbsp. garlic minced
1 tbsp. freshly chopped red onion
1 tsp. fresh lemon or lime juice
¼ cup parsley
¼ cup fresh cilantro or basil
½ tsp. dried oregano
2 tsp. dried Italian seasoning
1½ tsp. unrefined sea salt
1/8 tsp. black pepper
½ cup non-chlorinated water
1 cup sundried tomatoes (measured before soaking and soaked for an hour in non-chlorinated water)
1 tbsp. coconut oil or good-quality pure olive oil

Crust Directions
1. Combine the ground flax seeds, ground sprouted almonds, grated carrots, and bell peppers in a large bowl.
2. In a food processor, combine the soaked sundried tomatoes, garlic, parsley, cilantro, and sea salt. Blend until smooth. Add this mixture to the large bowl.
3. Add the remaining ingredients into the bowl and mix well.
4. Transfer the whole mixture back to the food processor and blend until smooth. This may take a couple of batches.

5. Take a Teflex sheet and spread the dough out into a 6-inch pizza crust as close to ¼ of an inch thick as you can. You may like it thicker, and that's fine.

6. Dehydrate the crusts for about 19 hours at 100°F, or until the crusts are solid but not hard.

Note: If you are not using already-sprouted almonds, then start this recipe the day before you want to make it, because you need to soak the almonds, separately, overnight in non-chlorinated water to remove the phytic acid and sprout them. Drain off the water after the soaking.

Do not sprout the flax seeds. They get gelatinous if soaked in water. It will make a better dough if you don't sprout them.

You can purchase pre-sprouted nuts, seeds, lentils, peas, beans, nut butters, and flours at many healthy grocery stores. You can also order them online from Blue Mountain Organics.

Pizza Cheese
Use a non-dairy cheese recipe of your choice.

Marinara Sauce Ingredients
1 red bell pepper, seeded
2 cups sun dried tomatoes
2 cups sundried tomato water (which you get from soaking the sundried tomatoes in 2 cups of non-chlorinated water for 2-4 hours)
¼ cup coconut oil or good-quality extra-virgin olive oil
1 minced clove of garlic
3 tbsp. dried Italian seasoning
½ tsp. freshly ground black pepper
½ tsp. unrefined, sea salt

Marinara Sauce Directions
Place all ingredients in a blender and blend until smooth.

Special Topping Ingredients
1 Diced bell pepper

1 diced zucchini

1 minced clove of garlic

2 diced mushrooms

4 chopped and pitted black olives

¼ tsp unrefined sea salt

1 tbsp. good quality, pure extra virgin olive oil

Special Topping Directions

1. Place all ingredients in a bowl and combine.

2. Then let it sit for 10 minutes or more.

3. Top the pizza marinara sauce with this mixture

Creating the Pizza

1. Take the pizza dough and spread the marinara sauce over it, then place small bits of the nut cheese over it.

2. Place the special toppings on top of that and serve at room temperature.

22

Dip

Cucumber Dip

Ingredients
½ cup sprouted cashews
1 cucumber
½ avocado
1 tsp. coconut oil
2 tbsp. dill
½ tsp. unrefined sea salt

Directions
Blend in blender or food processor until creamy. Serve with freshly sliced up veggies to use as chips.

Note: If you are not using already-sprouted cashews, then start this recipe the day before you want to make it, because you need to soak the cashews, separately, overnight in non-chlorinated water to remove the phytic acid and sprout them. Drain off the water after the soaking.

You can purchase pre-sprouted nuts, seeds, lentils, peas, beans, nut butters, and flours at many healthy grocery stores. You can also order them online from Blue Mountain Organics.

Hummus

Hummus is a traditional Mediterranean dip that is high in protein and nutrients. It also happens to be very easy to make. I typically make a large batch and continue to eat it all week with different fruits, and vegetables cut into slices and used as the "crackers." This recipe is my favorite.

Chickpeas can be sprouted by soaking overnight or longer in non-chlorinated water, until you see a little sprout (or tail) coming out of the chickpeas. Pour off the water you soaked them in. Sprouting the chickpeas will remove the phytic acid and make them more digestible.

Ingredients
3 cups sprouted garbanzo beans (also known as chickpeas)
1–3 cloves garlic (minced)
5 tbsp. freshly squeezed lemon or lime juice
¼ cup tahini (sesame seed butter)
1 tsp. cumin
1 tsp. unrefined sea salt
⅛ tsp. cayenne pepper
¼ cup parsley (fresh)

Directions
1. Combine all ingredients in a food processor and blend until creamy.
2. Serve with cut vegetables crudités as the dipping chips. *Examples*: sliced cucumber, carrot, celery, crooked neck squash, red or yellow bell pepper, green beans, and zucchini.

Variations: Use other bean varieties, instead of or in addition to the traditional garbanzo bean. You can also use cooked beans.

Pesto

This is one of my favorite ways to use fresh basil from my garden. It is so versatile. I use this pesto for many dishes: as a pasta sauce, to stuff mushrooms, to spread on tomatoes, as a salad dressing, on pizza, and as a topping for bread. The possibilities are endless!

When storing it, always cover the top with a layer of olive oil to seal it. Every time you use it, seal it back up with olive oil and clean the sides of the jar. Then it will keep for a long, long time.

Soak nuts 12–18 hours and then dehydrate them on low, if you wish to remove some of the phytic acid.

Ingredients
1¾ cup pine nuts
2 cup fresh basil
¼ cup walnuts
1/3 cup extra virgin olive oil
½ tsp. unrefined sea salt
½ tsp. black pepper

Directions
1. Combine all ingredients in food processor and process until smooth.
2. Place in a jar with a good-fitting lid. Clean the inside of the jar, all the way down to the top of mixture.
3. Cover top of mixture with at least ¼ inch of olive oil.
4. Store in refrigerator.

Guacamole

Serves: Four.
I use one avocado for each person I will serve.

This is one of my favorite foods. Serve it with salsa or pico de gallo. I frequently use freshly cut cucumbers, zucchini, or squash as my dipping chips.

Ingredients
4 avocados (pitted and peeled)
2–3 tbsp. fresh lemon juice
1 clove garlic, freshly minced
1 pinch unrefined sea salt
2 tomatoes, stems removed, chopped
¼ cup chopped red onion

Directions
1. In a large mixing bowl, combine the ingredients until creamy.
2. Serve cool or room temperature.

Note: When storing guacamole in the refrigerator, cover it with a thin layer of fresh lime or lemon juice to keep it from turning brown. Some people put the avocado pit in the guacamole when storing, which also helps keep it from turning brown. A trick we use in Texas is placing parchment or plastic wrap directly on the surface of the guacamole to keep oxygen out.

Pico de Gallo

Pico de gallo is a healthy and delicious condiment commonly served with Mexican food. Pico de gallo is easy to make, and you can keep it in the refrigerator for a few days in a well-sealed container.

Ingredients
8 tomatoes, diced
1 onion, diced
1/3 cup cilantro, chopped
2 (or more) jalapeños, seeded and minced
unrefined sea salt to taste

Directions
1. Combine all ingredients in a bowl. Reserve a few sprigs of the cilantro for garnishing, to make a pretty presentation.
2. Place in refrigerator for an hour, or overnight, to allow flavors to meld together.
3. Enjoy this with freshly cut veggies: orange, red or yellow bell peppers, cucumbers, celery.

Salsa

Here in Texas, we use salsa as a side dish for many of our meals. This is a very basic, easy recipe. I like to serve it with guacamole.

Ingredients
6 tomatoes
2 jalapeño peppers, de-stemmed
4 tbsp. fresh cilantro (optional)

Directions
Place all ingredients in blender and blend well.

Variation: Increase jalapeños for a hotter flavor.

Pâté

This is a delicious condiment I have even used as a main dish. It's also great for traveling when you need an easy meal to take on the road.

Ingredients
2 cups sprouted walnuts
¼ cup red onion
1 red bell pepper
1 teaspoon unrefined sea salt
2 stalks celery

Directions
1. Combine all ingredients in a food processor and blend until smooth.
2. Serve with sliced vegetable slices or in sliced celery sticks. You can also serve it on a plate as-is, over a salad, rolled up in a green leaf, or on crackers.

Note: Walnuts can be sprouted by soaking overnight or for 18 hours in non-chlorinated water. Pour off the water. If you want the nuts dry, then dry them in a dehydrator or a warm oven. Sprouting the nuts will remove the phytic acid.

If you purchase already-sprouted nuts, you can eliminate this step. You can buy them at many healthy food stores or online at Blue Mountain Organics.

23

Snacks

Veggies

These fresh veggies make the perfect snack!
-Fresh green beans
-Fresh snow peas
-Fresh okra
-Fresh cucumber
-Fresh celery
-Fresh tomatoes
-Fresh red, yellow, or orange bell pepper

Directions
1. Buy fresh organic vegetables.
2. Cut off stems and ends.
3. Sprinkle lightly with mineral-rich unrefined sea salt when you are ready to eat them. This helps you absorb the potassium more effectively.
4. Eat fresh and uncooked.

Notes: You can put washed and cut veggies in individual containers or baggies and store them in the refrigerator for the week. If you crave something a little more filling, have hummus with these veggies. Or, put a small amount of raw, sprouted nut or seed pâté or butter on the celery.

The green beans are an especially good choice, because they have an insulin-type effect that helps regulate blood sugar.

String Beans

Serves: Two.

String beans have an insulin-type effect that regulates blood sugar, and they are a healthy protein to have as a meal or snack.

Ingredients
¾ to 1 pound fresh string beans
2 tbsp. pure organic coconut oil, high-quality pure olive oil, or macadamia nut oil
1 ½ tsp. fresh, parsley (chopped)
1 tbsp. freshly squeezed lemon or lime juice
1 ½ tsp. freshly, made lemon or lime zest
½ tsp. unrefined sea salt
1/8 tsp. freshly ground black pepper

Directions
1. Place cleaned green beans in a large bowl and massage them with your hands using the unrefined sea salt for 4 or 5 minutes. This breaks down the tough skin and makes them more digestible.
2. Whisk together the remaining ingredients and add them to the green bean mixture.
3. Let this mixture sit and marinate for about an hour.
4. Serve at room temperature.

Kale Chips

This delicious, nutritious, fun and easy snack or side dish is made with a dehydrator. Kale shrinks a great deal, so use one bunch for each person.

Ingredients
1 bunch fresh kale per person
pure, organic coconut oil or extra virgin olive oil (about 1 tbsp.)
unrefined sea salt (about ¼ tsp.)
mesquite powder (about ¼ tsp.)
Ceylon cinnamon (about ¼ tsp.)

Directions
1. Cut kale in 2-inch-square pieces.
2. With clean hands, rub each piece with coconut oil or extra-virgin olive oil.
3. Sprinkle lightly with all of the seasonings.
4. Rub each piece again.
5. Place the pieces on dehydrator sheets with perforated holes. Spread them out so they can dry easily.
6. Dehydrate 8-10 hours until crispy.

Notes: I usually dehydrate chips for a few hours. It doesn't take that long with these little thin greens. These taste best when eaten right away. Store kale chips in an airtight container so they will keep for a few days.

Nut Pâté

This is an easy, rich, and savory snack or appetizer. I use it as a filling for my Nori Rolls with Nut Pâté (recipe in this book). You could also serve this with crackers or with chopped vegetables as a dip.

Start this recipe a day ahead of time, so you can soak the nuts in water to remove the phytic acid, or buy already sprouted nuts.

Ingredients
2 cups pecans, soaked 12–18 hours in pure, non-chlorinated water, drained and dried in a dehydrator or in an oven on low heat
1 red bell pepper, cored, seeded, and chopped
2 large stalks celery, chopped
2 tbsp. fresh lemon juice
1 tsp. unrefined sea salt
dash of mesquite powder (optional)

Directions
1. Combine all ingredients in a food processor.
2. Add a little water if necessary.

Variations: Use one cup of walnuts or two cups of walnuts, instead of one cup of pecans. Use lime juice instead of lemon juice.

Mushroom Nibbles

I love mushrooms, and I make these quick and easy nibbles all the time. I serve these as a quick bite for lunch or a snack. They are terrific as appetizers and/or a side dish. Serve them warm.

Ingredients
10 or more button or small cap mushrooms
enough soy sauce (organic and unpasteurized) to cover the mushrooms
¼ cup pesto (recipe in this book)
¼ cup raw, organic nut cheese

Directions
1. Brush off mushrooms and remove stems.
2. Soak mushrooms in soy sauce for two hours or overnight.
3. After soaking, place mushrooms in a baking dish.
4. Fill mushrooms with pesto and top with a dab of cheese.
5. Warm mushrooms in an oven, toaster oven, or warming drawer.

Notes: Soak the stems, too. Then chop them and save them to use in other recipes. When warming, keep the temperature under 118°F to keep the enzymes alive.

Variation: Fill the mushrooms with guacamole or hummus, instead of the pesto and nut cheese. They are delicious either way!

Trail Mix

I had trouble finding a trail mix I liked that didn't have some sort of sugar added to it, so I decided to make my own. Trail mix is wonderful to keep on hand as a snack when traveling, or at the office or school, or as an emergency food when running around on daily errands.

If you love chocolate, add some cacao nibs to this mix, and they will meld right in!

Ingredients
½ cup pecans
½ cup pine nuts
½ cup almonds
½ cup walnuts
½ cup pistachios
½ cup pumpkin seeds
½ cup sunflower seeds
½ cup coconut (fresh or dried), shredded
1 cup cherries or apricots (dried with NO added sugar), chopped
½ cup raisins (NO added sugar)
¼ tsp. sea salt
¼ cup raw cacao nibs (optional)

Directions
1. Use sprouted seeds and nuts in this recipe. You can purchase sprouted seeds, nuts, and grains; or, you can sprout them yourself as follows:

Soak all nuts and seeds 12–18 hours in water, drain, and then let them dry well. Dry them in a dehydrator for a few hours if you have one. If you don't, spread them on a cookie sheet and let them sit in a very dry, slightly warm oven (less than 118°F) for at least an hour.

2. Combine all ingredients in a bowl.

How to Store

Store the trail mix in an airtight glass container, or put it into small containers ready to grab quickly. Keep it in the refrigerator, so it will stay fresh longer.

Eat this mixture within a week. Since the nuts are soaked, they won't last as long. You can freeze it and then thaw out what you need.

Notes: Soaking the nuts and seeds makes them more digestible and helps eliminate the phytic acid and enzyme inhibitors. If you purchase already sprouted seeds and nuts, you can eliminate this step. You can buy them at many healthy food stores or online at Blue Mountain Organics.

24

Main Dishes

Veggie Shish Kebabs with Marinating Sauce

I love making this sauce and using it on my sliced or chopped veggies when I am grilling or broiling vegetables. This was a favorite dish of Larry Hagman's when I was his chef/nutritionist.

This marinade adds spiciness to the meal as well as the healthful properties of the spices and other ingredients. It will coat enough vegetables for four people. You need skewers (wood or metal) for this dish.

Ingredients
¾ cup coconut oil
1½ cup sprouted, Brazil nuts
4 tbsp. fresh lemon juice
2 tsp. freshly ground coriander seeds
2 tsp. ground cumin
½ tsp. turmeric powder
½ tsp unrefined, mineral rich sea salt
½ tsp. freshly ground, black pepper
¼ tsp. cayenne pepper powder
1 clove fresh garlic, finely minced
2 tbsp. freshly minced ginger root
¼ cup of fresh ginger juice (I juice my ginger in my juicer to get this fresh ginger juice)
½ bunch of cilantro
¼ cup fresh basil

Suggested vegetables, fruits, and mushrooms for shish kebabs: zucchini, red or yellow bell pepper, small cherry tomatoes, mushrooms, mango chunks, and pineapple.

Directions
1. Place all the marinade ingredients in a food processor and blend.
2. Cut vegetables into bite-sized pieces, 1 ¼ or 1 ½ inch wide and about ½ inch thick so they will cook fairly easily and be easy to eat.

3. Rub the marinating sauce on the freshly cut vegetables and fruits. Massaging them with cleans hands works best. Massage for about 5 minutes until they are coated well.
4. Let sit at least 30–45 minutes.
5. Skewer the veggies, fruits, and mushrooms.
6. Brush the vegetables with the leftover marinade.
7. Serve at room temperature.

Variation: These are also delicious lightly grilled or broiled as well.

Note: Brazil nuts can be sprouted by soaking overnight or for 18 hours in non-chlorinated water. Pour off the water. If you want the nuts dry, then dry them in a dehydrator or a warm oven, but drying them for this recipe is not necessary. Sprouting the nuts will remove the phytic acid and make them more digestible.

If you purchase already-sprouted nuts and seeds, you can eliminate this step. You can purchase sprouted nuts, seeds, nut butters, etc. from many healthy grocery stores or online from Blue Mountain Organics.

Veggie Pasta with Tomato Sauce

Serves: Two.

Pasta Ingredients
2–3 spiral-shredded zucchini or crooked-necked squashes.

Pasta Directions
1. Use a veggie slicer, spiralizer, or a vegetable peeler to create long, thin noodle-type shreds of the zucchini and/or squash.
2. Set aside until the sauce is ready.

Sauce Ingredients
2½ cups organic tomatoes, chopped
12 sun-dried tomatoes (soaked in olive oil or water to soften)
4 small organic garlic clove, minced
¼ cup extra-virgin olive oil or coconut oil
2 tbsp. parsley
1/8 tsp. cayenne pepper
½ to 1 dropper plain liquid stevia
½ tsp. whole sea salt (to taste)

Sauce Directions
1. Puree in a blender.
2. Serve over shredded zucchini or squash.

Lentil Salad Topping

I love this served over lettuces instead of salad dressing. You can make this with cooked sprouted lentils as well.

Ingredients
2 cups sprouted lentils
1 cup tomatoes, chopped
½ cup chopped cucumber
½ cup chopped red pepper
1 carrot shredded
1 avocado, pitted, peeled and cubed
1/3 cup chopped cilantro
1 tbsp. fresh lime juice
1 tbsp. extra-virgin olive oil
½ tsp. unrefined sea salt

Directions
Combine all ingredients and let sit for 30 minutes so the flavors meld together.
Serve scooped over lettuces.

Note: You can use sprouted lentils. Soaking the lentils makes them more digestible and helps eliminate the phytic acid and enzyme inhibitors. Soak all lentils overnight or for 12–18 hours in non-chlorinated water, then drain.

If you purchase already-sprouted lentils, you can eliminate this step. You can purchase sprouted nuts, seeds, nut butters, etc. from many healthy grocery stores or online from Blue Mountain Organics.

Tahini Patties

Serves: Two.

I love the unusual flavor of these patties. You can dehydrate them in an oven on very low, or even outside if you don't have a dehydrator.

Ingredients
1 cup sprouted almonds
1 cup sprouted walnuts
½ cup cilantro
¼ cup parsley
4 tbsp. fresh lemon or lime juice
2½ tbsp. tahini
1 tbsp. coconut oil or extra virgin olive oil
1½ tsp. cumin powder
1 tsp. unrefined sea salt
¾ cup pure water

Directions
1. Blend nuts in a food processor until they are a fine flour.
2. Add the rest of the ingredients into the food processor with the nuts. Blend well.
3. Roll tablespoon-size balls out, place them on a dehydrator mesh screen, and press down slightly.
4. Dehydrate at or below 115°F for 4 hours or longer. The longer you dehydrate them, the crispier they will be.

Note: Soaking the nuts and seeds makes them more digestible and helps eliminate the phytic acid and enzyme inhibitors. Soak all nuts and seeds 12–18 hours in water, drain, and then let them dry well. Dry them in a dehydrator for a few hours if you have one.

If you purchase already-sprouted nuts and seeds, you can eliminate this step. You can purchase sprouted nuts, seeds, and nut butters online from Blue Mountain Organics.

Raw Ravioli with Walnut Pesto

Serving Size: 12-16 ravioli

Ingredients
2 yellow summer squashes
4 cups basil, roughly chopped
¼ cup sprouted walnut butter
¼ cup sprouted walnuts
2 cloves garlic, finely minced
10 sundried tomatoes, chopped into tiny pieces
½ cup raw tahini
6 tbsp. non-chlorinated water
Unrefined sea salt
freshly ground black pepper

Directions
1. In a blender or food processor, blend the basil, minced garlic, walnut butter, and walnuts. If it is too thick, add a little more water. Add some unrefined sea salt and freshly ground pepper. Set aside.
2. In a small bowl, whisk together the tahini and the water, adding tablespoons of water as you go, until it is smooth. Then add the chopped sundried tomatoes and mix well until it forms a smooth paste.
3. With a good, sharp knife, slice the squash into very thin rounds ¼-inch thick or less, if you can. Take your time and be careful.
4. To make the ravioli, lay one round of squash on a plate. Add 1 teaspoon of the sundried tomato mixture. Top with another squash piece and seal the edges down with a finger or a fork. Repeat until all the squash rounds are used. Drizzle with the pesto sauce and a bit of raw tahini.

Note: You can use sprouted nuts, but they should be dry or dehydrated before you use them in this recipe for it to taste right and have the best consistency.

Soaking the nuts and seeds makes them more digestible and helps eliminate the phytic acid and enzyme inhibitors. Soak all nuts and seeds 12–18 hours in water, drain, and then let them dry well. Dry them in a dehydrator for a few hours if you have one.

If you purchase already-sprouted seeds and nuts, you can eliminate this step. You can purchase sprouted nuts, seeds, and nut butters from many healthy grocery stores or online from Blue Mountain Organics.

Nori Rolls with Nut Pâté

These are easy and delicious. The first time I made this recipe was when I needed a quick lunch to take with me on an airplane. This is a great finger food and makes a terrific appetizer.

Ingredients
2 nori sheets
1 cup Nut Pâté (Recipe in this book)
1–2 avocados, seeded, peeled, and sliced
1 carrot, julienned
½ cup sprouts (sunflower or broccoli)
½ cup soy sauce (unpasteurized, organic; for dipping)
¼ cup wasabi (optional)
¼ cup pickled ginger (optional)

Directions
1. Lay out a nori sheet (shiny side down) on a flat surface or a bamboo sushi mat that can roll up.
2. Spread half of the Nut Pâté on the nori sheet in a thick layer, leaving about a half-inch border around the outside edge.
3. Lay half of the avocado slices lengthways over Nut Pâté.
4. Lay half of the carrots lengthways in a thick layer on the avocado.
5. Lay half of the sprouts on the carrots and avocado in an even layer.
6. Take the end of the nori sheet closest to you and start rolling it away from you.
7. When you get to the end, seal the edge with a little water to make it stick.
8. Slice the roll into about 1-inch-thick rolls. Repeat with the second nori sheet and the rest of the Nut Pâté, avocado, carrots, and sprouts.
9. Dip in soy sauce and enjoy with wasabi and/or pickled ginger.

Notes: The nori will cut easier if you use a very sharp knife. Avocado is one of the two main ingredients in the recipe, so use a half or a whole avocado for each roll.

Creamy Raw Pasta

This is a nice alternative to pasta dishes.

Noodle Ingredients
2 zucchini
2 summer squash

Noodle Directions: With a vegetable peeler, peel zucchini and summer squash in long thick strips. These will be the noodles. Set aside.

Cream Sauce Ingredients
1 cup sprouted macadamia nuts
1 cup sprouted pine nuts
1 cup sprouted cashews
3 tbsp. lime or lemon juice
2 cloves garlic
2 tsp. unpasteurized Soy Sauce
1 or 2 tbsp. water
¼ tsp. unrefined sea salt

Cream Sauce Directions: Place all ingredients in a food processor and blend until creamy.

Combine the noodles and the sauce. It works best if you use your hands.

Note: You can use sprouted nuts, but they should be dry or dehydrated before you use them in this recipe for it to taste appropriately and have the best consistency.

Soaking the nuts and seeds makes them more digestible and helps eliminate the phytic acid and enzyme inhibitors. Soak all nuts and seeds 12–18 hours in water, drain, and then let them dry well. Dry them in a dehydrator for a few hours if you have one.

If you purchase already-sprouted seeds and nuts, you can eliminate this step. You can purchase sprouted nuts, seeds, nut butters, etc. from many healthy grocery stores or online from Blue Mountain Organics.

Grated Zucchini

Serves: Two.

This is my friend Maryann De Leo's recipe. She made this for me when I visited her in NYC. This recipe is on page 175 of our book we wrote for older people and people taking care of elderly parents, *Alive and Cooking: An Easy Guide to Health for You and Your Parents.*

Ingredients
2 zucchini (raw)
1–2 tbsp. extra-virgin olive oil
Unrefined sea salt to taste

Directions
1. Grate zucchini into short, thin strips. Don't grate the zucchini down to the seeds.
2. Make a mound of zucchini, and drizzle it with olive oil and sea salt.

Amanda's Veggie Sushi Rolls

Serves: One or two.

My daughter Amanda created this recipe. She says they are crazy delicious, and she makes them all the time.

I love to make this recipe when I want something healthy but filling. This dish can satisfy a salty and sweet-tooth craving. It's great for the end of the week when I'm using up a range of veggies in my fridge because you can always change up what you throw in the wrap, and it's easy to take to work!

Ingredients
One sheet of seaweed from a brand like Emerald Cove
Half an avocado, sliced
¼ cucumber sliced julienne style
Sprouts
Sprouted nuts or seeds (I like sunflower or pumpkin seeds.)
Your favorite nut butter or miso (I use sunflower seed butter with a dash of miso.)
Dash of nutritional yeast (optional)
Unrefined sea salt to taste

Directions
1. Tear the seaweed sheet into 2 or 3 strips.
2. Coat the beginning of each strip with the nut butter or miso.
3. Press sprouts and nuts onto the nut butter or miso.
4. Add cucumber and avocado slices on top of the sprouts on each of the strips.
5. Top cucumber and avocado with salt and nutritional yeast.
6. Roll each of the strips up into a wrap, adding more nut butter or miso to seal the end of the wrap to help hold it together and seal the end.
7. Cut the rolled sushi into small pieces with a sharp knife, and enjoy!

Notes: I rarely limit the wraps to just these ingredients, though I think they are a good baseline for the dish. Depending on what I have in my fridge I'll throw in carrots, radishes, romaine, celery, or anything else that might work!

I often cut these into bite-sized pieces with a sharp knife because, although delicious, the seaweed can be a bit difficult to bite through. Also, it can be a little messy (and turn your mouth green!), but I like to sprinkle chlorella and spirulina into the wraps for an extra dose of vitamins and protein.

25

Desserts

D esserts are not a good idea for anyone struggling with diet and diabetes, but I don't think having deprivation in our diet or life is good either. If we live with the feeling that we are deprived, then the emotional stress can build up until one day we explode. We might just break down and eat a whole cake! We do need to feel rewarded at times and participate in social celebration, and that can include sweets and desserts.

So, as you look at the choices you have for a dessert, keep in mind that there are some healthy, delicious desserts that can support well-being and won't destroy your health. If you do allow yourself a dessert, use a small plate, take a small portion, and eat it slowly with mindfulness and appreciation. You will eat less than you would if you ate mindlessly or gulped it down because of guilt. You may find you only want one bite.

Love yourself enough to allow room in your life for joy and celebration. Then, don't beat yourself up over eating something you know isn't good for you. Just move on with your new eating plan, and know it's okay to be flexible once in a while.

Mango Pudding

Serves: One to two.

Ingredients
2 ripe, unsweetened mangos, peeled and seeded
2-3 large, raw Swiss chard leaves, stems removed, torn into small pieces

Directions
1. Blend ingredients in a blender for a few minutes, until smooth.
2. Serve in individually sized bowls.

Note: Add a little non-chlorinated water or pure coconut water if it's too thick.

Fruit for Dessert

Fresh fruit wedges or fresh berries in their whole, unsweetened form are a healthy and delicious snack packed with nutrients that support our health.

A few good choices are:
-Orange
-Grapefruit
-Tangerine
-Berries
-Cherries (tart cherries are the best choice)
-Papaya
-Mango
-Apple
-Pear
-Bananas

If you want to heal your body of diabetes, only have one fruit each week as your special treat or dessert.

Consume fruit by itself. Always eat the whole fresh fruit with the fiber-rich goodness of the skin, if appropriate. Never drink pure fruit juice, because it is too high in natural sugar. It's better to eat the whole fresh fruit with the fiber.

Try to consume tree-ripened fruit, because it has natural immune system boosters.

Avoid bananas because most of their calories come from carbohydrates, with 34 grams per cup, and you want to avoid carbohydrates. According to MayoClinic.com, low-carb diets can help with weight loss by lowering your levels of insulin, which potentially helps you burn fat.

But, there are a few ways you can eat bananas. If you have a craving for ice cream, freeze bananas and eat small bites of them instead of ice cream. Bananas are delicious frozen, and a few bites help you avoid consuming something that is not as healthy.

Another healthy way to use bananas is in a smoothie. Make sure the banana is really clean, cut off the ends, and put the entire banana (with the fiber and nutrient-dense skin on it) in the blender. It tastes just the same, but it has the added nutrition and fiber. The banana skin has more nutrients in it than the fruit itself. The fiber and antioxidants in the skin can help support your adrenal glands.

Lightly adding some mineral-rich salt to fruit can help your body absorb potassium optimally.

Watermelon Drink

The hot months of summer are the perfect time to indulge in sweet, juicy, nutrient-rich watermelon. Watermelon is luscious and refreshing as a snack or as part of a fruit salad, dessert, or drink. One cup of watermelon has only 48 calories. However, it has high levels of nutrients, making it the perfect healthy treat. Watermelons are packed with Vitamin C, Vitamin A, Vitamins B6 and B1, potassium, and magnesium.

In addition, medical studies have shown watermelon can help with inflammatory conditions like asthma, atherosclerosis, diabetes, colon cancer, and arthritis. It is also high in the antioxidant lycopene, which has cancer-preventing properties and helps oxidize cholesterol.

Ingredients
1 watermelon
a few limes or lemons, freshly juiced
pinch of whole, unrefined sea salt

Directions
1. Cut watermelon into chunks and remove seeds.
2. Place watermelon chunks in a blender.
3. Add a splash of fresh lime or lemon juice and a pinch of sea salt.

Notes: Depending on the size of the watermelon, this can make a whole pitcher of drinks. You want to keep the fiber in this drink. It slows down the natural sugars from going into the blood stream too quickly.

Store whatever is not consumed immediately in the refrigerator.

Variation: Add some sparkling water and a sprig of mint for a fresh cocktail.

GMO corn, soy, and canola have been linked to kidney and liver disease and may promote diabetes and cancer.[212]

26

Remedies

Watermelon Juice Constipation Remedy

One cup of watermelon has only 48 calories. However, it has high levels of nutrients. Watermelons are packed with Vitamin C, Vitamin A, Vitamins B6 and B1, potassium, and magnesium.

Medical studies have shown watermelon can help with inflammatory conditions like asthma, atherosclerosis, diabetes, colon cancer, and arthritis. It is high in the antioxidant lycopene, which has cancer-preventing properties and helps oxidize cholesterol.

Avoid buying a seedless watermelon. Any food without seeds is genetically modified.

Ingredients
1 cup watermelon (cut into chunks)
1 cup water melon rind (cut into chunks)
¼ tsp. unrefined sea salt
½ tsp. cold pressed hemp or flax seed oil.

Directions
1. Make sure your watermelon is washed well and the rind is clean.
2. Place watermelon chunks in a blender or juicer.
3. Add the cold pressed oil and the sea salt.
4. Drink within 20 minutes. If you haven't gone within two hours, drink it once more.

Note: If you still haven't had a movement after drinking this remedy, you may need to get a colonic to help remove blockages from your intestinal tract. Avoid consuming any more food until you are regular once more, because you don't want to compound the problem by adding more food to what is already impacted in the intestinal tract.

Acid Indigestion Remedy

Ingredients

½ tsp. baking soda
1/8 tsp unrefined sea salt
1 cup non-chlorinated water

Directions

Mix, stir, and drink.

Eucalyptus Essential Oil

Many different cultures have used essential eucalyptus oils to help regulate blood sugar levels.

In 2015, Colombian researchers found that *Eucalyptus tereticornis* extracts increased glucose uptake in vitro (test tube study). Research also showed diabetic mice had reduced fasting glycemia, improved glucose tolerance, and reduced insulin resistance when using a variety of eucalyptus essential oils.[213]

In another study published in the *World Journal of Diabetes* reported that Eucalyptus globulus was the clear winner in this in vitro research study and found that the polyphenols and flavonoids in three eucalyptus species inhibited enzymes that played a role in type 2 diabetes.[214]

Some ways to use it:

- Add it in your bath water with Epson Salts.
- Use it in a humidifier.
- Massage your feet with the *Eucalyptus tereticornis* essential oil.

27

Exercise is Part of a Healthy Lifestyle

T his new healthy lifestyle plan also involves getting yourself moving. Exercise is important for everyone. We need to move! It is necessary for our health and well-being, and our lymphatic system depends on it to work properly.

So, start where you can. If you can't stand up, then move while seated. Exercise your arms and upper body, if that is all you can do at the moment. For example, while sitting at your desk or sitting in a car, stretch your arms. Stretch and move as much as possible.

If you can move more than that, then do what best fits your body for at least 30 minutes per day, four times per week. Those who can walk, walk for a minimum of 30 minutes per day (or at least four times per week), preferably in a brisk manner.

Studies show that when you exercise before breakfast, it stabilizes your blood sugar immediately and energizes you for the rest of the day. Studies show people who exercise before breakfast lose weight quicker.

If you add short bursts of high intensity to your workout, it can increase your fat burn by up to 36 percent. What does that look like? If you are walking, add a minute or two of jogging to your walk. If you are on a treadmill, intermittently add a minute or two of a faster, more intense pace to the workout. It is so easy to do, and *wow*, what a difference it can make!

Try picking up a new, fun form of exercise, such as dance classes, yoga, or even working in the yard. Anything to get your body moving!

When you feel ready, increase your exercise time to 40–60 minutes every day. Increase and expand your exercise routine, as you feel able. If you miss a day, don't get upset with yourself. Simply get back to your routine again tomorrow.

Always be kind to yourself. Just pick up where you left off and get going again. Ideally, we should exercise every single day, even if it's something as basic as walking. Getting the body oxygenated and the circulatory system going is important to maintaining an active metabolism and lymphatic system. It is also very helpful to our overall health and well-being.

The lymphatic system is comprised of a network of vessels similar to blood vessels that carry a clear fluid called lymph. There is three times the amount of lymph as blood, and it is a critical part of our immune system. Lymph nodes are where the lymph is filtered or cleansed along the way. When any part of this system gets clogged, it can cause inflammation, which leads to disease.

Some signs of a compromised or clogged lymphatic system include swollen hands or feet, painful swelling of the lymph nodes, any type of arthritis or bronchitis, lack of energy or mental clarity, trouble sleeping, cysts or fibrous tumors, an inability to recover quickly from viral infections, and—last but not least—cancer.

The heart pumps blood, but the lymphatic system doesn't have a pump to keep it moving. The movements of the body's muscles stimulate the flow of the lymphatic system. That is why exercise keeps the lymphatic system draining, healthy, and unclogged.

If you are unable to exercise, then lymphatic massages are important to keep the lymphatic system flowing properly and reduce inflammation caused by clogged lymph nodes. Regular lymphatic massages can also help someone lose weight.

In addition to exercising, start doing more weight training! It doesn't have to be much or too heavy. Find what works for you. Weight training increases bone density, and it improves muscle mass, balance, and connective tissue strength. It also increases your metabolism!

Weight training should be a priority if you really want to burn more fat. Lifting weights raises your metabolism long after you finish working out. It is estimated that your metabolism can stay elevated up to 39 hours afterwards!

Muscle is more metabolically active than fat, and each extra pound of muscle you gain burns 30 or more extra calories a day. It's estimated that a pound of muscle burns six calories at rest, compared to two calories burned by a pound of fat.

If you commit to this lifestyle (regular exercise, some weight lifting, and wholesome foods) and diet (completely vegetarian or vegan, gluten-free and mostly living, raw food), you can lose unwanted weight, get healthier, and feel invigorated. It depends on you!

"The best six doctors anywhere, and no one can deny it, are sunshine, water, rest, air, exercise, and diet."

—Wayne Fields

28

The Emotional Component of Diabetes

Our minds are very powerful, and our thoughts can manifest themselves in many ways in our health and our life. I have studied body-mind communication, becoming certified in this type of healing modality, and what I realize is that our health is directly affected by our emotions and our thoughts.

This may seem very esoteric to you, but I had a medical doctor tell me that when he went to medical school, one of the first things they were told was that 60 to 70 percent of the people coming into their office will not have physical ailments—that they are emotional and psychological traumas that manifest themselves as disease in the body. He told me the medical community has known about this body-mind communication for many years and realizes its power and relevance in human health.

So, in this last chapter, I would like to address our emotions and how they can contribute to our health and well-being. We create our own reality, and our thoughts can directly affect what we create in our present moment.

Many of us suffer from self-criticism, self-hatred, and negative self-talk. We are our own worst critics, like it or not. Releasing resentment and past negative experiences and letting go of things that cause us to feel pain or regret is possible, if we allow ourselves that precious gift. It is a choice. Releasing or forgiving does not condone what anyone has done, but it releases us from carrying an emotional burden which does not serve our best and higher self.

Self-approval and acceptance in the present moment are keys to positive changes. True health is a result of having true inner peace. *The Body Mind Workbook; Explaining How the Mind and Body Work Together* says:

> "Diabetes is due to a deficiency in insulin, so that the body cannot utilize the sugars in the bloodstream. The result is the inability to maintain sweetness.
>
> Excessive sugar in the blood causes excessive sugar in the urine, leading to a sense of inner sadness as the sweetness is lost and flushed away.
>
> If we are diabetic we may be starving in a sea of sweetness, thinking that none of the sweetness is available to us.
>
> This can give rise to anger and resentment, to thinking we are unloved when really there is too much love and we just do not know how to deal with it or express it.
>
> We may even feel we are being drowned in love.
>
> So, diabetes is directly to do with balancing the sweetness in ourselves and our world, and honoring the love both within and without. It is to do with being able to love others, to give of our own sweetness, so much as it is to do with being able to love ourselves and to receive the love from others."[215]

In Louise L. Hay's book: *You Can Heal Your Life*, she describes diabetes as: "Longing for what might have been. A great need to control. Deep sorrow. No sweetness left." Louise recommends a new thought pattern or affirmation: "This moment is filled with joy. I now choose to experience the sweetness of today."[216]

Look inside yourself and see if you are holding onto thoughts that do not serve your best and highest good today. Allow yourself room build new, more positive thoughts that move you forward with ease, grace, and joy.

Meditation on a daily basis has been shown to help ease depression, decrease anxiety, and create calm in the mind. I've embraced mediation on a daily basis and have found great peace in this practice. There are no limitations except the ones we place on ourselves. We can break free of limitations, if we choose to.

Taking that step to addressing the mental aspects of healing in deep emotional ways can be a new journey with surprises along the way. Reverend Scott once told me that color carries energy with it, and pink is the color of forgiveness and love. He said that if someone has caused me harm or is treating me in a mean or offensive fashion, then I should envision myself sending that person "pink."

I have been doing that ever since, and it is amazing how empowering it can be. I've told many people about it, and they have come back to me and told me how great it feels to be able to take that action and move on. You can send anyone pink, even that person speeding by you on the highway and cutting you off. Sending them pink is empowering and positively liberating.

As I come to a close on body-mind communication, I hope you will take some time to be quiet, sit back, and look into your life to see where there might be space in which you can adjust old thoughts that may not be serving your best and highest good. Take action, take a new path, release old hurts or grudges. Take in loving thoughts toward yourself and others, and let go of the negative thoughts you are able to at this time.

I pray for you and your family to have good health, joyful loving thoughts, and a healthy life.

"I have chosen to be happy because it is good for my health."

—*Voltaire*

Afterword

Writing this book has been such a joy for me. I have learned so much over the years, and now I find so much happiness in sharing this information with you.

As you embrace this new lifestyle and eating plan, the second edition of my cookbook *How to Be a Healthy Vegetarian* will help you continue eating a healthier diet that supports your well-being. It has more than 115 recipes that will support you on this journey to health through a plant-based eating plan.

How to Be a Healthy Vegetarian
Available at:
http://myBook.to/vegetarianbook

I pray you find health and happiness with the healthier eating plan and lifestyle! Bless you.

And remember: The main ingredient is always love!

"Today, more than 95% of all chronic disease is caused by food choice, toxic food ingredients, nutritional deficiencies, and lack of physical exercise."

—Mike Adams

About the Author

Nancy is a certified health counselor accredited by both Columbia University and the Institute of Integrative Nutrition. She holds a Certificate of Plant-Based Nutrition from Cornell University and the T. Colin Campbell Foundation, and is a board-certified health practitioner with the American Association of Drugless Practitioners.

Nancy studied with Natalia Rose and the Rose Program in Detoxification, and she is a certified raw food chef, instructor, and teacher with Alissa Cohen. Nancy is certified in Basic Intensive in Health—Supportive Cooking from the Natural Gourmet Institute for Food & Health in New York. She studied at Le Cordon Bleu culinary school in London, England; and at the Mediterranean Cooking School in Syros, Greece, with the Australasian College of Health Science.

Nancy recently studied Thai Cooking in Thailand, and Khmer Cooking in Cambodia. She also studied conscious farming (organic gardening) at the Tree of Life Rejuvenation Center with John M. Phillips of the Living Earth Training Center. Nancy is a Psychosomatic Therapy Certified Practitioner with the Australasian Institute of Body-Mind Analysis and Psychosomatic Therapy. Nancy is both a certified sports nutritionist and a certified personal trainer with American Sports and Fitness Association.

Nancy is the author of the #1 best seller *Raising Healthy Children* (winner of the Mom's Choice Award for Excellence), the second edition of the best-selling *How to Be a Healthy Vegetarian* (finalist in two categories of the Indie Book Awards), and *Lose Weight, Get Healthy & Never Have to Be on a Diet Again.* She co-authored *Alive and Cooking: An Easy Guide to Health for You and Your Parents.*

Nancy is featured in the documentary *Eating You Alive*, which also features Dr. T. Colin Campbell, Dr. Dean Ornish, and Dr. Caldwell B. Esselstyn, Jr.

She is a member of the National Speakers Association and a magazine columnist. Nancy holds a Bachelor of Arts degree from Hollins College (now University) in Roanoke, Virginia, and she holds a lifelong Texas teaching certificate for all grade levels. She is a certified wildlife rehabilitator. Nancy also served as secretary of the Earth Society, an affiliate of the United Nations.

Notes

[1] Mercola, Joseph. "The Deliberate Lies They Tell about Diabetes". http://www.mercola.com/diabetes.aspx#_edn5

[2] Lipman, T.H., et al. (June, 2013). "Increasing Incidence of Type 1 Diabetes in Youth." *Diabetes Care*.

[3] Nissan S.E., et. al. (June, 2007). "Effect of Rosiglitazone on the Risk of Myocardial Infarction and Death from Cardiovascular Causes." *New England Journal of Medicine*.

[4] JCI (October 1, 2010). *J Clin Invest, 120*(10): 3413–3418. DOI: 10.1172/JCI45094

[5] Mercola, Joseph. "The Deliberate Lies They Tell about Diabetes". http://www.mercola.com/diabetes.aspx#_edn5

[6] Ibid.

[7] Mercola, Joseph. "The Deliberate Lies They Tell About Diabetes". *Dr. Mercola's Newsletter*. http://www.mercola.com/diabetes.aspx?i_cid=cse-tbd-diabetes-content

[8] Malik, V.S., et. al. (November, 2010). "Sugar-sweetened beverages and risk of metabolic syndrome and type 2 diabetes: a meta-analysis." *Diabetes Care, 33*(11): 2477-83. DOI: 10.2337/dc10-1079

[9] Harvard T.H. Chan School of Public Health. (May 17, 2010). "Eating processed meats, but not unprocessed red meats, may raise risk of heart disease and diabetes". https://www.hsph.harvard.edu/news/press-releases/processed-meats-unprocessed-heart-disease-diabetes/

Micha, Renata, et. al. (June 1, 2010). "Red and Processed Meat Consumption and Risk of Incident Coronary Heart Disease, Stroke, and Diabetes Mellitus: A Systematic Review and Meta-Analysis." *Circulation, 121*(21). http://dx.doi.org/10.1161/CIRCULATIONAHA.109.924977

[10] Gerson website: http://gerson.org/gerpress/dr-max-gerson/

[11] Yokoyama Y, Barnard ND, Levin SM, Watanabe M. (Oct., 2014). "Vegetarian diets and glycemic control in diabetes: a systematic review and meta-analysis." *Cardiovasc Diagn Ther, 4*(5): 373-382. http://www.ncbi.nlm.nih.gov/pmc/articles/PMC4221319/

[12] Cousens, Gabriel. (2008). *There is a Cure for Diabetes*. Berkeley, CA: North Atlantic Books.

[13] Yokoyama et. al.

[14] Ibid.

[15] Anderson, James W. (Dec., 1990). "Dietary Fiber and Human Health." *HortScience, 25*(12): 1488-1495. http://hortsci.ashspublications.org/content/25/12/1488.full.pdf

[16] Ibid.

[17] Ibid.

[18] National Institutes of Health, Office of Dietary Supplements. "Chromium: Dietary Supplement Fact Sheet." http://ods.od.nih.gov/factsheets/Chromium-HealthProfessional/#h10

[19] Hendler, SS, & Rorvik, D. (2008). *PDR for Nutritional Supplements*. Physicians' Desk Reference Inc: Montvale, NJ. Includes the following relevant articles: Hendler, SS, & Rorvik, D, eds. (2001). "PDR for Nutritional Supplements." In *Medical Economics*. Montvale, NJ; Shils ME, Olson JA, Shike M. (1999). *Modern Nutrition in Health and Disease*, 9th ed. Williams & Wilkins: Baltimore, MD; R. Thiel. (2000). "Natural vitamins may be superior to synthetic ones." *Med Hypo*, 55(6):461-469.

[20] Brownstein, David. (2012). *Salt Your Way to Health*. 2nd edition. Medical Alternative Press.

[21] Ibid.

[22] Brown University. "Being a Vegetarian: What are the Health Benefits of a Vegetarian Diet?" http://brown.edu/Student_Services/Health_Services/Health_Education/nutrition_&_eating_concerns/being_a_vegetarian.php#4

[23] Esselstyn, Caldwell B., Jr. (2008). *Prevent and Reverse Heart Disease: The Revolutionary, Scientifically Proven, Nutrition-Based Cure.* Avery Trade.

[24] McDougall, John. "Nutrition in the Medical Clinic Part III" lecture. *Plant-Based Nutrition.* eCornell University.

[25] Campbell, T. Colin. (2010). "Principles of Nutritional Health. Plant-Based Nutrition." eCornell University and the T. Colin Campbell Foundation.

[26] Yokoyama, Y., Barnard, N.D., Levin, S.M., & Watanabe, M. (2014, October). "Vegetarian Diets and Glycemic Control in Diabetes: A Systematic Review and Meta-analysis." *Cardiovascular Diagnosis & Therapy,* 4(5), 373–382.

[27] Ibid.

[28] Nutrition Security Institute. "Average Mineral Content in Selected Vegetables, 1914–1997." (Data sources listed at the bottom of the chart: Lindlahr, 1914, Hamaker, 1982, US Department of Agriculture, 1963 and 1997.) http://www.nutritionsecurity.org/PDF/Mineral%20Content%20in%20Vegetables.pdf

[29] Nutrition Security Institute. "Eighty-Year Decline in Mineral Content of Medium Apple." (Data sources listed at the bottom of the chart: Lindlahr, 1914, Hamaker, 1982, US Department of Agriculture, 1963 and 1997.) http://www.nutritionsecurity.org/PDF/Mineral%20Content%20of%20One%20Apple.pdf

[30] Cousens, Gabriel and Rainoshek, David. (2008). *There is a Cure for Diabetes.* Berkeley, CA: North Atlantic Books. p. 192.

[31] George Mateljan Foundation. "What's New and Beneficial About Garlic." http://www.whfoods.com/genpage.php?tname=foodspice&dbid=60

[32] Ibid.

[33] Cousens, Gabriel and Rainoshek, David. (2008). *There is a Cure for Diabetes*. Berkeley, CA: North Atlantic Books; p. 201.

[34] Ibid.

[35] Micha, R., et al. (May 17, 2010). "Red and Processed Meat Consumption and Risk of Incident Coronary Heart Disease, Stroke, and Diabetes Mellitus." *Circulation*.

Harvard School of Public Health. (May 17, 2010). "Eating Processed Meats, but not Unprocessed Red Meats, May Raise Risk of Heart Disease and Diabetes." *Harvard News*.

[36] Hattersley, Joseph G. (2000). "The Negative Health Effects of Chlorine." *The Journal of Orthomolecular Medicine, Vol. 15, 2nd Quarter 2000*.
http://www.orthomolecular.org/library/jom/2000/articles/2000-v15n02-p089.shtml

[37] Sohn, Emily. (2010, September 21). "Chlorinated Pools May Increase Cancer Risk." *NBC News*.
http://www.nbcnews.com/id/39139307/ns/technology_and_science-science/t/chlorinated-pools-may-increase-cancer-risk/

[38] Connett, Paul. (2011, January 9). "50 Reasons to Oppose Fluoridation." Canton, NY: St. Lawrence University.
http://www.foodconsumer.org/newsite/Non-food/Environment/50_reasons_to_oppose_fluoridation_0109111037.html Originally published as Connett, Paul. (2004). Fifty reasons to oppose fluoridation. *Medical Veritas, 1:70-80*. In the introduction to the 2004 version it was explained that after over four years the Irish authorities had not been able to muster a response to the "50 Reasons," despite agreeing to do so in 2000. 2004 edition retrieved from
http://www.waterskraus.com/pdf/50%20Reasons%20to%20Oppose%20Fluoridation.pdf

[39] Ibid.

[40] Connett, Paul, et. al. (2005, April 8). *Revisiting the fluoride-osteosarcoma connection in the context of Elise Bassin's findings: part II*. Submitted to the NRC review on the Toxicology of Fluoride in Water.
http://oehha.ca.gov/Prop65/public_meetings/052909coms/fluoride/AEHSPFANFluoride2.pdf

[41] Ibid., page 4.

[42] Kumar, JV and Green, EL. (1998, February). "Recommendations for Fluoride Use in Children." *NY State Dental Journal*, p. 41-48. Qtd by Connett in *50 Reasons to Oppose Fluoridation.*

[43] Levine, 1976; Ferjerskov, Thylstrup and Larsen, 1981; Carlos, 1983; Featherstone, 1987, 1999, 2000; Margolis and Moreno, 1990; Clark, 1993; Burt, 1994; Shellis and Duckworth, 1994; and Limeback, 1999, 2000; Centers for Disease Control and Prevention, 1999. (All cited on p. 2, *50 Reasons to Oppose Fluoridation*, by Dr. Paul Connett.)

[44] Diesendorf, Mark. (1986, July 10). "The Mystery of the Declining Dental Decay." (Commentary). *Nature, 322*: 125-129. http://www.nature.com/nature/journal/v322/n6075/pdf/322125 ao.pdf

[45] Colquhoun, J. (1997, Autumn). "Why I changed my mind on fluoridation." *Perspectives in Biology and Medicine, 41*(1): 29-44. University of Chicago Press. Full text reprinted at http://www.fluoridation.com/colquhoun.htm

[46] Galetti, P and Joyet, G. (October, 1958). Effect of fluorine on thyroidal iodine metabolism in hyperthyroidism. *Journal of Clinical Endocrinology & Metabolism, 18*(10): 1102-1110. Reprinted at http://www.slweb.org/galletti.html

[47] Ditkoff, B. A. & Lo Gerfo, P. (2000). *The Thyroid Guide*. NY: Harper-Collins.

[48] Lin, F. F., et. al. (1991). "The relationship of a low–iodine and high–fluoride environment to subclinical cretinism in Xinjiang." *Iodine Deficiency Disorder Newsletter* 7.

[49] US Department of Health and Human Services (HHS). (2003, September). *Toxicological profile for fluorides, hydrogen, fluoride, and fluorine.* http://www.atsdr.cdc.gov/toxprofiles/tp11.pdf

[50] Hoover, R. N., et. al. (1990). *Fluoridation of Drinking Water and Subsequent Cancer Incidence and Mortality.* Report to the Director of the National Cancer Institute.

[51] Connett, P., et. al. (2005, March 2). *Revisiting the Fluoride-Osteosarcoma connection in the context of Elise Bassin's findings: Part 1*, page 1. Submitted to the NRC review panel on

the Toxicology of Fluoride in Water.
http://www.fluoridealert.org/wp-content/uploads/fan-bassin.2006a.pdf

52 Barclay, Eliza. (2010, March 5). "What's Best for Kids: Bottled Water or Fountains?" *National Geographic.*
http://news.nationalgeographic.com/news/2010/02/100303-bottled-water-tap-schools/

53 "Drinking Water at Schools Contains Lead, Pesticides, Other Toxins: Study." (2009, September 25). *New York Daily News.*
http://www.nydailynews.com/life-style/health/drinking-water-schools-lead-pesticides-toxins-study-article-1.404089

54 Naidenko, Olga, et. al. (2008, October 15). "Bottled Water Quality Investigation: 10 Major Brands, 38 Pollutants." *EWG (Environmental Workers Group).*
http://www.ewg.org/research/bottled-water-quality-investigation

55 Ibid.

56 "Cleveland Takes Offense at Fiji Water Ad." (2006, July 20). *The Washington Post.* http://www.washingtonpost.com/wp-dyn/content/article/2006/07/20/AR2006072000322.html

57 Vandenberg, L. N., et. al. (2012, June). "Hormones and Endocrine-Disrupting Chemicals: Low-Dose Effects and Nonmonotonic Dose Responses." *Endocrine Reviews, 33*(3): 378-455. http://www.ncbi.nlm.nih.gov/pmc/articles/PMC3365860/

58 Ibid.

59 Le, Hoa H., et. al. (2008, January 30). "Bisphenol A is released from polycarbonate drinking bottles and mimics the neurotoxic actions of estrogen in developing cerebellar neurons." *Toxicology Letters, 176*(2): 149-156.
http://www.ncbi.nlm.nih.gov/pmc/articles/PMC2254523/

60 Milman, Oliver. (2014, December 10). "Full Scale of Plastic in the World's Oceans Revealed for First Time." *The Guardian.*
http://www.theguardian.com/environment/2014/dec/10/full-scale-plastic-worlds-oceans-revealed-first-time-pollution

61 Ibid.

62 Dr. Pollack. (January 29, 2011). "Water: The Single Most Important Element for Your Health." *Dr. Mercola newsletter.*

http://articles.mercola.com/sites/articles/archive/2011/01/29/dr-pollack-on-structured-water.aspx

[63] Martin Chaplin, BSc, PhD, CChem, FRSC. "Water Memory." Water Structure and Science. *London South Bank University.* http://www1.lsbu.ac.uk/water/memory_of_water.html

[64] Emoto, Masaru. "Water Crystals." Retrieved from http://www.masaru-emoto.net/english/water-crystal.html

[65] Howell, Edward. (1985). *Enzyme Nutrition.* Avery Publishing Group Inc.

[66] Cheung, Anthony. "Digestive Enzymes." *Enerex.* http://www.enerexusa.com/articles/digestive_enzymes.htm

[67] Ibid.

[68] Ibid.

[69] Ibid.

[70] Ibid.

[71] Azulay, Sol. (1997, November). "There's More to Sprouts than Just a Little Crunch in Your Salad." *San Diego Earth Times.*

[72] Ibid.

[73] Adlerberth I, Hansson LÅ, Wold AE. "The ontogeny of the intestinal flora." In: Sanderson IR, Walker WA, editors. (1999). *Development of the gastrointestinal tract.* Hamilton: BC Decker; pp. 279–92.

[74] Larsen, N. et al. (February 5, 2010). "Gut microbiota in human adults with type 2 diabetes differs from non-diabetic adults." *PLoS One,* 5(2): e9085. doi: 10.1371/journal.pone.0009085.

[75] Azulay, Sol. "Sprouts in the News." *International Specialty Supply.* http://www.sproutnet.com/Sprouts-in-the-Press

[76] Staciokas, Linden. (2010, April 21). "Growing Sprouts Is Easy, Nutritious Way to Satisfy Veggie Cravings." *Fairbanks Daily News-Miner.* http://www.newsminer.com/features/food/growing-sprouts-is-easy-nutritious-way-to-satisfy-veggie-cravings/article_fcdbf007-b718-5962-a8cb-d9904df23774.html

[77] Phillips, John. (2009, January). "Conscious Gardening Workshop at Tree of Life." *Dr. Cousens' Tree of Life Center US.*

[78] Chavan, J. and Kadam, S. (1989). "Nutritional improvement of cereals by sprouting." *Critical Reviews in Food Science and*

Nutrition, 28(5): 401-437. Abstract available at
http://www.ncbi.nlm.nih.gov/pubmed/2692609

79 Kearns, Cristin E., et. Al. (September 12, 2016). "Sugar Industry
and Coronary Heart Disease Research: A Historical Analysis of
Internal Industry Documents." *JAMA Internal Medicine.*

80 BBC News. (2005, January 10). "Olive Oil Acid 'Cuts Cancer
Risk.'" http://news.bbc.co.uk/2/hi/health/4154269.stm

81 Whoriskey, Peter. (Feb. 10, 2015). "The US government is poised
to withdraw longstanding warnings about cholesterol." *The
Washington Post.*
http://www.washingtonpost.com/blogs/wonkblog/wp/2015/02/
10/feds-poised-to-withdraw-longstanding-warnings-about-
dietary-cholesterol/

82 Mercola, Joseph. "Here's the Smarter Oil Alternative I
Recommend to Replace Those Other Oils in Your Kitchen."
http://products.mercola.com/coconut-oil/

83 Johnson, Lorie. (2013, January 1). "Coconut Oil Touted as
Alzheimer's Remedy." *CBN News.*
http://www.cbn.com/cbnnews/healthscience/2012/january/coc
onut-oil-touted-as-alzheimers-remedy/

84 Mercola, Joseph. "Here's the Smarter Oil Alternative I
Recommend to Replace Those Other Oils in Your Kitchen."
http://products.mercola.com/coconut-oil/

85 Mercola, Joseph. "Vegetables and Olive Oil May Cut
Rheumatoid Arthritis Risk."
http://articles.mercola.com/sites/articles/archive/2008/01/02/v
egetables-cut-arthritis-risk.aspx

86 World's Healthiest Foods. (2011, September 27). "Why I Never
Cook with Extra Virgin Olive Oil by George Mateljan." Video at
https://youtu.be/3B4cte5aviM

87 National Consumers League. (2015, May). "Olive oil
mislabeling: Are consumers catching on?"
http://www.nclnet.org/evoo

88 McDougall, John. (2003, December). "A Brief History of
Protein: Passion, Social Bigotry, Rats, and Enlightenment." *The
McDougall Newsletter,* 2(12).

http://www.nealhendrickson.com/mcdougall/031200puprotein.htm

89 Centers for Disease Control and Prevention. "Protein." http://www.cdc.gov/nutrition/everyone/basics/protein.html

90 D'Adamo, Peter J., & Whitney, Catherine. (1999). "Blood Type O, Food, Beverage and Supplement List." *Eat Right 4 Your Type.* Berkley Books.

91 Ibid.

92 Mangels, Reed. "Protein in the Vegan Diet." *Vegetarian Resource Group.* http://www.vrg.org/nutrition/protein.php

93 Navratilova, Martina. (2009, May 22). "Eat the Right Kinds of Protein: Don't Overdo Protein; Do it Right. Here's How." *AARP.*

94 Bennett, Jannequin (November 6, 2001). *Very Vegetarian.* Rutledge Hill Press. Foreword by Carl Lewis.

95 McDougall, John. (2003, December). "A Brief History of Protein, Passion, Social Bigotry, Rats, and Enlightenment." *The McDougall Newsletter, 2*(12). http://www.nealhendrickson.com/mcdougall/031200puprotein.htm

96 Golubic, Mladen. (2014, April 4). "Benefits of Plant-based Diets." *Cleveland Clinic.* http://my.clevelandclinic.org/health/transcripts/1602_benefits-of-plant-based-diets

97 Weil, Andrew. (2005, March 21). "Vegetarians: Pondering Protein?" http://www.drweil.com/drw/u/id/QAA142995

98 Ibid.

99 Gordon, Dennis. (1996, March). "Vegetable Proteins Can Stand Alone." *Journal of the American Dietetic Association, 96*(3).

100 Mangels, Reed. "Protein in the Vegan Diet." *Vegetarian Resource Group.* http://www.vrg.org/nutrition/protein.php

101 Tuso, Philip J., et. al. (Spring, 2013). "Nutritional Update for Physicians: Plant-Based Diet." *Perm J 17*(2): 61-66.

102 Leson, Gero, & Pless, Petra. (1991). *Hemp Foods and Oils for Health.* Sebastopol, CA: Hemptech. Gero Leson, DEnv, is an environmental scientist and consultant with extensive experience in food and fiber uses of hemp and other renewable resources.

103 Consumer Reports. "Alert: Protein Drinks: You Don't Need the Extra Protein or the Heavy Metals Our Tests Found." http://www.consumerreports.org/cro/magazine-archive/2010/july/food/protein-drinks/overview/index.htm

104 WebMD. "Whey Protein." http://www.webmd.com/vitamins-supplements/ingredientmono-833-WHEY%20PROTEIN.aspx?activeIngredientId=833&activeIngredientName=WHEY%20PROTEIN

105 Golubic, Mladen. (2014, April 4). "Benefits of Plant-based Diets." *Cleveland Clinic.* http://my.clevelandclinic.org/health/transcripts/1602_benefits-of-plant-based-diets

106 Damato, Gregory. (2009, May 27). "GM-Soy: Destroy the Earth and Humans for Profit." *Natural News.* http://www.naturalnews.com/026334_soy_Roundup_GMO.html#ixzz1RzIZAWwh

107 Fallon, Sally, & Enig, Mary G. (2000, April–May). "Newest Research on Why You Should Avoid Soy." *Nexus, 7(3).* http://www.eregimens.com/therapies/Diet/Soy/NewestResearchonwhyYouShouldAvoidSoy.htm

108 Damato, Gregory. (2009, May 27). "GM-Soy: Destroy the Earth and Humans for Profit" *Natural News.* http://www.naturalnews.com/026334_soy_research_Roundup.html

109 Ibid.

110 Mercola, Joseph. (2012, June 9). "New Evidence Against These Cancer-causing Foods - and the Massive Cover-up Effort." http://articles.mercola.com/sites/articles/archive/2012/06/09/monsanto-roundup-found-to-be-carcinogenic.aspx

111 Bellé, R., et. al. (May 9, 2012). *Journal of Toxicology and Environmental Health, Part B: Critical Reviews, 15(4): 233-237.* http://www.tandfonline.com/doi/abs/10.1080/10937404.2012.672149

112 Mercola, Joseph. (2009, January 9). "Learn the Truth About Soy. Just How Much Soy Do Asians Eat?" http://articles.mercola.com/sites/articles/archive/2000/01/09/truth-about-soy.aspx

[113] Ibid.

[114] Sheegan, Daniel M., & Doerge, Daniel R. (1999, February 18). *Letter to Dockets Management Branch (HFA-305).* The letter was posted on ABCnews.com as "Scientists Protest Soy Approval."

[115] Bellatti, Andy. "You Ask, I Answer: Soy Protein Isolate." *Medpedia.* Belatti is a commenter on the original article by Kelsey Lepp. http://smallbites.andybellatti.com/you-ask-i-answer-soy-protein-isolate/

[116] Rutz, Jim. (2006, December 12). "Soy is Making Kids 'Gay'." *WND Commentary.* http://www.wnd.com/2006/12/39353/

[117] Cousens, Gabriel. (2008). *There Is a Cure for Diabetes.* Berkeley, CA: North Atlantic Books.

[118] PRWeb. (2014, July 23). "Teraganix Opens New Arizona-based Agricultural Products Supply Facility." http://www.prweb.com/releases/TeraGanix/new-production-facility/prweb12034078.htm

[119] Kearns, Cristin E., et. Al. (September 12, 2016). "Sugar Industry and Coronary Heart Disease Research: A Historical Analysis of Internal Industry Documents." *JAMA Internal Medicine.*

[120] Ibid.

[121] Fulgoni, V, 3rd. (2008, December). "High-fructose corn syrup: everything you wanted to know, but were afraid to ask." *American Journal of Clinical Nutrition, 88*(6), 1715S. http://www.ncbi.nlm.nih.gov/pubmed/19064535

[122] Conklin, Michele. "Q&A with Dr. Richard Johnson." Colorado University, *CU Medical Today.*

[123] Mercola, Joseph. "The Deliberate Lies They Tell About Diabetes". *Dr. Mercola's Newsletter.* http://www.mercola.com/diabetes.aspx?i_cid=cse-tbd-diabetes-content

[124] Ibid.

[125] Ilardi, Stephen. (2009, July 23). "Dietary Sugar and Mental Illness: A Surprising Link." In *The Depression Cure. Psychology Today.* http://www.psychologytoday.com/blog/the-depression-cure/200907/dietary-sugar-and-mental-illness-surprising-link

126 Goulart, Frances Sheridan. (1991, March 1). "Are You Sugar Smart? Linked to Heart Attacks, Kidney Disease, Diabetes and Other Diseases, Sugar Is to the 90s What Cholesterol Was to the '80s (Includes 9 ways to Cope with Sugar Cravings)." *American Fitness*. http://www.highbeam.com/doc/1G1-10722552.html

127 Ibid.

128 Ibid.

129 Edwards, Michael. (2007, June 12). "Healthy Sugar Alternatives: Understanding Both Healthy & Not So Healthy Sugars with Their Glycemic Index and Load." *Organic Lifestyle Magazine*. http://www.organiclifestylemagazine.com/blog/healthy-sugar-alternatives.php
This is a good source for the glycemic index of various sugars.

130 Horton, Jenn. (Reviewed by Kathleen M. Zelman, MPH, RD, LD on July 22, 2014). "The Truth about Agave." *WebMD*. http://www.webmd.com/diet/the-truth-about-agave

131 *Berkeley Wellness Alerts*. (2010, December 17). "Not Such Sweet News about Agave."

132 Occupational Safety and Health Administration (OSHA). *Regulations (Standards - 29 CFR)*. https://www.osha.gov/pls/oshaweb/owadisp.show_document?p_table=standards&p_id=10078

133 Tandel, Kirtidia R. (2011, October-December). "Sugar substitutes: Health controversy over perceived benefits." *Journal of Pharmacology and Pharmacotherapeutics, 2*(4), 236-243.

134 MedlinePlus. "Methanol Poisoning." http://www.nlm.nih.gov/medlineplus/ency/article/002680.htm

135 Gold, Mark. (January, 2003). *Recall aspartame as a neurotoxic drug: file #4: reported aspartame toxicity reactions*. http://www.fda.gov/ohrms/dockets/dailys/03/jan03/012203/02p-0317_emc-000199.txt

136 Ibid.

137 Smith, Michael W. (2014, October 13). "What is Stevia?" *WebMD*. http://www.webmd.com/food-recipes/what-is-stevia

[138] Gare, Fran. (2003). *The Sweet Miracle of Xylitol.* Basic Health Publications, Inc.

[139] *Weekly World News.* (1995, January 17). "Cinnamon and Honey."

[140] Gittleman, Ann Louise. (1996). *Get the Sugar Out,* p. 15. New York: Three Rivers Press.

[141] National Institutes of Health, Office of Dietary Supplements. "Chromium: Dietary Supplement Fact Sheet." http://ods.od.nih.gov/factsheets/Chromium-HealthProfessional/#h10

[142] Hendler, SS, & Rorvik, D. (2008). *PDR for Nutritional Supplements.* (2008). Montvale, NJ: Physicians' Desk Reference Inc.
Shils ME, Olson JA, Shike M. (1999). *Modern Nutrition in Health and Disease,* 9th ed. Williams & Wilkins: Balt.
R. Thiel. (2000). "Natural vitamins may be superior to synthetic ones." *Med Hypo,* 55(6): 461-469.

[143] Hofmekler, Ori, et al. (1998). "Vitamin Poisoning: Are We Destroying Our Health with Hi-Potency Synthetic Vitamins?" "Human plasma and tissue alpha-tocopherol concentrations in response to supplementation with deuterated natural and synthetic vitamin E." *Am J Clin Nutr,* 67: 669-684.

[144] Nuzum, Daniel. (2014). The Truth about Cancer, "The Quest for the Cure." Complete Transcripts, pp. 194-195. *Episode 9, Proven treatments protocols.* TTAC Publishing, LLC.

[145] Ibid.

[146] Agricultural Research Service. "What We Eat in America, NHANES 2001–2002, 1 Day, Individuals 1+ Years, Excluding Breast-Fed Children and Pregnant or Lactating Females." http://www.ars.usda.gov/SP2UserFiles/Place/12355000/pdf/0102/usualintaketables2001-02.pdf

[147] Nielsen, Forrest. "Do You Have Trouble Sleeping? More Magnesium Might Help." *USDA's Agricultural Research Service.* http://www.ars.usda.gov/News/docs.htm?docid=15617&pf=1&cg_id=0

[148] Ibid.

[149] "Diabetes risk may fall as magnesium intake climbs." (September 24, 2010). *Reuters.* http://www.reuters.com/article/us-diabetes-magnesium-idUSTRE68N4ZA20100924

[150] Brownstein, David. (2012). *Salt Your Way to Health,* p. 17. (2nd edition.) Medical Alternative Press.

[151] Ibid., pp. 120,107, 87.

[152] Ibid, p. 26.

[153] Ibid., p. 53.

[154] Geleijnse, J.M., et. al. (1994, August 13). "Reduction in Blood Pressure with a Low Sodium, High Potassium, High Magnesium Salt in Older Subjects with Mild to Moderate Hypertension." *British Medical Journal, 309:* 436–40. http://www.bmj.com/content/309/6952/436

[155] Centers for Disease Control and Prevention (CDC). "Folic Acid." http://www.cdc.gov/ncbddd/folicacid/index.html

[156] Mercola, Joseph. (2002, January 30). "Vitamin B12: Are You Getting It?" http://articles.mercola.com/sites/articles/archive/2002/01/30/vitamin-b12-part-three.aspx

[157] Carmel, R. (2008). "How I treat cobalamin (vitamin B12) deficiency." *Blood,* 112: 2214-21.

[158] Group, Edward. (November 11, 2014). "Vitamin B12 Benefits: 4 Types and Their Health Benefits."

[159] Norris, Jack. "Vitamin B12: Are You Getting It?" *Vegan Health.* http://www.veganhealth.org/articles/vitaminb12

[160] Goulart, Frances Sheridan. (1991, March 1). "Are You Sugar Smart? Linked to Heart Attacks, Kidney Disease, Diabetes and Other Diseases, Sugar Is to the '90s What Cholesterol Was to the '80s (Includes 9 ways to Cope with Sugar Cravings)." *American Fitness.* http://www.highbeam.com/doc/1G1-10722552.html

[161] Wilson, Lawrence. (2014, October). "Vitamin D." *DrWilson.* http://www.drlwilson.com/ARTICLES/VITAMIN%20D.htm

[162] Douillard, John. (2010, March 4). "Sun Exposure: Don't Be Fooled by Your Sunscreen." *Lifespa.* http://www.lifespa.com/dont-be-fooled-by-your-sunscreen/

[163] Wilson, Lawrence. (2014, October). "Vitamin D." *DrWilson.* http://www.drlwilson.com/ARTICLES/VITAMIN%20D.htm

[164] Science Daily. (March 17, 2015). "Recommendation for vitamin D intake was miscalculated, is far too low, experts say." *Creighton University.* https://www.sciencedaily.com/releases/2015/03/150317122458.ht m

[165] Cooney, R.V., et al. (March 1, 1993). "Gamma-tocopherol detoxification of nitrogen dioxide: superiority to alpha-tocopherol." *Proc Natl Acad Sci U S A, 90*(5): 1771–1775. http://www.ncbi.nlm.nih.gov/pmc/articles/PMC45961/

[166] Akilen, R, et al. (July 5, 2010). "Glycated haemoglobin and blood pressure-lowering effect of cinnamon in multi-ethnic Type 2 diabetic patients in the UK: a randomized, placebo-controlled, double-blind clinical trial." DOI: 10.1111/j.1464-5491.2010.03079.x Abstract available at http://onlinelibrary.wiley.com/doi/10.1111/j.1464-5491.2010.03079.x/full

[167] "Eating mushrooms daily 'may cut breast cancer risk by two thirds'." (16 March, 2009). *The Telegraph.* http://www.telegraph.co.uk/news/health/news/5000582/Eating-mushrooms-daily-may-cut-breast-cancer-risk-by-two-thirds.html

[168] Craig, Winston J. (11 March, 2009). "Health effects of vegan diets." *The American Journal of Clinical Nutrition, 89*(supplement): 1627S-1633S. http://ajcn.nutrition.org/content/89/5/1627S.full.pdf

[169] Lo, H.C, and Wasser, S.P. (2011). "Medicinal mushrooms for glycemic control in diabetes mellitus: history, current status, future perspectives, and unsolved problems (review)." *Int J Med Mushrooms, 13*(5): 401-26.

[170] Seto, S.W. (May, 2009). "Novel hypoglycemic effects of Ganoderma lucidum water-extract in obese/diabetic (+db/+db) mice." *Phytomedicine, 16*(5): 426-36. doi: 10.1016/j.phymed.2008.10.004.

171 Soo, Teow Sun. (2004). "Effective dosage of the extract of ganoderma lucidum in the treatment of various ailments." *Mushworld*.

172 Bundy R., et al. "Turmeric extract may improve irritable bowel syndrome symptomology in otherwise healthy adults: a pilot study." Itokawa H., et al. (September 17, 2008). "Recent advances in the investigation of curcuminoids." *Chin Med*, 3: 11. Nagabhushan M. and Bhide, S.V. (1986). "Nonmutagenicity of curcumin and its antimutagenic action versus chili and capsaicin." *Nutr Cancer;* 8(3): 201-10.

173 Zanotto-Filho A, et al. (June, 2012). "The curry spice curcumin selectively inhibits cancer cells growth in vitro and in preclinical model of glioblastoma.". *J Nutr Biochem*, 23(6): 591-601. doi: 10.1016/j.jnutbio.2011.02.015.

174 Smith, Jeffrey M. "Can Genetically-Engineered Foods Explain the Exploding Gluten Sensitivity?" *Institute for Responsible Technology*. http://responsibletechnology.org/media/images/content/Exploding-Gluten-Sensitivity_.pdf

175 Ibid.

176 Navert, B., & Sandstrom, B. (1985, January). "Reduction of the phytate content of bran by leavening in bread and its effect on zinc absorption in man." *British Journal of Nutrition*, 53(1): 47-53.

177 Bohn, T., et. al. (2004, March). "Phytic acid added to white-wheat bread inhibits fractional apparent magnesium absorption in humans." *American Journal of Clinical Nutrition*, 79(3), 418 – 23.

178 Trinidad, P., et. al. (2002). "The Effect of Coconut Flour on Mineral Availability from Coconut Flour Supplemented Foods." *Philippine Journal of Nutrition*, 49: 48-57.

179 Nagel, Ramiel. (2010, Spring). "Preparing Grains, Nuts, Seeds and Beans for Maximum Nutrition." *Wise Traditions in Food, Farming and the Healing Arts*, the quarterly journal of the Weston A. Price Foundation.

180 Nazor, Nina. "All About Insulin." *People and Diabetes*. http://peopleanddiabetes.com/id26.html

[181] Johnson, Dr. Ben. Qtd. in Bollinger, Ty. (2014). *The Quest for the Cures... Continues.* (Film transcript, p. 188.) TTAC Publishing.

[182] Steury, Tim. (Winter, 2009). "Is organic more nutritious?" *Washington State University.* http://wsm.wsu.edu/s/index.php?id=749

[183] Bassler, Dr. Anthony. (2004, January). "A Common Mistake that Prevents Most People from Losing Weight...and How to Avoid It! Why This Simple 'First Step' Should Be Part of Any Weight Management, Anti-Aging and Health Improvement Program." *Vegetarian Times.*

[184] Jensen, Bernard. (1980). *Tissue Cleansing through Bowel Management.* Escondido, CA: self-published.

[185] Anderson, Richard. "Colon Plaque-Mucoid Plaque." *Cleanse.net.* http://cleanse.net/mucoid-plaque
Dr. Richard Anderson, ND, NMD, is the author of *Cleanse and Purify Yourself* (Avery Trade, revised edition 1998).

[186] Yerba Prima. *Kalenite pill product website.* http://www.yerba.com/kalenite-cleansing-herbs/

[187] Ibid.

[188] Arizona State University. (2008, April 7). "'Healing Clays' Hold Promise in Fight Against MRSA Superbug Infections and Disease." *Biodesign Institute.* https://biodesign.asu.edu/news/%E2%80%9Chealing-clays%E2%80%9D-hold-promise-fight-against-mrsa-superbug-infections-and-disease

[189] El, Akilah M. (2011, June 9). "The Health Benefits of Bentonite Clay." Celestial Healing Wellness Center: *The Natural Health and Holistic World According to Dr. Akilah El.* http://docakilah.wordpress.com/2011/06/09/the-health-benefits-of-bentonite-clay/

[190] Jensen, Bernard. (1998). *Dr. Jensen's Guide to Better Bowel Care: A Complete Program for Tissue Cleansing through Bowel Management.* Avery.

[191] Ibid.

[192] Sterling, Joseph. (2004, March). "The Silent Killers: The Secret World of Parasites." *Secrets of Robust Health,* 5(1). (Reprints 5th

anniversary edition).
http://www.healingwatersforhealth.com/GetAttachment.pdf

[193] Dyer, Diana. (Feb. 22, 2009). "What's in Kale? USDA Nutrient Content Data." *365 Days of Kale*. http://www.365daysofkale.com/2009/02/whats-in-kale-usda-nutrient-content.html

[194] Wigmore, Ann, and the Hippocrates Health Institute, Inc. (1985). *The Wheatgrass Book: How to Grow and Use Wheatgrass to Maximize Your Health and Vitality*. Avery Health Guides.

[195] Jensen, Bernard and Goldman, Leslie. *The Healing Power of Chlorophyll from Plant Life (Magic Survival Kit Book 1)*, 2nd Revised Edition. Jensen Enterprises.

[196] Mercola, Joseph. (2011, November 13). "Benefits of Juicing: Your Keys to Radiant Health." http://articles.mercola.com/sites/articles/archive/2011/11/13/benefits-of-juicing.aspx

[197] Bolen, Jim. "Histamine/Anti-histamine and the Dangers of Taking Anti-histamine." *Water Cure*. http://www.watercure2.org/histamines.htm

[198] Batmanghelidj, Fereydoon. (2000). *ABC of Asthma, Allergies and Lupus, First Edition*. Global Health Solutions, Inc.

[199] Pitchford, Paul. (2002). *Healing with Whole Foods*. North Atlantic Books, pp. 224–5.

[200] Ibid., p. 246.

[201] Ibid., p. 537.

[202] Ibid., p. 545.

[203] Baliga MS, et al. (2013). "Ocimum sanctum L (Holy Basil or Tulsi) and its phytochemicals in the prevention and treatment of cancer." *Nutr Cancer* 65(Suppl 1): 26-35.

[204] Agrawal, P. et. al. (September, 1996). "Randomized placebo-controlled, single blind trial of holy basil leaves in patients with noninsulin-dependent diabetes mellitus. *Int J Clin Pharmacol Ther* 34(9): 406-9.

[205] Gholap S, et al. (2004). "Hypoglycaemic effects of some plant extracts are possibly mediated through inhibition in corticosteroid concentration." *Pharmazie* 59(11): 876-8.

Khan V, et al. (2012). "A pharmacological appraisal of medicinal plants with antidiabetic potential." *J Pharm Bioallied Sci 4*(1):27-42.

Bergland C. (2013). "Cortisol: why 'the stress hormone' is public enemy no. 1." *Psychology Today.* 2013 http://www.psychologytoday.com/blog/the-athletes-way/201301/cortisol-why-the-stress-hormone-is-public-enemy-no-1

[206] Vivoch J, et al. (2006). "Evaluation of in vitro antimicrobial activity of Thai basil oils and their micro-emulsion formulas against Propionibacterium acnes." *Int Journal of Cosmet Sci 28*(2): 125-33.

[207] American Gastroenterological Association. *Food Allergies.* https://www.gastro.org/patient-center/diet-medications/AGAPatientBrochure_FoodAllergies.pdf

[208] Ibid.

[209] Aliaga, L., et. al. (2000). "Influence of goat and cow milk on the digestive and metabolic utilisation of calcium and iron." *J Physiol Biochem 56*: 201-208.

Park, Y.W., et. al. (1986). "Bioavailability of iron in goat milk compared with cow milk fed to anemic rats." *J Dairy Sci 69*: 2608-2615.

Barrionuevo, M., et. al. (2002). "Beneficial effect of goat milk on nutritive utilization of iron and copper in malabsorption syndrome." *J Dairy Sci 85*: 657-664.

Prosser C et al (2003). "Digestion of milk proteins from cow or goat milk infant formula." Abstract and poster paper presented at the New Zealand Pediatric Conference, Queenstown, August 2003.

Bevilacqua, C., et. al. (2001). "Goats' milk of defective alpha(s1)-casein genotype decreases intestinal and systemic sensitization to beta-lactoglobulin in guinea pigs." *Journal of Dairy Research 68*: 217-227

Jensen, Bernard Jensen. (1994). *Goat Milk Magic.*

[210] Elliott R., et al (1999). "Type I (insulin-dependent) diabetes mellitus and cow milk: casein variant consumption." *Diabetologia, 42*: 292-296.

[211] Carter, P., et. al. (August 18, 2010). "Fruit and vegetable intake and incidence of type 2 diabetes mellitus: systematic review and meta-analysis." *BMJ 341*: c4229. DOI: 10.1136/bmj.c4229.

[212] Samsel, Anthony, and Seneff, Stephanie. (March 24, 2015). "Glyphosate, pathways to modern diseases III: Manganese, neurological diseases, and associated pathologies." *Surg Neurol Int 6*: 45. DOI: 10.4103/2152-7806.153876

[213] Guillén, Alis, et. al. (July, 2015). "Antihyperglycemic Activity of Eucalyptus Tereticornis in Insulin-Resistant Cells and a Nutritional Model of Diabetic Mice". *Advances in Pharmacological Sciences*, 2015(9). http://dx.doi.org/10.1155/2015/418673

[214] Dey, B., et. al. (April 15, 2014). "Exploration of natural enzyme inhibitors with hypoglycemic potentials amongst Eucalyptus Spp. by in vitro assays." *World J Diabetes*, 5(2): 209-218. https://www.ncbi.nlm.nih.gov/pubmed/24748933

[215] Shapiro, Debbie. (2002). *The Body Mind Workbook; Explaining How the Mind and Body Work Together*. Vega, Chrysalis Books: UK; p. 127.

[216] Hay, Louise L. (1999). *You Can Heal Your Life*. Hay House, Inc; p. 189.

Made in the USA
Charleston, SC
22 November 2016